BEYOND THE
IVORY TOWER
The Autobiography of
Sir Cyril Philips

The Radcliffe Press
London · New York

TO DORCAS AND JOAN

Published in 1995 by
The Radcliffe Press
45 Bloomsbury Square
London WC1A 2HY

175 Fifth Avenue
New York
NY 10010

In the United States of America
and Canada distributed by
St Martin's Press
175 Fifth Avenue
New York
NY 10010

A full CIP record for this book is available from the British Library

A full CIP record for this book is available from the Library of Congress

ISBN 1–86064–016–8
Library of Congress Catalog card number: available

Copy-edited and laser-set by Selro Publishing Services, Oxford
Printed and bound in Great Britain by WBC Ltd, Bridgend, Mid Glamorgan

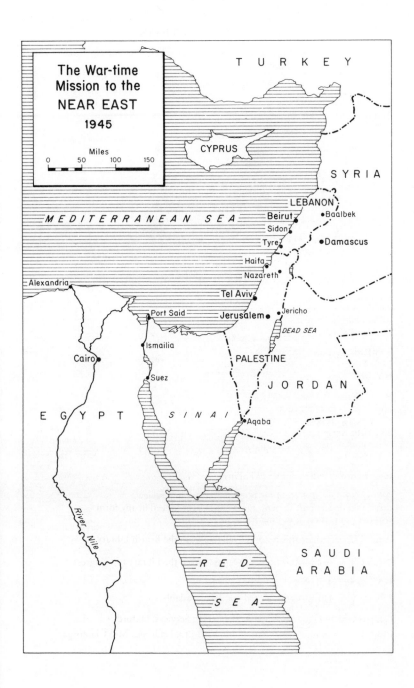

The War-time
Mission to the
NEAR EAST
1945

Miles

0   50   100   150

TURKEY

CYPRUS

SYRIA

MEDITERRANEAN SEA

LEBANON

Beirut   ●Baalbek

Sidon

Tyre   ●Damascus

Haifa

Nazareth

Tel Aviv

Alexandria

Port Said   Jerusalem   ●Jericho

DEAD SEA

Ismailia

Cairo   PALESTINE

Suez   JORDAN

EGYPT   SINAI

●Aqaba

River Nile

SAUDI
ARABIA

RED

SEA

The War-time
Mission to
ITALY
1945
- - - Winter line 1944-45
Miles
0 20 40 60 80 100 120

AUSTRIA

L. COMO
L. GARDA
Milan
Verona
River Po
Trieste
Venice
Bologna
Faenza
Forli
Rimini
Pesaro
YUGOSLAVIA
Pisa
Florence
Leghorn
Ancona
Perugia
Macerata
Assisi
A P E N N I N E S
ADRIATIC SEA
CORSICA
Rome
Anzio
Cassino Foggia
Bari
Caserta
Naples
Avellino
VESUVIUS
Salerno
Amalfi
Taranto
SARDINIA
Gulf of
Taranto
TYRRHENIAN SEA
Palermo
ETNA
SICILY
IONIAN SEA
TUNISIA
MEDITERRANEAN SEA
GOZO MALTA

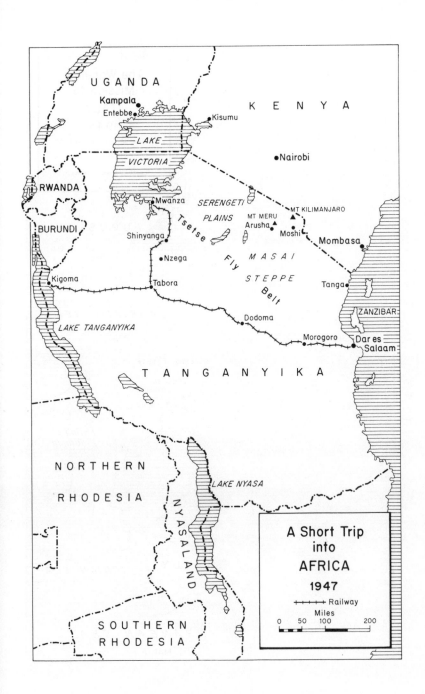

UGANDA

Kampala
Entebbe
Kisumu

K E N Y A

LAKE

VICTORIA

Nairobi

RWANDA

Mwanza

SERENGETI
PLAINS

MT KILIMANJARO

BURUNDI

Shinyanga

Tsetse

MT MERU
Arusha
Moshi

Mombasa

Nzega

Fly

M A S A I

S T E P P E

Kigoma

Tabora

Belt

Tanga

LAKE TANGANYIKA

Dodoma

ZANZIBAR

Morogoro

Dar es
Salaam

T A N G A N Y I K A

N O R T H E R N

LAKE NYASA

R H O D E S I A

N Y A S A L A N D

A Short Trip
into
AFRICA
1947

+++++ Railway

Miles

0   50   100   200

S O U T H E R N

R H O D E S I A

Contents

Acronyms and Abbreviations

ABCA	Army Bureau of Current Affairs
ACPO	Association of Chief Police Officers
ADC	aide-de-camp
AEC	Army Educational Corps
AFHQ	Armed Forces Headquarters
AJS	A. J. Simpson
ARP	air-raid precautions
BBC	British Broadcasting Corporation
BWP	British Way and Purpose
C-in-C	Commander-in-Chief
GWR	Great Western Railway
HM	His Majesty's
IRA	Irish Republican Army
LSE	London School of Economics and Political Science
MO	medical officer
NATO	North Atlantic Treaty Organization
OCTU	officer cadets' training unit
PACE	Police and Criminal Evidence Act
RAF	Royal Air Force
TOET	test of elementary training
TWI	training within industry
UGC	University Grants Committee
USSR	Union of Soviet Socialist Republics
WEA	Workers' Educational Association
WO	Warrant Officer
YMCA	Young Men's Christian Association

Glossary

achcha	all right
ayah	woman employed to look after small children, in both Indian and European households
baba	child
baraza	meeting
bhisti	Muhammadan water-carrier
bukra	tomorrow
burkha	material covering face, veil
charpoy	common Indian bedstead
chatty	an Indian pot for water
contessa	countess
dhobi	washerman
Dozent	university teacher (Ger.)
goonda	minder
gram	rough pulse normally fed to horses
hackery	bullock-cart
jao	get out
juldi	quick
khana	meal, usually dinner
lathi	bamboo pole, heavily ringed and ferruled
maalesh	what does it matter?
maidan	large level area, plain or parade ground
mehtar	sweeper
memsahib	term of respect used for a European married woman
mufti	Muslim religious authority, legal expert and adviser on the law of the Koran

Glossary

Namaste	Indian Buddhist salutation
neem	margosa tree
pawn	betel leaf, used to make a concoction to chew
peepul	Indian tree resembling the banyan
souk	market
topi	pith helmet
tulli	conical shaped cottages built of stone
vino	wine
wallah	common expression meaning 'fellow' or 'fella' associated with a vocation

Acknowledgements

This story would be far from complete without putting on record the debt I owe to Miss Nora Shane, who worked with me as secretary through the 20 years of my directorship of the School of Oriental and African Studies; and who, along with Miss Heather Thompson of the Senate House of the federal University of London, contrived to impose some order on the concluding five years I served as vice chancellor. Nor through so busy a period could my personal research in history have been kept alive without the devoted cooperation of Miss Doreen Wainwright.

After spending some 50 years in academia it was never going to prove easy to manage a successful transition into the very different domains of the police and the criminal justice system, and quite impossible had I not been buoyed successively by the knowledge, expertise and valued friendship of Christopher Train and Peter Bolton of the Home Office, Michael Sayers of the Lord Chancellor's Department and Christopher Dyment now of the Law Commission. In them I enjoyed the civil service at its best.

In the preparation of my manuscript for publication, I am indebted to Mrs Christine Lewis for her patience well beyond the call of duty, and to Dr Lester Crook and Mrs Selina Cohen, who with sure judgement have smoothed rough edges and rounded off many an awkward corner.

Phil Philips

1

Growing up in Bihar

Neither Father nor Mother ever explained, and I never discovered why, in the early autumn of the year 1920 they suddenly made up their minds to pack up and leave England for India. Unlike many British families we had no tradition of service there, though Mother's father, Owen Kimberley, who in early life had been a soldier in Queen Victoria's army, may have served in the east. Whatever the truth of the matter, he could certainly spin a good old yarn about snow-white elephants, man-eating tigers and sacred cows, gaudy Hindu gods and Muslim holy men and his own colourful life 'somewhere east of Suez, where the best is like the worst, where there aren't no Ten Commandments and a man can raise a thirst!'

Both my parents had left school at the age of nine — Mother, named Mary, who had been born in August 1888 in Woolwich within, as she always proudly claimed, 'the sound of Bow bells', going on to earn a living doing piecework in daytime making gussets for leather gloves in Dent's factory in Worcester and, in the evenings, selling biscuits at a stall in the market. Father, by name William and always called Will, who was born in 1884 in Glamorgan, started as a tea boy in the railway yards of the Great Western Railway at Worcester, soon, for his meticulous hard work, being promoted to be an engine cleaner. Growing into a slim, athletic figure just under six feet tall, with a sharp-cut grey face and dark wavy hair and a splendidly moulded moustache, the possessor, too, of a sweet tenor voice, he became widely known as a concert singer. But despite his popularity he remained reserved, preferring always through the rest of his life to be a 'loner'. By comparison, Mother was outgoing and confident of her charms. Full-bosomed, short and strong of stature, agile in movement, her round rosy face with deep-set neurotic grey eyes surmounted by a wavy mass of brown hair gave her a bouncy yet striking appearance. She liked to flirt and always found it easy to get on with men. She led and dominated her husband and, from the start, took complete, though erratic and wasteful, control of all their financial and practical affairs. Although forming opposites in character and outlook, they got on quite well together and were regarded by their friends as a handsome, lively, attractive pair.

They had first met and married in Worcester early in 1912, the year of my birth. Father continued to work on the railway to which he was passionately devoted, steadily making his way as a fireman on the footplate and, by the end of the Great War of 1914–18, had been promoted to a driver, mainly of tank engines, in which capacity he then transferred to the shunting yards of the large soap manufacturing firm of Lever Brothers at Port Sunlight, just outside Birkenhead.

There he soon somehow fell foul of the local railway union boss and in the row that followed, according to Mother's account, found himself set up and taken to court for allegedly stealing small amounts of soap and coal. By a timely stroke of good luck, at a charity concert where he was singing he happened to meet the well-known union general secretary, Jimmy Thomas (later to become a notorious Chancellor of the Exchequer), from whom he managed to get a letter of support, which at the trial helped him to get an acquittal.

After this he never had a good word for the unions and later, at the time of the general strike of 1926, happening to be on leave in England, he took great satisfaction in volunteering to run a strike-breaking passenger train service between Birkenhead and Chester, which, with the help as firemen of a wealthy young stockbroker and an accountant, both from Liverpool, and quite undeterred by a threatening visit by a group of five irate union members followed by a brick through our front downstairs' window, he maintained throughout the strike.

About the same time as his case came to court Mother found she was pregnant; and Father, seeing an advertisement for engine drivers for the East Indian Railway Company in India, applied for, and after interview was offered, a job in Bengal, which Mother eagerly encouraged him to take, though, as both confessed later, neither of them had much idea where India was, let alone what life would be like there.

So in the autumn of 1921, soon after the birth of a baby daughter, Peggy, he set off alone for Calcutta, leaving Mother to sell the furniture, pack up and follow with the two children. As we saw him off, tears coursing down his cheeks, he gave me a small Oxford Bible with a fervent 'God Bless!' as if he never expected to see me again. Within a fortnight of his arrival we got a cable telling us not to leave because he had been posted to the small railway junction of Asansol on the borders of Bengal and Bihar, in the heart of the Ganges' plain, about 130 miles upcountry from Calcutta, where conditions would be extremely primitive and unsuitable for us. But for Mother there was no turning back. Without a home of her own, her meagre possessions already packed and our passages booked, she was not prepared to cancel a voyage to which by this time she was obviously looking forward. One month later, in December, with my sister not yet one and myself aged eight, we went down to the Birkenhead docks to take ship on the Ellerman Line's *City of Poona*.

For me the gangway to that liner led to fairyland. Even though travelling steerage in a cramped cabin in the ship's stern, above the heavy monotonous thump of the ship's propeller, I was exchanging life in a small, grubby, terraced back-to-back house in Birkenhead for what seemed a grand floating palace where everything in sight shone brightly. Never before had I seen gleaming white washbowls, flush lavatories, a capacious bath with hot running water and electric light at the touch of a switch, or dreamed of stewards in starched white uniforms with polished brass buttons serving early morning tea and bearing loaded trays of food as we sat at table faced by a bewildering choice of knives, forks and spoons. At a stroke we entered a world which previously I had only glimpsed with wonder in early Hollywood films.

3

That ever-changing, enchanting voyage lasted for six glorious weeks, *en route* taking us to Gibraltar, Malta, Port Said, Suez, Aden, Colombo and Madras, presenting a dazzling kaleidoscope of people of every colour and dress, crowded bazaars where men wore turbans and fezzes and women covered their faces or shrouded themselves completely in tent-like *burkha*s.

With the best of intentions, when wandering round the large Simon Artz department store in Port Said, Mother was persuaded into buying me a large *topi*, fully an inch thick, although quite light, which afterwards in the midday sun I always had to wear. Because of its clumsy size it was forever toppling off and, even when more or less brought under control, its wide brim created a severely blinkered world.

At each port we went ashore, first having to climb gingerly down the shaking ladder on the ship's side before jumping into a small rowing boat. At Aden, deep in the forbidding dark crater of an extinct volcano, the ship took on coal, borne in heavy baskets on the heads of an endless, chanting line of coolies, and covering everything in a layer of choking black dust.

In the clear waters of Suez we could see the sinister, waving shapes of the sharks. I watched several of the crew prepare to catch them, tying ropes to large steel hooks baited with lumps of meat, and listened mouth agape as they told yarns of a previous voyage when, as a shark took the bait, one of their shipmates got his leg trapped in a loop of the fast-tightening line.

This was 'the stuff that dreams are made of', well beyond the reach of satire, far removed from life in the grimy, shipbuilding town of Birkenhead. There on Tranmere Hill, in a complex of mean little streets, my family had shared its small terraced house with mother's 60-year-old parents and her younger brother, Ben, and his new bride, Millie. With only three bedrooms, a kitchen and parlour, ill-lit by gaslight, we were thrown together, the grown-ups seemingly always at each other's throats. Grandfather, once a square, well-muscled figure, now bent and hesitant, had become almost a recluse, defeated by life, his brooding face drawn down into a large, sagging, tobacco-stained moustache. Long out of work, he mooned about his bedroom, sorting through piles of the *Sporting Times* and forever thumbing the pages of a small brown horse-racing form book, occasionally jotting down points, comparing weights and records, checking the state of the course for the day, making his selections and then, jamming on his cloth cap, suddenly darting out of doors to lay his bets. Waiting and watching in the kitchen, Grandma, her beaky, frustrated face alert, poised on tiptoe like a sparrow on spindly legs, always followed, vainly calling after him not to be such a fool.

Every Saturday afternoon she took me to the film matinée at the local cinema, on the way buying a 'pennuth' of acid drops to suck and a bag of locust bean-pods and tiger nuts to chew, and always staying on to see the programme, especially *The Perils of Pauline*, twice over. Week by week we hung on each episode as Pearl White, the devil-may-care gorgeous blonde, escaped from one death-defying hazard after another.

At home, Mother's brother, Ben, dominated and terrorized the household. Physically short and heavily muscled like his father, he earned a boring living as a salesman in one of the new wireless shops and got his excitement in the evenings and weekends at the local football club, Tranmere Rovers, where occasionally he played on the right wing. In appearance older than his years, he had, on the outbreak of war in 1914 at the age of 16, bluffed his way into the Gunners, serving virtually uninjured throughout, but emerging dissatisfied and embittered, always grumbling and swearing, and, like his father, a born gambler. Every Friday, payday, he came home the worse for drink, usually first picking a row with his wife Millie, whom he punched and pushed around; and once, when she locked herself into the bedroom, he smashed the door down to get at her. On one unforgettable Saturday night, following a row at the match, he dragged down the tall kitchen dresser, bringing Grandma's precious crockery crashing to the red-tiled floor.

When the worst of these stormy 'barneys' was over, Grandfather would quietly emerge from his bedroom carrying a small, brown hand-painted concertina and, gathering us round the fire in the kitchen, gradually got us to join in a singsong, always starting with his favourite, 'Rock of ages, cleft for me', and, best of all, because we could stamp and clap in unison, going on to 'Where are the boys of the old brigade?' He invariably ended with the forlorn 'Keep the home fires burning', which for some reason we all knew by heart.

> Keep the home fires burning, while your hearts are
> yearning,
> Though your lads are far away they dream of home;
> There's a silver lining through the dark cloud shining,
> Turn the dark cloud inside out, till the boys come home.

Afterwards, somehow or other, everyone carried on as if nothing untoward had happened.

Whenever possible I spent most days out of doors, often in the local Mersey Park hanging around any group lucky enough to have a football or a cricket bat; and on summer evenings playing hopscotch or skipping in the street, or occasionally tagging along with an older group of boys who formed the Whitfield Street gang, which was bent on taking over the territory of the neighbouring Mill Street lot. Thereabouts the streets were roughly surfaced with small, impacted, granite stones, easily dislodged and readily usable as formidable missiles. Skirmishes were frequent, usually lasting until someone was hurt, or a window broken, or a policeman, or rumour of one, appeared. A running fight one evening took us to the vicinity of the local park, which was bounded by cast-iron railings topped by pointed armorial spikes, which, when sharply tapped, broke off to form handy, vicious weapons, one of which badly gashed my mouth so that I had to be carted off to hospital. Oddly enough we never got run in by the police, who seemed quite content to chase us home.

Father greatly admired the police and was deeply shocked when, in 1919, just before Easter, large numbers of the Liverpool force, who in fact had a genuine grievance over poor pay, went on strike. Predictably, rioting soon broke out and, for several nights running, there was a good deal of looting in the city's shopping centre. On Easter Monday morning, evidently curious to see what was going on, Father took me across the river to Liverpool. On the ferryboat we passed two grey battleships, anchored in mid-stream, before tying up beside a destroyer at the landing stage. On Pier Head, lines of marines stood with fixed bayonets and, in Lord

Street, goods and broken glass from looted shops covered the pavements, a tailor's dummy sprawled from a shattered shop front and next door, outside a music shop, the severed strings of a smashed piano plaintively twanged in the breeze. On guard in St George's Square stood several massive grey-green tanks, the first I had ever seen. Boarding a tram to the Scotland Road area, where a colony of the Liverpool Irish lived, we could see piles of brickbats collected on every street corner, ready to hand, so Father said, for that night's rumpus. In fact, during the strike rioting went on for three days and nights until the troops were ordered out to clear the streets at bayonet point, one man being shot dead in the ensuing mêlée.

Afterwards Father, who had a yearning to be a policeman, always spoke with bitterness about the manner in which those on strike were subsequently treated, being dismissed with ignominy and loss of pension, and humiliated by having to return their uniforms to collecting carts paraded around the city streets. As we made our way home, he kept telling me, 'Now you know what people are really like!'

Against this background the Mersey Park elementary school, which I attended with its solid, polished, red-brick walls and grey-tiled gables, standing between two large playgrounds surrounded by cast-iron railings, formed an oasis of discipline, good behaviour and kindness. Discipline was asserted first thing every morning by the deputy headmaster, grey-haired with enormous shaggy eyebrows and a boxer's broken nose, standing at the gates, cane in hand, ready to punish those who came late, one stroke for every tardy minute. Inside, by comparison, all was kindly calm, presided over by the headmaster, Richard Hughes, who resembled a big brown bear — burly, stooping, his large shining bald pate held to one side — peering enquiringly though his pince-nez and never passing by without a reassuring nod. On the eve of my departure for India he called the whole school together and, to my astonishment, formally presented me with three small volumes from Herbert Strang's Literary Series, *Stories from Grimm*, *Tales from Hans Andersen* and Daniel Defoe's *Robinson Crusoe*, each identically signed and inscribed in his own perfect copperplate handwriting, 'With all good wishes for your future career'.

7

Somewhat battered and dog-eared, but still with their challenge and inspiration undimmed, they lie before me as I write.

By the time the good ship *City of Poona* was steaming through the gales and fog of a wintry Bay of Bengal, all this had long since faded. On board I had soon found for myself a hideaway and perch on a metal girder in the stern, beside a porthole window, so that as the ship pitched and rolled in rough weather and the massive propeller alternately thrashed the air and plunged deep into the sea, I watched enthralled as streams of green and blue iridescent bubbles and the occasional fish flashed by. There I was enclosed within my own world of sounds: the thrashing of water round the propeller, the distant thudding of the engines and the muted roar of the ventilation. Approaching Calcutta through the Sunderbunds, the swampy wilderness of the Hugli delta, we were shrouded in a warm brown mist, the ship's foghorn dismally booming. On deck there was a sudden hubbub and a burst of excited voices caused me to rush to join the crowd on the taffrail, just in time to see two grey British destroyers emerge close by, steaming downstream. On both, at the salute, lines of white-uniformed sailors were on parade and, on the bridge of the leading ship, stood a small group. An excited cry went up, 'It's the Prince of Wales!', and we cheered as the slim figure saluted. Afterwards I was told that the tall figure beside him was his aide-de-camp, Lord Louis Mountbatten, whose career later became entwined with India and whom, in that context, I was to get to know well.

His Royal Highness, no doubt with a deep sigh of relief, was leaving India after a difficult tour, marred by the early stirrings of Mahatma Gandhi's nationalist, non-cooperation movement. Both he and Lord Louis were reported as 'liking the tigers and hating the politicians'.

When, later that afternoon, we reached the port of Calcutta, it was strike-bound, completely at a standstill. With difficulty the crew berthed the ship and the passengers, watched sullenly by a silent crowd of coolies on the dockside, struggled in the clammy heat to get their luggage ashore. Happily, Father was there to meet us, accompanied by a driver with a four-wheeled cart, drawn by a miserable skeleton of a horse; and, fragile transport though it seemed, our trunks and cases were soon piled high and we were on our way to Howrah railway junction. That night we boarded the train, which took us across the plains of the Ganges river to the small railway town of Asansol on the borders of Bihar and Bengal, which was to be our home for the next five years.

At dawn, in a cool grey mist, we pulled into Asansol station under a tremendous clattering as a family of monkeys scampered across the station's corrugated iron roof, scolding us for disturbing them. Undisturbed and unmoving along both platforms lay rows of sleeping figures, covered head to foot in grey and brown blankets, forcing us to step over them in order to reach an ancient dust-covered taxi to take us to our bungalow home.

It was in fact not so much a bungalow as a ground-floor apartment taking up one quarter of an ugly, box-like, flat-roofed, two-storeyed, brown-bricked building situated in the middle of the railway cantonment. It consisted of no more than two large rooms, each about 25 feet square, sparsely furnished, the living room with only a bamboo table and chairs, a sideboard and two armchairs, without pictures or floor covering, and the bedroom with two large beds, each with a mosquito net. Most of our clothes had to be kept in tin trunks pushed into a small adjoining windowless boxroom, where they soon turned green with mould. Extra living space was afforded on the south and hot side by an arched veranda, partly shielded from the sun by bamboo lattices, which extended along the length of the apartment. Each of the main rooms contained a single large central fan and a small electric light, scarcely strong enough to pierce the gloom, and, as we soon discovered, prone to frequent breakdown.

The whole grim building, which included our place, stood in a large compound extending about 70 yards in each direction, bounded by broken wire and concrete fencing, and intersected by large, open storm drains, the land itself brown and bare without a shrub or flower and long since stripped of every blade of grass by the cows, goats and chickens, which roamed freely and, if the lattice door was left open, invaded the veranda where indiscriminately they devoured everything within reach — pot plants, newspapers and washing. Well to the north, about half a mile away, a line of trees, mainly aromatic *neem*s, leafy *peepul*s and the drooping casuarinas, and a constantly rising cloud of brown dust and a distant hum of voices marked the Grand Trunk Road, the stamping ground of Rudyard Kipling's famous boy hero, Kim, which reached all the way from Calcutta past Asansol and upcountry to Benares, the holy city, to Delhi and Lahore, thence on to Peshawar and the Khyber Pass. Although strictly forbidden to go anywhere near it, I always felt conscious of its menacing presence, for along it throughout the day, taking advantage of the shade provided by the lines of trees, moved a multitude of people, pack animals and squealing *hackeries*, or bullock-carts. Alert for the slightest hint of food, the aggressive pariah kites hovered overhead and every post, roof and railing around provided a perch for hundreds of squalling crows and the occasional predatory vulture.

With no piped water in the bungalow, the nearest supply was a ground pump in the neighbouring compound from which, twice a day, the *bhisti*, carrying a goatskin slung on his back, brought water to fill our tin bath. Water for drinking, kept cool in an earthen *chatty*, of course had first to be boiled. A small cement-lined room with a narrow air hole near the ceiling served as a bathroom; and for a bath we simply poured water over ourselves from a bucket.

Our *bhisti*'s arrival on his morning round formed one of the events of my day, for to me he seemed,

> Of all them blackfaced crew,
> The finest man I knew.

Over six feet tall and strong, he juggled easily with the heavy goatskin on his back, never spilling even a drop of water. Always chewing *pawn*, the Indian equivalent of chewing gum, he went to a lot of trouble to show me how to make it, taking a small, heart-shaped green leaf on which to mix a betel nut and mint with a dash of white quicklime, which, when chewed, quickly stained lips and teeth blood-red. Such a flow of saliva was created that he constantly had to spit, making the spotted ground look as though a rain of blood were falling.

Although the winter months were tolerably, often enjoyably, warm and sunny, from April onwards the sun's monotonous yellow glare and clammy heat kept us penned indoors. Even with the wooden and matting lattices closed, dust and sand blew through and by day and night insects, mainly ants, swarmed in. Above all I hated the blister-flies and the small red ants, whose stinging bites usually festered into sores and, if I omitted before going to bed to wash my face and hands, in no time at all, in their search for food, they found their way on to the bed and over me. Like a hot blanket, night fell early, tempting us to open wide the doors for air, despite the incoming swarm of moths, beetles and mosquitoes, which were welcomed only by the gecko lizards on the walls, tongues flicking, always darting here and there and sometimes, in their eager dash for prey, falling off and, as they hit the floor with a loud plop, parting company with their long tails. Outside, the howling of the jackals and the chirping of the crickets in summer and the constant, monotonous croaking of the frogs in the monsoon never ceased.

As the sultry summer deepened, sandstorms, especially in the afternoon, gradually increased in intensity, their approach marked by great purple clouds on the horizon, promising, though never delivering, imminent rain. Sheet lightning flickered across the horizon, usually culminating in blinding blue flashes with deafening crescendos of thunder. But in late June, with the coming of the monsoon rains, we heralded a world magically reborn, blissfully standing for hours under the gushing drain pipes, our prickly heat rash, which we called 'the red dog' and which had got steadily worse through the summer, being marvellously cooled and soothed. Within hours, from the seemingly dead ground vivid green grass sprouted and covered the parched earth.

It was enthralling to watch Indians washing and bathing, for they adored the water which rendered their lives tolerable; as we acknowledged every morning at school in a thanksgiving chant, first in Hindi and then in English:

> Water, stored in wells and tanks,
> Filling Ganga's, Jumna's banks,
> Water, giving daily food,
> Fruit and flowers and precious wood.
> Water, laughing, water, weeping,
> Water, waking, Water, sleeping,

11

Father, Mother in the blending
Hail, O, Hail, be never ending.

We had two servants, a 30-year-old, low-caste, worn-looking *ayah*, Lita, always dressed in a plain, rather grubby *sari*, who shopped and cooked for us as well as caring for her husband and two young children; and a pitifully thin, outcast sweeper, Devi, who, whenever he caught sight of me invariably bowed low muttering '*Achcha, Baba, achcha*', 'All right, child, all right!' Apart from continually disturbing the perpetual sand and dust in the flat, to him fell the very important job of emptying the privy pot, which he did twice a day on to an open-fenced concrete platform, situated no more than 30 yards from the flat. There also was deposited the daily household waste and, although this dunghill was sprinkled morning and night with powder of lime, it generated and attracted swarms of flies, which must have caused most of the illnesses which persistently laid us low. There never seemed to be a day when someone in the family was not ill with a high temperature, the only treatment for which was the detestably bitter quinine. Even this did little to moderate the inexorably eviscerating routine of fever — shivering bouts, burning skin and fitful dreaming — before the heavenly, profuse release into sweating and quiet, merciful sleep.

My legs and arms, splotchy with sores from insect bites, were forever being coated by Mother with a violet-staining iodine, as a preliminary to lancing with sharp-pointed scissors and soothing with leaves of the *neem* tree. Life became one repeated round of quinine, aspirin, iodine and castor oil, the daily dose of one or other being treated as if it were a religious ritual. Toothache, from which I suffered through eating too many rich Bihari sweetmeats, left the most poignant memory and legacy for, lacking a local dentist, the only palliative was a mouthful of oil of cloves, quickly followed by a visit to the doctor, who never hesitated to whip out the offending tooth; as a result of which, by the time we returned to England, I had lost most of my teeth.

Ayah, with her family, worked and lived in the cookhouse situated at the edge of the compound, about 30 yards from the house. Consisting of one room no more than 20 by 10 feet, it contained at one end a brick oven with a charcoal fire and at the other a door with a small open aperture, so it was always smoke-filled and stiflingly hot. Apart from a pile of cooking pots and pans, her only furniture consisted of a single *charpoy* with a wooden frame and rope matting. Ayah's husband, a *mehtar*, or sweeper, who worked for another family, rarely seemed to be around but always appeared when we were to have chicken for dinner and then, with evident relish, brandishing a large knife, he would chase and seize one of the fowl on the compound and, taking care only to half-cut its throat, throw it down, laughing and clapping while the wretched bird fluttered and squawked around, spraying blood all over the place, until it finally collapsed.

After breakfast every morning Ayah was given detailed instruc-tions on the daily shopping to be done in the bazaar, which was about half a mile away. Mother herself never went there and it was declared out of bounds for me. Except for the fruit, luscious mangoes, melons and lychees, our food was monotonous and unappetizing, for the most part consisting of tough horse and goat meat, camouflaged in hot curries and rice and occasionally, only in winter, including some vegetables.

Around the cookhouse, drawn by the smell of cooking, the yellow, pariah dogs gathered, most of them diseased, perpetually cringing, snarling, yelping and copulating, and as the day warmed up moving off to the roads where, deaf to the lorries, they curled up and went to sleep. Now and again, one would be run over, the carcass then thrown into the ditch to be picked over and disposed of by the hovering vultures.

One evening an agitated, demonstrating crowd gathered and swarmed shouting around the cookhouse. Inside lay Ayah's 13-year-old daughter who, some months previously, had left to get married but had just been carried back on a makeshift stretcher seriously ill. During the night Mother was awakened and taken to her and, when she came back, I heard her telling Father that the young girl had been assaulted, presumably by her husband, her face badly bruised and her left arm broken, and that she could actually see maggots crawling from between her legs. Three days later in great agony the girl died and, although the police were called, no action was taken.

Perhaps we were unfortunate in living in Bihar, notoriously the most crime-ridden and worst-administered province of British India, where, for example, to ensure that evidence in criminal cases was duly forthcoming on the day of trial, witnesses were habitually kept in gaol, some to linger there for years, some to be totally forgotten, and the police, in their zeal to obtain confessions, were known to have resorted at times to breaking the limbs of suspects and even on some occasions putting out their eyes.

My parents were not alone in the European railway community in despising and detesting Indians, showing no wish whatsoever to get to know them, never deigning to mix except at work and making not the slightest effort, as Father put it, 'to learn the lingo'. Mother always kept her distance, but on the footplate Father obviously got on well with his Indian crew of three.

About a mile away from our bungalow, on the western outskirts of the town, stood a white-towered Roman Catholic mission school, Asansol College, which was run by a community of Christian Brothers, mostly Irish with a few Anglo-Indian priests. Almost all the children of Europeans living on the debilitating Ganges' plain were sent away to school in the high hills, and later to Britain, but my parents wanted to keep me and my sister with them and, although we were Anglicans, albeit token, sent me as a dayboy to the college where, in a class of some 25, I was the only European. With their close-cropped hair and brilliant white cassocks neatly buttoned to the neck, the Brothers looked clean and efficient. On a golden waist belt they each carried a short, thick, black leather tawse, or strap, which was freely used to maintain a very strict discipline. Since it seemed less sharply painful than the more familiar cane, I did not feel as intimidated by it as the rest of my classmates and, foolishly showing this, soon fell foul of my form master, Brother Ignatius. Even-handedly he picked out his favourites and victims, and to his beatings my instinctive response was to refuse to learn. Anyway, I was so often absent through illness, incidentally soon becoming anaemic and taking on the appearance of a 'pale for-pyned ghost', that the brothers soon became sorry for me and mostly left me alone. Between illness and truancy I went to school less and less and no one, neither my parents nor the college, seemed to mind.

Whenever possible, early in the morning I used to play and wander round with Ayah's eldest son, Ram, who was about my own age and as thin as a stick with a shrill piping voice to match. Whenever possible we called on the grain *wallah*, who sat day and night at the nearby crossroads amid the surface roots of a large banyan tree, surrounded by sacks of cereals and nuts and trays of sweetmeats, able for a few pice to fill my trouser pockets with *gram*, a rough pulse normally fed to horses and providing a long, satisfying chew.

Although polluted by the bullocks which wallowed in the muddy shallows, we often swam in the man-made local tank or lake beside the *maidan*, around which Indian women and *dhobi* washermen were always clustered beating their washing on piles of flat stones. On the far side there was a constant procession of Indians, each carrying a little brass washing pot, making their way to defecate and bathe. Beyond that again lay the burning grounds for funeral pyres, where crowds of mourners stood around shaking bells and banging drums, the Muslims forever chanting '*Hosein, Hasan, Hosein, Hasan*'. In the distance lay a tangled, jungly wilderness, vivid in spring with 'flame of the forest' trees, on the edge of which the local women scavenged for firewood and where, with my Indian friends, I sometimes hunted the large, repulsive-looking, though harmless, green forest lizards, which we called 'bloodsuckers' because they had such erect, blood-red necks.

Warned to keep away from this area, we went there rarely, but one day Ram's pye dog, yapping loudly, rushed deep into the undergrowth only suddenly to go quiet. As we repeatedly called him the silence grew and, crossing a small stream, Ram shook his head at me, pointing to large pad marks in the sandy bed of the stream, slowly filling with water. As we listened there was a noise like a cough, then a piercing yelp. '*Juldi, jao*,' 'Quick, get out,' shouted Ram, and we both took to our heels, never to see the pye dog again.

In the hot and sultry afternoons my play area on the veranda became such an oven that I often sought refuge close by in the European Institute, which, on dust-covered shelves and tables, contained higgledy-piggledy a little-used collection of books. Most consisted of light romantic novels, but there were older, tattered leather-bound works, including memoirs and recollections of the British soldiers and civilians who had served on the North-West Frontier and in the high mountains around Afghanistan, some of whom, in the shadowy conflict with the Russians glorified in *The Great Game*, had become legendary. I remember tracing on the end maps Colonel James Kelly's heroic race in 1895 with a ragtag force across the snow-covered mountains to save a beleaguered British force in Chitral, and in another volume reading how in 1904 Francis Younghusband had pioneered his way across the Tibetan plateau, capturing the highest fortress in the world before entering the forbidden holy city of Lhasa. But it was the futile, sad fate of two British officers, Captain Arthur Conolly and Colonel Charles Stoddart, kept for months by the Emir of Bokhara in a deep, dry well there, filthy, lice-ridden and starving, ordered to dig their own graves before being beheaded, which really moved me and lingered longest in my memory.

Many years later, journeying by car across the northern Punjab, I came on a vast, forbidding, rock-strewn, tree-less, arid plain, which reached to the far horizon where a hill stood out, black and rugged, topped by a tall obelisk. Wondering what on earth in that empty quarter could have deserved such commemoration, I slowly made my way towards it and, in the fierce sun, disregarding the risk of snakes, climbed up a mass of boulders to the summit. There, amid the debris of a long since shattered stone plinth, I found and pieced together the broken fragments of a plaque on which was recorded the deaths in 1847 of two teenage British army lieutenants who had been caught and slaughtered by Sikh guerrillas, their bodies no doubt soon picked clean by the vultures and covered by the brown, swirling dust. Like Conolly and Stoddart they had presumably been on duty, but for what purpose so far from headquarters in that godforsaken deserted wasteland, passed my understanding.

To me these godlike heroic figures of *The Great Game*, 'whose shoulders held the sky suspended', belonged to another world, as remote as Nordic warriors in Valhalla. Why had they braved, endured and sacrificed so much to protect and expand an Indo-British raj, which, so far as I could see, was such a wretchedly dirty, impoverished and miserable place, its peoples seething with hostility? Their motives were as puzzling to me as my parents' presence in India. When asking about them at home, neither of my parents had the remotest idea what I was going on about; indeed, Father never missed a chance of making fun of the often hollow and absurd pomp and exaggerated ceremonial of the British governors in Delhi and Calcutta. He took a special pleasure one day in calling my attention to a newspaper photograph of the funeral cortège of a British general, on whose bier was displayed a white-plumed cocked hat, which he laughingly said must be 'emptier than ever'. But what really got his goat was the nationalist leader Mahatma Gandhi's encouragement of thousands of the National Congress followers to lie down on the railway tracks in order to bring the railway system to a standstill, while at the same time roundly condemning it as 'the evil and dangerous tool of imperialism' and making everyday use of the trains to spread his own gospel of nationalism.

In 1948, after Gandhi's assassination, he thought justice was finally done when it was announced that the Mahatma's ashes would have to be carried by train to their last resting place. And he always enjoyed telling how hundreds of white-capped Congress *wallah*s, trapped on a mile-long, rickety monsoon railway bridge over the swollen Ganges river, were clinging for dear life, some unsuccessfully, to the railway track sleepers and railings while his train remorselessly passed over and past them, his orders, for reasons of safety, forbidding him on bridges to bring his heavily loaded train to a halt. One of Father's friends reassured him with the thought that anyway the victims would have been happy to drown in Mother Ganges, the holy river.

My happiest hours were spent on the playing fields of the local *maidan*, fielding at the cricket nets and occasionally being allowed to bowl, where I caught the attention of the local sporting hero, Clarrie Turner, who captained Asansol's European hockey and cricket teams. An Anglo-Indian himself, one of a family of four brothers, all of whom had taken degrees at Calcutta University, he had become the manager of the local electricity generating station and took a leading part in running the Asansol European Institute's social programme, especially the popular Friday night film shows, the big social event of the week, which all the local Euro-

peans and Anglo-Indians religiously attended. Just above medium
height, very dark-skinned, almost black, with a flashing white
smile and infectious laugh, beautifully lithe and buoyant on his
feet and an absolute charmer, he was much sought after by the
ladies. I think he felt sorry for my family, becoming especially
fond of Mother who, no doubt bored with Father's frequent long
absences, adored his gaiety and extravagant attentions, and often
welcomed him to an afternoon siesta. Years later, in an unforeseeable, unforgettable way, he was to exert a decisive influence on
my life.

Against a background of increasing communal violence, rivalries
in football, cricket and hockey, some of them ugly, between the
competitive teams, European, Hindu and Muslim, often turned
into battles on the *maidan*. At one football final between the local
European and Muslim teams, several thousands of Indians gathered around the pitch, one side being reserved for the 200 or so
European spectators — men, women and children — including
ourselves. From the start feelings were tense and, as foul followed
foul, the crowd became rowdy, threatening to invade the pitch until, after a particularly vicious tackle in the far corner, a hail of
stones was thrown and the enraged Indians rushed forward, completely engulfing the players and the dozen or so khaki-uniformed
Indian police on duty. After a moment's hesitation, then seemingly
with one accord, the European men grabbed the upright steel
chairs on which their womenfolk had been sitting, and, from their
side of the pitch, charged the Indian mob, which promptly turned
tail and fled up the road into the bazaar.

Panic-stricken, Mother grabbed my small sister and myself and
hurried us home where she at once started to barricade the doors
and hunt for weapons; but all remained quiet, and that evening a
small group of Europeans called to reassure us that police
reinforcements had arrived and all was calm. Afterwards no one
mentioned the episode, nor was it reported in the papers.

Spurred by Gandhi's call for non-cooperation, animosity
towards Europeans, even among the servants, grew steadily, and
endemic terrorism in Bengal and Bihar flourished, with two
civilians in Calcutta being shot and a magistrate in Asansol
murdered. Prompted by his public denunciation of the railway

system as 'a source of evil' and a call for action, the terrorists, often referred to in the European press as the 'Irishmen of India', promised to bomb it out of existence. Protesters along the track took to stoning passing trains and, after suffering a serious eye injury, Father built a strong wire-meshed frame to protect his footplate, and was glad to have his locomotive fitted with a powerful searchlight to illumine the track ahead, and, as an added safeguard against the bombers, always to have a light engine running a mile in front of his express.

On the 300–400-mile stretch of line he normally covered, trains were often derailed by Bengali terrorists, killing and wounding hundreds of Indians and scores of Europeans. One dreadful night, while crossing a bridge just outside Asansol, a passenger train driven by one of Father's friends, Sandy Gregg, was blown up, Sandy being instantly killed by a steel bar which pierced his chest.

Nevertheless, from the moment his coolie box *wallah* called at the bungalow an hour or so before Father was due to report for duty, to collect the heavy teak *khana* box containing enough food and several changes of clothes for the next 24 hours, Father was impatient to get to work. He loved his engine, even more than his wife, and was proud to be part of a system he thought was the best thing the British had given India.

Almost always driving high-speed expresses, sometimes down line to Calcutta, but more often upcountry to Patna and Benares, and despite the terrorists, he managed on those long runs speeds well over 100 miles an hour. Much though he admired British railway engines — the four-cylinder GWR King class being his favourite — he was critical of their use on Indian tracks. Built to run on crowded, sharply curved and often steep English gradients, he thought they were too small and quite unsuited to pull the very long trains and enormous loads along the straight, level stretches of the north Indian plains. About as appropriate for their purpose, he used to say, as British-style democracy was for India. Engines often broke down far from the repair sheds, largely through the dreaded 'red-hot boxes' and the fusing of over-heated ball bearings in the wheels, which caused axles to collapse, but, unlike most of his colleagues and largely through his own foresight and ingenuity, he rarely suffered these failures.

On every run- he made use of lengths of rubber hoses to keep a constant flow of cold water from the tank pouring across the points of friction, and, for areas of greatest stress and heat, such as the smaller front-wheel 'bogies', he invented a constant oil-drip, consisting of a wooden peg with a spiralling groove filled with cotton waste to carry a slow, steady flow of oil on to the working parts.

Among his colleagues he gained a reputation for being the complete driver whose engine never broke down and, at their special request, ran courses of instruction on maintenance, which were so much appreciated that they presented him with a suitably inscribed gold watch-chain medallion, praising him as an instructor, which became his most prized possession and which, in his last illness just before dying, he gave me. While on leave, his company sent him to inspect their new locomotives then being built in the workshops in Newton-le-Willows in Lancashire, and, as an unaccustomed treat, took me with him so that I was able to drive one of those gleaming monsters backwards and forwards along the test track, steam, smoke and power surging out of every nook and cranny as I pulled levers, adjusted gauges and endlessly blew the whistle. Thrilling though all this was, I then realized that I had no wish to follow in his footsteps.

Although many times offered promotion, he always refused, well content to remain on the footplate; and, remarkably, for the heat and strain were excessive, he stayed on the job until he left India for good just before the outbreak of war in 1939. Regularly chosen to drive 'special' trains carrying VIPs, especially the viceroy and the governor of Bengal, who usually in transit took time to inspect the engine and thank the crew, he got to know some of these exalted personages quite well. On one long run across Bengal to Howrah, the viceroy, then Lord Linlithgow, and his two young sons joined him on the footplate, both boys to their delight being invited by Father to handle the controls. Many years later one of them, Lord Glendevon, who was then writing a study of his father's viceroyalty, later published under the title *The Viceroy at Bay*, invited me to help check its accuracy and was obviously quite startled, yet pleased, when I asked about that trip.

Understandably, Father showed not the slightest interest in

travelling for pleasure, so the family remained, winter and summer, in the debilitating climate of Asansol.

Vividly memorable, therefore, was the tour one December the newly appointed, enthusiastic local Anglican padre, Alfred Earl, organized for his troop of Boy Scouts, of which I was a junior member, to visit the legendary battlefields of the great Indian Mutiny of 1857. An evangelist by nature, he abhorred the Hindus' worship of their many gaudy gods and their treatment of outcasts, and I remember him assuring us that the Indian Buddhist salutation, the *Namaste*, with hands brought reverently together, much admired and copied by Europeans, had come into general use by caste Hindus because they wished to avoid contact with non-Hindus. In his eyes a peaceful, prosperous future for India depended on the maintenance of British rule, inspired by Christian teaching.

So far as I know, he made no Indian converts, which was not surprising, for the terrorists' campaign had virtually eliminated social intercourse between Indians and Europeans, except at work, and the European Christian community would no more have tolerated Indians in the church than in the European Institute.

Every inch the muscular Christian himself, he was never more completely in his element than when standing, immaculate in a new Scoutmaster's uniform, atop the 60-foot high walls of the Red Fort in Delhi, dramatically pointing to the exact place where the sepoy mutineers had first stormed in from their garrison at Meerut. In the midday sun he marched us across the scrub-covered ridge outside Delhi where the Europeans who survived the first wild onslaught of the mutineers took refuge, whence also the final savage, successful British attack to recapture the city was launched. We stood in turn in each of the Lahore, Kabul and Kashmir wall gates of Old Delhi while he reverently described how British heroes, notably the great John Nicolson, had sacrificed their lives in forcing entry, and, as he talked, got us to push our fingers deep into the old shot and shell holes still there in the crumbling brickwork.

We arrived by train at Agra in early dawn, the air cold, the sky ice blue, and across the white, rime-covered mud flats of the River Jumna we could see emerging from the rising mist the slender minarets of the Taj Mahal glinting in the morning sun. At Lucknow, the Union Jack, which Earl proudly reminded us was never lowered, drooped languidly over the shell-shattered ruins of the Residency, where the governor, Henry Lawrence, and his mixed garrison of British and sepoy troops had held the mutineers at bay for 87 days. We went into the room where he had been struck dead by a shell to read his simple epitaph, 'HENRY LAWRENCE, WHO TRIED TO DO HIS DUTY, MAY THE LORD HAVE MERCY ON HIS SOUL', and climbed the grass-covered trench mounds, looking down the dark well into which the mutineers had thrown their British victims — men, women and children, some dead, some still alive — and cooled our feet in the stretch of river where, despite the promise of safe conduct, the remainder of the besieged European garrison had treacherously been slaughtered. But in all his vividly rendered stories of desperate courage, the Reverend Earl never found place for the many Indian sepoys who gave their lives in defending British families, nor referred to the ferocity and wanton pillaging of the conquerors in finally suppressing the uprising.

Someone ought to have told him that the really deadly enemies of the British were not, as he appeared to believe, racial and religious hatred, but the diseases of fever, cholera, malaria and venereal infection, and that only 600 of the 9500 British soldiers who died in the great mutiny of 1857 were in fact killed in action. In his saga, the bravery of the warriors always took centre stage, not the endurance of the women, which really formed the true heroism. In our own sojourn in India, which went far to wrecking our family life, it was Mother who sacrificed, suffered and endured the most.

In recent years I have watched with mixed fascination and disbelief the frequent indulgent presentations on Western television and in the movies of what purports to have been the character and style of British life in India in the last decades of the raj. In this long-running, nostalgic, imperial melodrama, the British are invariably pictured in spacious, handsome bungalows set in wide expanses of well-watered green lawns, bordered by a profusion of colourful poinsettias, hibiscus and roses, all devotedly tended by immaculately clad Indian servants. While their menfolk are away on parade, or at district headquarters, or on the occasional foray up the Khyber keeping the empire secure for Britain, the *mem-sahib*s, usually garbed in elegant jodhpurs, pass the mornings riding horseback over verdant hills and the evenings at dinner in the club and dancing to dreamy, romantic music.

In adding in this manner one more false layer, one more refracting glass to the British perception of their forbears' experience in India, we further distort reality, for it is false to pretend that the much-vaunted 'jewel in the crown' of the imperial raj had ever formed a central or lasting or pleasing concern of the British public at home. It is wrong, too, especially after the terrible Amritsar massacre of 1919, to play down the racial hostility which repeatedly broke the bland, official crust. Where, too, in this picture is the British underclass, which, among other things, provided the rank-and-file soldiers and kept the trains running? Where are the broken families, the cesspits, the fevers and the populous graveyards with which my family became so familiar? As far back as Edmund Burke's day, the subject of India became the signal to empty the House of Commons and, even in the heyday of Queen Victoria's empire, the Duke of Wellington declared it was a place in which to look for honours and a fortune and otherwise to be quickly forgotten. When the long-delayed time to quit came in 1947 the British public gave a sigh of relief, soon making India, perhaps because it had formed the keystone, the focus of its sense of imperial guilt.

In our own life in Asansol, where for much of the year not a blade of grass was to be seen, I can recall little that was clean, or civilized, still less beautiful. Life was ugly, often brutal and unbearable. That my family should have stayed on was as puzzling to me as the British disinclination to quit. Although assured that it was the Indian civil service, 'the guardians', 'the heaven-born' from the cadre of district officers up to governors who were holding the raj together, dispensing even-handed justice and making life tolerably better for the Indian, I never actually saw any one of them, my only glimpse of any so-called upholders of the *pax Britannica* being a few bullying, *lathi*-wielding Indian police. Far from forming a 'steel frame', British rule and society were no more than a crust resting and sliding uneasily on the surface of India, yet no one in Asansol could have remained for one moment unaware of the constant, brooding presence of the tall, swaggering Marwari moneylenders, strolling around in pairs, always attended by a gang of 'minders', the *goonda*s, who, despite the British, really held in thrall the Indian town and country folk. But perhaps that overlarge *topi* of mine unduly blinkered me, and in any event it would be absurd to expect a callow youngster to get a good view, or even much of a view, from what was little more than a backyard, especially a backyard of empire.

2

The Struggle for a Schooling

None of us wanted to go back to Tranmere in Birkenhead, but, for want of better, that was where Mother, my sister and I landed up in the early winter of 1925, leaving Father behind in India. It was the grinding, insupportable burden of perpetual illness in Asansol and the belated realization that some regular schooling for my sister and myself had soon to be found, that broke Mother down and finally drove her back. In our absence, her family had dispersed; her father to his grave, her mother, who had gone blind, to an old people's home in Cheshire, her brother Ben and his wife, Millie, to join the rest of the family in Australia.

In a cold mist and drenching, incessant rain we trailed miserably round Tranmere looking for lodgings until an elderly, warm-hearted widow, living alone in a decrepit old house overlooking Mersey Park, took pity on us, finding room in the basement and giving us, too, a shared use of her own bathroom and kitchen.

A place was soon found for me at the local central school near Tranmere Rovers' football ground, but, after I had taken the entrance test, the headmaster summoned Mother to tell her that it was a great pity I had missed the 11-plus examination because, in his view, I was bright enough for a grammar school, mentioning also that a few fee-paying places were still available in a small, new school which was just opening in neighbouring Rock Ferry. But having spent rather a lot on the voyage home she could not afford this and at once turned for help, oddly enough, not to my father, but to our family friend and my sporting hero back in Asansol, Clarrie Turner, who promptly responded by promising to pay the annual fee of ten guineas for at least a year ahead and, into the bargain and out of the kindness of his heart, arranged to have a brand-new Raleigh bicycle sent to me on which to get to school.

Through the following couple of years I had to struggle to find my feet in this new grammar school in Rock Ferry, physically fit though evidently causing some concern because always looking so pale, and scholastically bumping along at the bottom of my class, far behind in most subjects, especially in Latin and French. However, term by term, perhaps bent on repaying Clarrie Turner's generosity, and bit by bit I made my way and, at 16, was able to achieve a creditable all-round result in the matriculation examination.

Gradually the family got settled, but just after Mother had put together the necessary £25 as a deposit for a mortgage on a semi-detached house on a new estate in the nearby suburb of Bebington, we suffered a crippling setback when Father in Asansol had to be rushed into hospital, desperately ill with cholera. For several months, hovering between life and death, his weight falling from 12 to 4 stones, he seemed certain to die but, to everyone's astonishment, including the doctor's, tenaciously held on and slowly clawed his way back to health. Although during this harrowing period, which lasted over a year, his firm continued to employ him, it was at first only on half then on quarter pay, so for 18 months Mother found herself with less than £2 a week and only by borrowing and renting out rooms was she able to keep going.

But we all paid a price. Lonely, frustrated and miserable, she became depressed and angry, continually writing to importune any prominent person whose name she happened to catch sight of in the daily paper, to local worthies like Lord Derby and Lord Leverhulme, and not hesitating to put her plight even to the prime minister and the Archbishop of Canterbury. Her moods swung bewilderingly from extreme to extreme. So far as I was concerned, there were times when she praised me to the skies, wearing me like a medal on her chest, and even going to endless trouble to get books for me from the Birkenhead public library, out of which she copied long extracts thinking to help my studies, at other times going to excessive lengths to humiliate me.

In the family's straitened circumstances, as soon as I had passed the matriculation examination I needed to get a paid job, which I succeeded in doing as a junior clerk in the accounts department of the Birkenhead town hall, but fortuitously my stay there was short-lived.

Closest among my classmates in school, and in some respects also my chief rival, was Alec Ramsay, fair-haired, tall and hefty in comparison with my shorter, compact Welsh stature. Cavalier in temperament, he got a lot of fun out of my more cautious, republican inclination and reactions, yet we remained good friends, so often together on the playing fields and in class as to be generally dubbed Jonathan and David.

I much envied Alec's secure, solidly middle-class background, especially admiring the *gravitas* of his father, who was a solicitor, and also Alec's razor-sharp mind and evident easy ability to excel in any school subject he chose. But beneath his effortless superiority lurked an indolent and wayward disposition, forming a constant source of exasperation to his serious-minded Presbyterian parents. To my embarrassment they often held me up as a worthy exemplar, going so far as to pay for me to accompany Alec on several school trips. When Mr Ramsay learnt that after matriculating I was leaving school and therefore would not be joining Alec in the sixth form, he called on Mother to persuade her to let me stay and then intervened successfully with the headmaster to offer a free school place for the next couple of years. For Mother this must have posed a difficult decision, perhaps eased by the fortunate, timely news of Father's recovery and return to full pay.

If the Ramsays hoped that my companionship would prove a lasting, steadying influence on Alec they must have been disappointed for, after achieving a brilliant result in the higher school certificate examination and winning a state scholarship, he apparently made little of his subsequent time at Cambridge University. As for me, I thanked my lucky stars, for, without the timely successive interventions of first Clarrie Turner and then Alec's father, I would not have been able to continue schooling to the age of 18, or to escape from our miserable home life.

Surprisingly, so far as I know, Clarrie never again attempted to make contact with us. Twenty-five years later, soon after the war had ended, by which time I had become a professor in the University of London and was making a first research visit to India, I made up my mind to try to see him again and, through the good offices of the firm he had once managed, discovered that he was still living not far from Asansol. With difficulty, finally managing to reach him by telephone, I found him strangely reluctant to meet, but by arranging an early morning break in my overnight rail journey from Delhi to Calcutta, finally persuaded him to join me briefly on Asansol railway station. At first sight I did not recognize him. Gone was the splendidly erect athletic figure, gone was the sporting hero of my youth; instead I saw a bent, grey-faced ghost of a man, hobbling with the aid of a stick, smoking and coughing persistently in the cool dusty air. As I took his hands I saw that they were gnarled and knotted with arthritis.

'How are your dad and sister?' he asked. 'Very well,' I assured him, hastening to add, 'And Mother, too.' 'But what about you?' I asked. 'I'm finished,' he replied. In silence we walked slowly up and down. Never asking what I was doing in India, he went on smoking and coughing, growing increasingly restive, constantly looking around towards the station entrance. Suddenly he drew himself up, offering a quick nostalgic glimpse of the man I once knew, and in a tone of finality said, 'I must go.' Unsteadily he moved off, slow as a tortoise, pausing to wave his stick before disappearing. By this time the sun was rising and a warm wind tugged at the station posters, fluttering some wastepaper caught on the telegraph wires and blowing fine dust in my face. Later from Calcutta I wrote but received no reply.

In the sixth form at school I at first found the relatively relaxed style of work much to my liking, allowing plenty of opportunity to read widely, but soon, with little clear guidance from over-stretched teachers, several of whom had never previously handled work at this level, I began to lose all sense of direction. Looking back it is easy to see that a school with fewer than 300 pupils in a poor Birkenhead district could never have hoped to create a strong sixth form or to provide disciplined teaching at that standard and in a wide range of subjects.

Although already having achieved examination results in the sciences and mathematics sound enough to justify continuing with them to the university entrance standard, I was advised to join Alec in committing myself to the arts' side, not fully realizing how decisive later this might prove in choosing a career. Although I never mentioned it at the time, I rather fancied becoming a doctor, perhaps even doing research on the human brain, so it came as a sober awakening later to realize that, without advanced study of the natural sciences, entrance to medical school was out of the question, even though in fact I could never have found the money for the long, five-year course. But few, if any, of the school's staff had any experience of sixth-form work, and several plainly regarded it as a soft option giving them time to catch up on other work.

Most of the instruction was pedestrian, with little or no attempt at giving personal tutoring, even though the class was extremely small. In history it amounted to little more than copying notes from the blackboard and learning by heart long passages from the routine textbooks, with no direction or encouragement to read any of the great or even well-known historians. Gibbon, Motley, Macaulay and even Trevelyan were never mentioned. The English master, Stanley Ellams, contented himself with exhorting us to continue reading ever more widely, yet giving little guidance, so I found myself puzzling over Bradley's exotic theories about the real meaning of Shakespeare's plays when I should have been studying the texts of the plays themselves. When at the end my disappointing examination result was queried, an external examiner commented that what I had written, though able, was irrelevant.

It was a bitter lesson I never forgot. From that day onwards, in dealing with any question, the practice of turning first to the basic original texts became a mark of my academic progress.

In none of our courses was there a hint that a good education should include some familiarity with the best in human character and achievement, some inspiring vision of greatness; and never once did the headmaster, R. J. Griffith, whose own academic field was said to be modern languages, find the time to pay us a visit, let alone give a lesson.

In my second and final year in the sixth form, election by the seniors as head boy unhappily involved regular meetings with the headmaster, who soon made it plain that he did not much like me. Somewhat incautiously, I got embroiled in what turned into vexatious tussles with him over, for example, his sudden, inexplicable, much-resented decision to abandon the periodic reporting to the assembled school of our hard-won, prized results in rugby, or, on another occasion, over his censorship of sketches Alec Ramsay and I had written for an end-of-term school party, some of which admittedly had made light-hearted fun of the staff.

Although a short, stocky, unimpressive figure, Griffith seemed to tower like a god. Forever slowly running his hand over his carefully coiffured iron-grey hair, he ostentatiously cultivated a modulated, suave and judicious manner, using his deep, melodious Welsh voice to enhance the effect, pausing often to indulge in a knowing, slowly expanding smile which revealed a row of gold-filled teeth. Dapper in dress, usually wearing a dotted bow tie with a matching silk handkerchief and, in winter, often appearing in light grey spats, carrying gloves of the same colour and flourishing, too, a black, silver-knobbed walking stick, he resembled a peacock strutting in a kitchen garden.

One of the masters, James Murray, who was sometimes given to exaggeration, later assured me that Griffith, in recruiting staff for his new school, had set out to confirm his own authority by deliberately picking second- and even third-raters, of whom he then cheerfully added, 'And I was one.' Be that as it may, what they may have lacked in academic distinction and intellectual presence, they made up for in enormous enthusiasm for team games and athletics, and exotic amateur theatricals, inculcating 'the stiff upper lip', exhorting us to 'play up and play the game' and always to put the interests of the team and school first. In my complete agreement and satisfaction with these activities, and compared with the uncertainties and miseries of life at home, my school became the enjoyable centre and haven of my life. But there was nothing there to reconcile the ideals that were preached with my growing awareness that in fact self-interest and material satisfaction were what seemed to drive most people. For me this long remained an unresolved dilemma, adding to my general sense of insecurity.

In his role as headmaster, while always making great play of his close ties with the school's governors, some of whom were also town councillors, he showed little interest in the future of his boys, making no attempt to provide information on openings in higher education or in careers generally. Stanley Ellams, a former graduate of Selwyn College, Cambridge, urged me to try for a scholarship there but, in my total ignorance of possibilities, it looked too daunting a prospect and, anyway, I could see no way of finding the money for the railway fare or lodgings. I was told that the best way of making sure of a university place was to win one of the very small number of national state scholarships, but the headmaster was adamant, no doubt rightly, that if so, I must remain in the sixth form for three rather than the customary two years, which was out of the question.

Looking back, it is easy to see that growing up as part of a relatively poor community, which was slipping deeper into economic recession, and at school conditioned to keep our place and accept our lot in life, we were encouraged to develop an unassertive, unambitious outlook and to be grateful for the smallest of mercies. In Britain we inherited a political, economic and constitutional tradition based on practices of hierarchy and undue deference. If any of the better things in life were to come my way, if there was to be any beckoning future, I knew that it would only be through personal austerity and hard work; and, perhaps naïvely, I clung to the belief that with goodwill and application all obstacles could be overcome.

Now, unhappily, even the good memories of school are soiled. Some ten years or so after the war, as a distinguished old boy, I was invited back by the then headmaster to speak at my old school. In the interval it had several times metamorphosed before becoming a mixed comprehensive. Although the two original, attractive, grey-stoned buildings still stood out, they had been cluttered by an array of cheap, prefabricated huts, their windows and walls plastered with posters. Much of the surrounding woodland had gone and the once neat paths had been reduced to stretches of pure mud, and the remaining area defaced by coke tins, broken glass and empty crisp packets. At the assembly, which I had come to address, an unwilling crowd of boys and girls

31

slowly drifted in, shouting, talking and fooling, followed by a sheepish trickle of parents. In the absence of chairs all stood around in groups. Gone was the civilized sense of discipline and order I remembered. Gone were the dark suits, white shirts and neat ties of yesteryear; they were replaced by crumpled anoraks and scruffy jeans. Putting aside my obviously irrelevant prepared speech, I chatted casually for a few minutes, for good measure throwing in a few stories and jokes, and then, feeling like an alien from another world, made my escape as soon as I decently could.

Earlier, when strolling around with the headmaster, I had found myself by some mischance in the basement of Ravenswood, one of the two original buildings, where astonishingly in an abandoned room there still remained the small history museum, which 30 years previously Alec Ramsay and I had lovingly collected and displayed. The whole assemblage stood quite undisturbed by war and time. Still discernible were the once white replica of the Taj Mahal, the scenes of Wellington and Napoleon at Waterloo, a sketch of Gladstone and Disraeli in debate, but all now covered in layers of dirt and festooned by a musty tangle of cobwebs. These were the dust and ashes of my school and my youth.

In confusion about my own future, both at school and at home, I learnt from a chance visitor from the University of Liverpool that I might get a place there by applying to the Department of Education for a teacher training bursary, which would cover the fees for a first degree course provided I still continued to live at home. I duly applied and, achieving the required result in the higher school certificate examination, including a distinction in history, was able to join the history school of that university in October 1931.

Contrary to expectations, I was living by that time not at home, as anticipated, but in digs in Liverpool, for, as soon as my place at the university was assured, Mother decided once again to sell up our home and, taking my sister with her, to return to India to rejoin Father. Within a year, however, not finding Asansol any more enjoyable or salubrious than previously, she hurriedly returned, so that we came together again, this time in a two-roomed, rented flat, which we were lucky to find over a news-agent's corner shop in the suburb of Bebington.

Although I had found life in lodgings near Sefton Park in Liverpool highly instructive, at times hilarious, for most of my fellow boarders were travelling salesmen, replete with racy stories and unbelievably exotic, sexy experiences, it had hardly proved a congenial setting in which to pursue systematic academic study. In that first year my only memorable achievement was to win a place in the university's rugby three-quarter line alongside the famous centres, Heaton and Leyland, both then playing for England, but it was short-lived for, hard put to find the travelling expenses for the obligatory twice-weekly fixtures, I had to pull out. Luxuriating, too, in the liberal atmosphere of the university, I over-indulged in joining every available university society, never missing a chance of a party or a dance, and giving such cursory attention to lectures and tutorials as in the third term to be abruptly called to account by the tolerant head of the History Department, Professor George Veitch, who simply warned me, 'Work or get out.'

Mother's return therefore coincided with a crisis in my academic fortunes; and because she came back penniless, at once plunged us into a nightmare of overwhelming debt, marked by weekly, itemized calculations and a gruelling stocktaking of what she owed, always ending with the despairing cry, 'What am I to do?' Making things worse, on the voyages to India and her unhappy sojourn there, she had discovered how to drown her sorrows, also gradually taking her into a private world, spending more and more time in bed so that she rarely attempted to get up until late in the day.

In the difficult year that followed I managed in my spare time to earn some money by part-time gardening and house-painting in Rock Ferry, and enjoyed a stroke of fortune in landing a lucrative assignment to produce an anonymous weekly article on university affairs for the reputable *Liverpool Daily Post*, for each of which I received a princely £5. By talking around I soon discovered rich seams of semi-confidential information on topics that were about to appear on the university's agendas, such as hush-hush proposals to rebuild the students' union and to create a new university library. But after several coups of this kind, innocuous though they really were, the vice chancellor, Sir Hector Hetherington, and the pugnacious, legendary registrar, Stanley Rumbold, who seemed to run the university, let it be publicly known that the author, if a student and if discovered, would at once be sent down.

This posed a risk I dared not run and, to my regret, brought my lucrative journalistic career to an abrupt close.

Lack of money dominated my life. I was receiving from the teacher training grant £24 a year, which I shared with Mother, so all I possessed for my own general expenses was £1 a month, about a shilling a weekday, half of which I needed for the daily bus fare and cross-Mersey ferry to Liverpool; and the remaining sixpence for a sandwich and a bun for lunch in Reece's café or, when the weather turned cold, a plate of hot chips in the union refectory. At the start of one awful, unforgettable month I somehow lost my pound note.

From this disaster and exactingly austere regimen, I was rescued by a young woman fresher with the delectable name of Dorcas Rose, whom I had met in preparing an entertainment for the History Society. A budding comic actress, who had already starred in the winning cast in a national drama festival at Blackpool, she was playing in two sketches I had written for the occasion. With a beautifully articulated, sweet voice, a finely moulded head held erect on a slender neck, moving with the grace of a dancer, she captivated me; and in rehearsing together over several weeks we fell in love. It was the best thing that ever happened to me; and vivid still is the memory of our first tentative kiss on the dark balcony of the old brown-tiled Victoria Hall, before running hand in hand, elated and breathless, right down Brownlow Hill, past the olive oil and wine cellars and across the town to Pier Head.

Realizing how hard-pressed I was for money, she prepared every day a packet of sandwiches to share for lunch, thus discreetly contriving for me some financial margin. That this did not extend to provide holidays or entertainment hardly mattered while we could enjoy together, close at hand, the bright-yellow gorse-covered heaths and long sandy beaches of the Wirral coast, and the occasional sixpenny seat on the benches in the gods at the Liverpool Playhouse, where Diana Wynyard and the Wyndham Goldies then reigned supreme.

And as we got to know each other better I grew to admire her sense of fun and honesty of purpose, her dedication in running Saturday play groups in Toynbee Hall for poor children; and her buoyant, courageous spirit, which never failed to lift me when I felt down. She was my first girl, bringing loving kindness into my life and, through thick and thin, through the strains of war and peace, and the rest of her life, she so remained. In that first wonderful year together, the most carefree of my life, we truly found 'the riches of heaven's pavement'. But no silver lining lacks its cloud. With the laconic comment, 'You makes your bed!' Father distanced himself and, from the start, Mother so bitterly resented my love for Dorcas, in effect deliberately creating and fomenting an open, suppurating sore, which, whatever we did, never healed, not even with the passage of time, not even 40 years later when she lay on her deathbed.

Spurred no doubt by romantic excitement I began at last to find my academic feet, winning the Bishop Chavasse Prize medal for the best performance in Part 1 of the history honours examination and gaining the much-desired privilege in the third and final year of presenting a dissertation on a subject of my own choice. This suited me down to the ground because by this time I was becoming aware that a career as a professional historian might well lie within my reach. As a student I sat admiringly at the feet of Dr May McKisack, a forthright, demanding tutor in medieval studies, and of Dr G. C. Allen in modern economic history, both of whom I was to meet again later as professorial colleagues in London, the former in her lectures first setting up a clear target then, like a machine gun, hitting it remorselessly and repeatedly, the latter in a relaxed, quiet style, raising question after question, posing theory against theory in reaching balanced, yet always tentative conclusions. But most impressive and appealing to me were the carefully structured analyses of George Veitch, the head of the department, an unprepossessing, lumbering, lovable bear of a man, always dressed in suits too large for him. He was a surprisingly effective teacher, admirably marshalling his material, relieved by a rich vein of humour, to bring alive his own researches into the struggle for English parliamentary reform in the late eighteenth century. At the end of each term Veitch and his wife, who were childless, invited the students to a party at his house, making us feel we were part of his family, winning my affection and inspiring me to follow in his footsteps.

In one of his lectures he happened to mention the extent to

which personal fortunes made abroad in the West Indies and India, notably in the latter, for instance, by Robert Clive, were later used to purchase seats in the unreformed House of Commons, which, in the light of my Indian background, at once appealed to me as a suitable topic for my proposed dissertation. Enough published material for the purpose lay readily to hand in the Liverpool libraries, but I soon discovered that the richest stores were to be found in the manuscript archives of the British Museum and India Office Library in London, and fired by Veitch's own extensive, profitable use of first-hand manuscript sources, I was able, using prize money won in the Royal Empire Society's essay competition, to spend ten blissful days working there. It was thrilling to handle and read the original letters of the great Robert Clive, Warren Hastings, William Pitt, the prime minister, and to trace their relationships and use of patronage in the management of politics. In those few days I gained the inspiration and impetus to try to equip myself as a historian.

But to gain the chance to do this, it was essential for me to achieve nothing less than a clear, first-class degree in the final examination, which fortunately, with hard work, came my way, bringing, too, the invaluable bonus of an award of the Gladstone research fellowship of £100 for each of two years, which I was free to use at a university of my own choice.

First, however, there was the need to fulfil my obligation to undergo formal training as a teacher, which among other duties required me to spend six weeks in an elementary school situated as it happened in that poverty-stricken Scotland Road area of Liverpool, which as a young boy I had once visited with my father. In the intervening years it seemed that little had changed; groups of unemployed men in overalls still clustered on street corners and around every pub, women in black shawls gossiped in doorways and dirty, raucous children raced through the streets. Under an experienced teacher, Charlie Cook, who enjoyed the distinction of holding a first-class honours degree in physics from the University of Manchester, I worked with a class of forty 11-year-old boys, lively, undisciplined and cheeky, barely kept down by Cook's free use of the cane. Cuts and bruises on their faces, arms and legs indicated what a rough, street life they led; and only one or two had footwear, although Cook told me they received each month a free issue of boots, which, within a few days, were usually and promptly pawned by the parents.

Holding their attention for about ten minutes, or at most fifteen, was about as much as I could manage, and if Cook happened to leave the classroom, they soon got out of hand, jumping up and down and, in frenzied unison, shouting and banging their desktops. I was mortified to discover that without a cane there was little or nothing I could do to control them. It was in fact enough to survive.

One morning a young woman teacher in the adjoining classroom began to scream piercingly and, although Cook did his best to quieten her, even slapping her face, nothing sufficed to stop her. Ultimately, the headmaster arrived, promptly dispatching me for a glass of water, which I held out for her to drink, only to be pushed aside by the head who grabbed the glass and dashed the contents into her face. This, too, had little effect, and she was led away, her screams echoing down the corridors. Meanwhile the boys in the classroom rampaged wildly, delighted with what they obviously regarded as a triumph. She never returned.

Cook, who must have been an agnostic, got rid of some of his frustration on the mainly Irish Catholic boys by poking a lot of fun at formal religion, usually in stories he told and acted so well as to capture their interest. With a rich store of anecdotes about the papacy, one of his favourite openings was to announce, 'I'll tell you a story about a pope', which always produced an instant, unaccustomed silence. One day, for example, he related the incident in which the medieval Pope Gregory ordered Kaiser Heinrich to do penance by walking barefoot in midwinter across the Alpine passes to appear before him at Canossa. Falling on his knees before the class, much to the boys' delight, Cook then described Heinrich's plight, wearing soaking wet sackcloth coated in ashes, knee-deep in snow, feet bleeding, as he bowed his head in obeisance. Pausing dramatically, raising his arms, Cook then asked, 'And what was going through Heinrich's mind?' At the back of the class, a skinny arm went up and a thin, fluted voice piped out, 'Keep yer pecker up, 'Enry.' It was a precept tailor-made for that school.

By this time I had ascertained that the most suitable place at which to pursue the research that was beginning to take shape in my mind would be the London School of Oriental Studies, a constituent college of the University of London, but knowing that my fellowship would scarcely cover fees and upkeep there I sought and obtained a loan of £30 to be repaid within three years from the Cheshire County Council, despite my former headmaster's refusal to support my application, and then had the good fortune to land a job in the evenings for a fee of £30 pounds with the Workers' Educational Association in Rock Ferry to give a course of 12 lectures on international affairs.

Through the following cold winter in the unheated classroom of a local elementary school, situated in the shadow of Cammell Laird's shipyards, I lectured to a group of about 30 local workers, some of whom came with their wives. Mostly middle-aged, grey and grizzled, neatly and soberly dressed, wearing cloth caps, and the women in dark, woollen shawls, one and all showed a passionate interest in the subject, especially the couple whose son was then fighting for the republicans in Spain, and another whose brother had been wounded there. Although they took for granted that both sides in the Spanish civil war were committing appalling atrocities, it seemed to make not one jot of difference to their belief in the superior virtues and ultimate victory of the communists and the anticipated triumph of communism worldwide. I could not but admire the quiet, tolerant confidence they showed in speaking of subjects, most recently the general strike of 1926 in Britain, of which they had such bitter, personal experience. In the face of their experience I felt inadequate, ignorant of life and humble. They seemed to appreciate my book learning and were tickled pink when I persuaded the editor of the local *Birkenhead News* to publish a summary of the weekly lecture along with their attributed comments in discussion.

One incident in particular at my expense gave enormous pleasure. Being invited to a public dinner by the mayor of Birkenhead, I warned that in the following week I would be turning up in a black tie and dinner jacket. On the night they duly paid exaggerated deference to my hired outfit 'You're like the proverbial colonial officer,' one said, 'keeping up appearances in the jungle.'

Halfway through my lecture, a grey-haired, dark-suited stranger entered and quietly took his place at the back. At the close I had to leave promptly for the dinner, only in the following week to be greeted by the class with the news that the stranger had turned out to be the local WEA inspector, whom afterwards they had apparently tried to convince that it was my invariable habit to turn up dressed like that; but we never enjoyed the pleasure of seeing his report.

The excitement and sense of achievement engendered by this course and the active, vivid response of the class did much to restore my morale as a teacher, so recently and rudely shaken; from this time onwards I knew that I would be happy facing the challenges of teaching; I now understood that it required both hard work and high artistry to interpret and vitalize the minds and spirits of students and to engage and retain their interest in a common pursuit for understanding, and even a small measure of success proved exhilarating and deeply satisfying. Many years later, in conversation with a famous prima donna when the subject of the art of teaching happened to crop up, I ventured the teasing, but somewhat incautious, comment that teaching had claims to be the greatest of the arts and that the demands on the lecturer, who has both to prepare and deliver a lecture, could well be greater than those on the singer, for example, who simply interprets, however movingly, what someone else has composed. I added that it was ironical to compare the customary few seconds of polite applause, which usually follows a lecture, however gifted, with the prolonged, rapturous clapping and repeated laudatory encores and bouquets of flowers which concert goers habitually confer, getting some quiet amusement from her indignant, almost horrified rejection of what she obviously regarded as heresy.

In the following summer, soon after I had applied to the London School of Oriental Studies,* I happened by chance in Liverpool to run into Dr May McKisack, one of my Liverpool tutors, who, enquiring about future plans, urged me not to rule out Cambridge or Oxford and gave me an introduction to Dr J. R. M. Butler,

---

* On the initiative of Lord Hailey, then chairman of Governors, it became the School of Oriental and African Studies in 1938.

senior tutor of Trinity College, whose published work on the Reform Act of 1832 I knew and respected. So, on my journey south, I made a special detour to Cambridge, only to learn from Butler that he could think of no suitable specialist there to act as supervisor, and anyway that little relevant material on my subject was in fact held in the Cambridge libraries. Gathering, too, that the position was not all that different at Oxford, I went directly to the school in Finsbury Square, London, where I found a warm welcome, discovering however, to my astonishment, that I was the first and only British student registering for a degree in British-Indian history. At a period when the keystone of the British empire, the acclaimed raj, had come to be seen and was widely lauded as the 'jewel in the crown', I found it incredible, though no doubt revealing of the nature of empire, that the three premier British universities had been and were still paying so little attention to the study of the dependent Indian peoples. As for myself, it made me wonder whether I was wandering into an academic cul-de-sac.

At the school I was at once taken in hand by the formidable, acidulous Henry Dodwell, the only professor of history there, who had previously served as curator of the Madras Records Office, where he had first made his name with a study of the early English and French combatants in India, Dupleix and Clive, fortified subsequently at the school by his role in editing the two modern volumes of the new, definitive *Cambridge History of India*. From conversation in the college I soon gathered that, although widely respected for his scholarship, he was deeply disliked by colleagues in the same field for his uniformly scathing and dismissive criticisms of their work, and feared as an inveterate controversialist and opponent with a mind as unyielding, sharp and cutting as a diamond.

Working side by side under him, my two fellow research students, both of whom were Indians, also obviously went in fear and not without good reason, for he treated all of us with contemptuous discourtesy. Once a fortnight he brought us together in a seminar, never announcing the subject beforehand, but at the start of each occasion picking on one of us to introduce some topic, selected by himself, making it obvious that he was ready to take over from the unprepared and usually hesitant speaker; and with obvious relish he would then proceed to display his own undoubtedly cogent powers as a lecturer. Every sentence he uttered had the character and carried the force of a precise examination question, the cumulative effect battering us into silent submission.

The study of Oriental subjects in Britain owed much to the German philological tradition of teaching and scholarship in which each professor and head of department arrogated, and was afforded excessive deference by, his chosen circle of *dozenten*. A tradition of unrelenting, unpleasant, often personal controversy had also carried over, and Dodwell and his peers at the school indulged themselves to the full. I recall in a corridor coming across him and Dr Vesey-Fitzgerald, the red-faced professor of Indian law, engaged eyeball to eyeball in a shouting match over the validity of the charges brought against Warren Hastings on his impeachment in 1788; and on another occasion I witnessed at lunch a poisonously bitter dispute with the director, Sir Denison Ross, over the attribution of a quotation in Thackeray's novel *Vanity Fair*. They reminded me of strident cocks crowing and strutting on their own middens.

However, my personal feelings towards Dodwell soon became ambivalent because, although overbearing, he was obviously delighted after many years to have at last attracted a British student. Also, when he gathered that I was hard pressed for money, without another word he promptly persuaded the school to give me a gift of £30; following that, in my second year, with the offer of an assistant lectureship in Indian history for three years at the princely salary of £250. Excited not only by the thought that with continued application a university career now lay within my reach but also that with Dorcas I could contemplate the prospect of getting married within a year or two, we were walking on air. But there was a cautionary postscript to this euphoria, for, when the imminence of war with Nazi Germany led me in due course to tell him that I was proposing to get married, he stared in astonishment, as if seeing me clearly for the first time, before exclaiming, 'Good God!' and never referred to the subject again.

Although in size small with an academic staff of just over 30, the school, since its establishment in 1917, had attracted a nucleus of highly gifted scholars with established international reputations — mostly self-absorbed specialists whom it was difficult to get to know. They must have formed the biggest single bunch of eccentrics in Europe. Besides the director, Sir Edward Denison Ross, remarkable for the facility with which he was able to pick up a speaking knowledge of any language, this group included the reclusive Harold Bailey, born in the Australian outback and, perhaps for that reason, without a single word of small talk, now deeply versed in the early languages of central Asia, H. A. R. Gibb, the foremost European Arabist of the day, Ralph Turner, a Sanskritist and outstanding lexicographer of the Indo-Aryan languages, and Lloyd James, a phonetician, famous as a contemporary 'Professor Higgins', who was then engaged in training BBC announcers in King's English. Always audible throughout the school was the harsh voice of Vladimir Minorsky who, while serving in the tsar's consular service, had escaped from the clutches of the Bolsheviks and who, whenever we met, treated me like a fellow conspirator, again and again warning me against the director, whom he said was 'mean and treacherous'. More intriguing was a younger man, Dr Heyworth Dunne, an Arabist, who entertained me alone at dinner in a large luxurious house in Hampstead, where he apparently lived, surrounded by silver Islamic metalwork, blue Persian vases and a truly impressive library. On close acquaintance I found him disturbing, for he kept wanting to touch me and his eyes were a strange murky colour, difficult to identify, rather like a stagnant pond under a dark grey sky, deep set in a smooth glazed face. From his habit of clicking his heels and from his square-shaped head and *en brosse* hairstyle he appeared to me the very model of a traditional German, a Junker. Later I even began to wonder whether he was a spy, for on the eve of war he disappeared from London, turning up briefly in Cairo only to disappear again, this time, so far as I know, permanently. More approachable by far were two charming, gifted, warm-hearted, middle-aged women, both of whom took a motherly interest in me — Professor Eve Edwards, a sinologist, plump and jolly, and Dr Ida Ward, meagre and sharp as a sparrow, who in her own work was breaking new ground in creating alphabets and grammars for some of the lesser, still unwritten, West African languages. Also on the staff, but remotely ensconced on an island home in a Scottish loch, was the sinologist Sir Reginald Johnston, best known as the tutor to the last emperor of China, who, after his appointment as professor, to my knowledge, never once set foot in the school, though to make amends, when he died he bequeathed his private library to the school, much of which was found to consist of erotica.

Several newly arrived apprehensive Jewish fugitives from Nazi Germany added to the school's exotic, esoteric character, notably Walter Simon and Walter Henning, both passionate scholars and both still struggling to learn English. The latter became a good friend. I found his work especially intriguing because his own special area of study was the Sogdian language of central Asia, of which apparently only some hundreds of words were known. He lost his temper over my amusement at his translation of one manuscript fragment which appeared in an issue of the school's journal as 'the clouds scudding across the sky', only to be discreetly amended in the next as 'dropping the frogs' legs into the cauldron'.

On the odd day out I went walking with the teacher in Sanskrit, one C. A. Rylands — I never found out his Christian names — whose consuming interest lay in the study of the wild flowers mentioned in ancient Indian texts. Always dark-suited and dressed as if for the office, he yet never wore socks and always kept his trousers pulled right up so that his bamboo-thin legs stood out like white sticks. With a long sharp nose pointing to the ground and a stilted habit when walking of raising his knees high, he was the image of a black stork. On being told one day that I had been injured in a bad fall out of an apple tree, Rylands paused, deep in thought, before enquiring, 'Did he say what sort of an apple tree?'

Finding it necessary for my own research to acquire a reading knowledge of Marathi, an important language of western India, I sought out the lecturer in the subject, Miss Hester Lambert. Middle-aged, with grey hair pulled tightly into a sober bun over a deeply lined face from which all vitality had long since been squeezed by the combined ravages of the Indian sun and her unrequited struggle to convert the heathen, she accepted me, her only student, as a soul ripe for rescue. She always used a narrow table, so that we sat face to face, eyeball to eyeball, and, as I soon found, she had a fixation about eyes. No more than five minutes into the first lesson, she suddenly declared, 'Time for cupping!' Startled because coming from so unlikely a source, this injunction at first seemed somewhat improper; I then learnt that it was her invariable practice every five minutes to pause and cover the eyes by hand in order to rest them. For the student, too, this was apparently obligatory, so in this staccato manner the lessons stuttered on and, although I have long since lost my Marathi, I have never forgotten the cupping.

A large circular walnut table in the small senior common room, where lunch was served daily, provided a social forum for the staff and gave me an opportunity of getting a little closer to these academic giants, especially Denison Ross, the director, although in my first acquaintance with him I got off completely on the wrong foot. Ross happened to mention casually in discussion that he was eager to get hold of a novel, *The Well of Loneliness*, by Mrs Radclyffe Hall. Knowing nothing of the book I yet remembered seeing that morning in Foyle's in Charing Cross Road on my way to lunch a full window display of the book, vivid in a bright green jacket. I therefore promised to get him a copy and straightaway went back to Foyle's only to find that the display had been completely cleared, the book apparently having just become the subject of a law case. My face must have fallen because, as I turned away, a young salesman sidled up and whispered that if I badly wanted a copy he would secretly get me one for £5, which he duly did that evening. The following morning therefore I proudly handed in the volume to Ross's office, but perhaps because, as I later discovered, it dealt with the subject of homosexuality he never acknowledged it, nor did I get my fiver back.

Ross, who out of doors affected a black, voluminous velour hat and swung a malacca cane, wore brightly coloured shirts, silk ties and handkerchiefs, and suits with exaggeratedly square shoulders, giving him a rakish look. He was something of a socialite and social climber, attracted to those at the top like iron filings to a magnet, and regularly holding, for example, a coffee morning at the school for each season's débutantes. With his disproportionately large head, short pear-shaped stumpy body and very small pointed feet, he struck me as the likely original for Fougasse's famous cartoon figure in *Punch*. One day, for no apparent reason, he took me on one side whispering, 'You know I am really a big man with big ideas struggling to get out of a small body.' My supervisor, Dodwell, who had been a rival for top jobs in India, hated Ross, dismissing him as 'a pompous little ass' whom he alleged had found fame and a knighthood by cultivating Lord Curzon, especially by singing at viceregal parties in his light contralto voice accompanied by his wife at the piano. Before he retired from the school Ross commissioned a bust of himself cast in bronze, copies of which he distributed to select institutions like the British Museum and the Royal Asiatic Society, but years later I still found a few left over in the school's cellars. Under him the school languished, its annual income of around £40,000 scarcely changing through his 20 years' reign; and I was not surprised that on being offered the British ambassadorship in Turkey he went off saying, 'At long last I've got a worthwhile job.'

The very small number of students at the school, for the most part serious-minded aspiring Asians, mainly Indians, were more often that not treated by the staff as second-class citizens, not even enjoying a students' union, though occasionally we arranged tea parties at which I was glad to meet two other young English students who later made their mark as internationally recognized scholars, Nancy Lambton in Persian, and Bernard Lewis in Near Eastern history. Efforts I made to arrange student gatherings and to form a union were actively discouraged, especially by the professor of Burmese, J. A. Stewart, a close friend of the director, who, perhaps still living his years as an official in Burma, said he would get the union banned as 'destructive and subversive'.

One of these occasions brought me into confrontation with Ralph Turner himself, who in 1937 had succeeded Ross as director. Since one of the burning political issues of the day was the future of Palestine and there were a number of Jews and Arabs from that area at the school, I had organized a gathering of students to debate the question, inviting two of them, Abbas Eban (later Israel's foreign minister) and Al Husseini (nephew of the grand *mufti* of Jerusalem), to open the proceedings. Just before the start of the meeting Turner summoned me and, in tones of mixed anger and anxiety, told me at once to cancel the meeting, warning, 'If you proceed, be it on your own head.' A packed meeting in fact enjoyed a brilliant and memorable occasion, the case for each side being so admirably put that we decided at the close that no vote could adequately or fairly reflect so complex a matter. We then went our separate ways in the same sensible, calm, informative and uplifting manner in which the debate had proceeded.

Husseini later came to a notorious end, for soon after the war began, after achieving a creditable degree in history at the school, he escaped the clutches of the British security services to make his way through Eire to join Lord Haw-Haw's team of Nazi broadcasters in Berlin, and, when that city fell to the Russians, escaped again to the Near East where he was later executed for the part he was alleged to have played in the assassination of the king of Jordan.

Single-minded in pursuing my own work, I concentrated my weekly teaching into two days in order to spend the rest of the time preparing my thesis, which I proposed to complete within three years. Although strenuous, this regimen was rewarding, for the archives of the East India Company, which I was studying in the India Office in Charles Street and in the Western manuscript division of the British Museum, offered a unique treasure house of evidence on the experience of the British in Asia, and in delving ever more deeply into them I enjoyed the most fruitful, satisfying years of my life as a scholar.

Situated on the top floor of the India Office overlooking St James's Park in a beautifully proportioned yet book-cluttered room, with in winter a glorious coal fire burning in the large fireplace at one end, I was able to make myself so much at home that, in the absence of professional library staff, and usually attended only by a lowly messenger, Greenway, who although lacking formal educational qualifications of any kind, from long service knew the collections intimately, I was able to roam and read at will among the archives themselves.

At lunch I was often joined by two fellow research students, both Indians — melancholy, lovable and sweetly austere Pratul Gupta, who later became vice chancellor of the Tagore University at Santiniketan, and older bustling Suray Kumar Bhuyan, who returned to his backward province of Assam to create an Institute of Historical Research. They both became lifelong friends. But more often than not I was the only reader in the library, my loneliness assuaged by the anticipation of a fortnightly Sunday railway excursion trip from Euston to Liverpool, costing only ten shillings, to spend the day with Dorcas, who by this time was teaching in Liverpool, devotedly saving every penny towards our marriage and in her spare time typing the draft chapters of my thesis.

On these journeys I sometimes found myself in the same compartment as a race gang from Camden Town; it included several retired jockeys who always played poker and I was soon roped in as stakeholder and adjudicator. Once aware that I was going to see my fiancée, they made it their business to instruct me in what they obviously regarded as my incomplete sex education. Drawing largely on their experience of horses, they lectured me on how to consummate the marriage, but I must confess that their advice, which included all kinds of odd manoeuvres and postures, seemed more calculated to lead to marital conflict than conception. In return they much liked my true story of a medical research team in a small town in the American Midwest that set out to establish the correlation, if any, between male circumcision and cancer of the cervix in women. After questioning some of the wives about the penile status of their husbands, one of the team became uneasy at some of the findings and went back to check, only to discover that a high percentage of the women originally questioned had only the haziest notion of the meaning of circumcision, some assuming that it meant sterilization, some even that it involved total amputation, which he maintained accounted for their initial, often inexplicably exaggerated, hysterical responses.

On the return journey I always caught the overnight milk train, arriving at Euston at about 5.00 a.m., thence making my way in the cool morning air by the first early tram up Highgate Hill and on foot to my lodgings in Muswell Hill, where I snatched a couple of hours' sleep before going into town for a 9.00 a.m. lecture at the college and getting ready to plunge back into research.

In choosing a field of research I had to bear in mind that there were still no departments or posts in British universities offering a career specifically in Indian history, and that appointments in British imperial history, which offered the only other direct route into my field of choice, were still few in number. Moreover, the entrée scholars like Henry Dodwell and Ralph Turner, for example, had enjoyed through an early career in the Indian education service was no longer open to British candidates. I therefore had to make sure of finding a topic which, while maintaining interest in India, would at the same time keep open the door into English or European history, in which fields far more job prospects existed.

In fact, virtually by chance in having picked as the subject of my undergraduate dissertation the role of the newly rich so-called 'nabobs' in returning from India and buying their way into the unreformed British parliament, I had already found an appropriate field. I therefore decided to continue within the broad sweep of English parliamentary history to investigate the subject of Indian politics in London in the period at the close of the eighteenth and start of the nineteenth centuries when British dominion in India was growing most rapidly.

While still struggling to find my feet on the lower rungs of the historians' ladder, I set out to exploit this material in competing for national essay prizes, soon winning a welcome cheque from the Royal Empire Society and also the highly coveted Alexander Prize medal of the Royal Historical Society, the latter carrying with it the daunting privilege of reading my paper to the assembly of fellows of the society. In the discussion, which by custom followed the lecture, the lead was taken by two of Britain's leading historians, Professor Richard Pares of Oxford and Professor (later Dame) Lillian Penson of London, who had come to prominence for her work in both imperial and modern diplomatic history and who, for the rest of her life, included me among the group of young scholars on whom she kept a benevolent, encouraging eye. Marvelling at the way she mobilized fact and argument in debate, and at her total dedication to her responsibilities, I sat at her feet eager to learn and with growing affection and admiration as she moved from one senior appointment to another, culminating in her election in 1948 as vice chancellor of the University of London, the first woman to achieve this eminence in Britain and the commonwealth.

Later, as she approached retirement, regret that she had for many years given second place to her own historical research began to dominate her thoughts, particularly that she had failed to produce the definitive study of Lord Salisbury's foreign policy on which she had long set her mind. It was therefore no surprise that, when invited to give the university's annual prestigious Creighton history lecture, she chose that as her subject. But as the realization grew that the years the locusts had devoured could not be recovered, to my growing dismay, late at night for weeks on end, she telephoned me, pouring out her often tearful woes and sense of frustration at the gulf which had opened between the book she had hoped to write and the lecture she was actually able to produce. On the eve of the occasion, suffering a massive stroke from which she never recovered, she reached a sad, tragic end.

Some time later, discussing the subject of such sad demises with James Callaghan, the former prime minister who, referring to his own recent retirement, told me *en passant* that he was thinking of writing his memoirs, I commented on the frequency with which political memoirs, Winston Churchill's being a good case in point, seemed to reach a close not 'in fire but in dust and ashes'. I casually asked what he regarded as his own greatest achievement in office, what he expected to be best remembered for? 'Cats' eyes,' he said, 'Cats' eyes in the roads. I was minister of transport when they were introduced.'

In the summer of my third year of research, by a herculean effort often involving a working day of 16 hours, I duly managed to complete and present my thesis for examination, being then called to the customary viva voce before an academically appropriate, yet formidably daunting, examining board consisting of Professor (later Sir) Lewis Namier, Professor Lillian Penson and my formal supervisor, Professor Dodwell. None of them were in the habit of taking criticism or opposition lightly and from the start I got the unsettling impression that they were already at loggerheads. Namier started by revealing that he had put to work on my thesis a group of his own research students at Manchester in checking the minutely detailed information I had compiled on East India membership of the House of Commons, and then proceeded to take me laboriously through one relatively minor error after another, only after about ten minutes to be sharply pulled up by Professor Penson complaining that he had long since made his point.

As they went on bickering I sat back helpless, yet lucky in that temporarily they seemed to have forgotten me. At one point, to illustrate his argument, Namier cited a piece of eighteenth-century doggerel, immediately being challenged on its accuracy by Dodwell; and, although acutely aware that in fact both had got it wrong, I felt it prudent to stay silent, although, had they thought to ask, I would have been delighted to give the correct version which ran:

> When Macreth served in Arthur's crew
> And said to Rumbold 'Black my shoe'
> His quiet reply was 'Yea, Bob'.
> But when returned from India's strand
> And grown too proud to brook command
> His stern reply was 'Na-Bob'.

Bad-tempered and cantankerous to the end, the viva altogether lasted for nearly three hours, their catalogue of criticism leaving me exhausted.

When finally dismissed I hung about the corridor outside, assuming that one or other in leaving, perhaps my supervisor, would give me some inkling of the outcome, but, obviously preoccupied, all three swept past without a word.

I feared the worst. Moreover, the long summer vacation had already started and in the weeks that followed, receiving not a word from either Dodwell or the university, I felt it necessary to turn my mind actively to the question of looking for an alternative career, perhaps in educational administration. But just before the start of the new session I received news from the university Senate House that I had passed, followed by a note of congratulation from Dodwell and a letter from Namier asking whether I would be interested in having my thesis published in Macmillan's Modern History Series, of which he was the general editor; and, if so, inviting me to call on him in Museum Street where apparently, in his capacity as secretary of the Palestine Agency, he had an office. Since at that time it was difficult to get any research thesis published, and quite impossible without a subvention, which I could not provide, I leapt at the chance.

Elated, but with some trepidation, I therefore duly presented myself at what I found was not so much an office as a large, barely furnished room containing no more than a white deal table and a couple of upright wooden chairs. No one appeared and for 20 minutes I sat twiddling my thumbs wondering why Namier, whose books on the structure of politics tended to discount the influence of political ideas, should devote so much of his own time to Zionism. Suddenly the great man himself, a burly untidy figure with a face that was all nose and jowls on a head like a boulder on a hilltop, marched through the doorway waving aloft a newspaper cutting which he threw on the table before me, bellowing in his rough, guttural Polish voice, 'If you want to know how to write, read this,' before at once lumbering out again. Dutifully I read the article, which was in fact the turnover piece from that morning's *Manchester Guardian*, written by him on the worsening Sudeten Czech crisis. A few minutes later he came back, impatiently pushing aside the article before telling me that he wanted my thesis completely rewritten for publication, with a broader, more popular title like *The East India Company*, and curtly dismissing my plea that the precise subject was in fact *Indian Politics in London*, which personally I thought would make a better title. Although I resented his boorish, overbearing behaviour, he was after all the Pied Piper calling the tune, so I acquiesced submissively, but ever afterwards, partly because of his habit of signing his correspondence in bold, very large and crudely printed letters, L. B. NAMIER, I always thought of him as 'L. Bloody Namier'!

By the following Easter, having duly rewritten the text, though in the process having to render the style even denser and not altogether to my liking, I was able to parcel up the typescript and, with loving care and high hope, dispatch it to the publishers, then, with a sigh of relief, depart with Dorcas to the high hills for a couple of days' walking in the Lake District. Unbelievably, on our return, lying on the front doormat, apparently unopened, was the identical brown paper parcel and, with it, a brief letter from

Macmillan's signed by Harold Macmillan (the later prime minister) saying that, arising from a dispute on general policy, Namier had resigned as editor and that to their regret my book could not therefore be published by them. However, Namier stood by his word and through his intercession got Manchester University Press to take the book. Some months later it duly appeared, as it happened in the same fateful week in which all eyes were fixed on the British army's evacuation from Dunkirk. Reflecting at that juncture that four years' work seemed likely to sink without trace, I got a tiny drop of comfort from the thought that copies of the book probably stood a better chance of surviving the war than we did.

My personal relations with Lewis Namier, resumed after the war, seemed doomed to remain brittle. After I was demobilized, he took it for granted that I would edit the volume on the eighteenth century in his projected, massive history of Members of Parliament; when I declined on the grounds that in my new job I was necessarily turning actively to Indian history proper, he became offensively petulant. Some years later it fell to my lot as host to welcome him when he came to the University of London to deliver the annual Creighton history lecture and to lead him on to the platform; but in mounting the steps he accidentally dropped his bundle of notes and, surprisingly and foolishly for a man of his experience, started to speak without reordering them, in the process completely losing his way and his confidence; he therefore ended up giving a lamentably confused, disappointing performance. I do not think that he deserved the extraordinarily high reputation as a great historian that some accorded him in his lifetime, for although displaying in his studies of politics and parties in the parliaments of the eighteenth century a mastery of detailed analysis and demonstrating the rich pickings to be found in primary manuscript sources, he lacked that sweep of narrative, that sense of scope and span which I believe the truly great historians have displayed. Personally he was a boor and a bully.

While my book was being printed I suffered a short period of anguished doubt, precipitated by a warning from one of my colleagues in London, Dr W. P. Morrell of Birkbeck College, who had asked to read the typescript. Commenting at some length, he expressed concern that, if published in its existing form, it might well bring my academic career to an abrupt close. In particular, he had in mind my two chapters (with which in fact I was particularly pleased) that scrutinized in detail the early diplomatic performance, in their capacity as presidents of the India Board, of the two later famous foreign secretaries, Lord Castlereagh and George Canning. In their respective well-known magisterial studies of these foreign secretaryships, the two celebrated historians Professor Sir Charles Webster of London and Professor Harold Temperley of Cambridge had each included introductory general pieces describing the previous roles of these statesmen as presidents of the India Board, in the process understandably committing a number of minor errors of detail. However, to a young, ardent and ambitious researcher trying to make his mark, this seemed too good an opportunity to miss, so I revelled in putting these established writers straight, turning my footnotes, as Morrell vividly remarked, into 'a bloody battlefield'. 'If you publish this as it stands', he concluded, 'they will destroy you, and Temperley in particular, who is an inveterate hater, will see to it that you never again get an academic post.'

Taken aback by this sudden, unexpected, unwelcome glimpse of the dark underside of academe, I wavered for some days before deciding to stick to my criticisms while toning down the gleeful manner in which I had pounced on what after all were minor mistakes. But I need not have worried, because on publication Charles Webster, whom I found to be a kindly, magnanimous man, could not have been warmer in his praise, and fate seemingly took my hand, for Harold Temperley happened to die just before the book appeared.

3

Waiting for the Call-up

While I was single-mindedly getting my book ready for publication, the subject dominating everybody's thoughts was whether, in the face of Hitler's policy of aggression in central Europe, war could any longer be avoided. Crisis followed crisis and by September 1938, certain that war was imminent and that widespread, devastating bombing of our cities would follow, Dorcas and I made up our minds at once to bring forward our projected marriage. While people queued for gas masks in the streets outside, we solemnly took our vows in the vast, empty church of St John's, Wallasey, accompanied only by Dorcas's parents and by my Mother, who at the last minute was with difficulty persuaded to come. Father was still in India.

Afterwards, by stages taking one bus after another, we made for the Lake District, spending our wedding night at Kendal and going on next day to Buttermere. No sooner had we arrived than the news broke of the prime minister's dash to Munich and triumphant claim of 'peace with honour'; and, although under no illusion about its real meaning, we selfishly blessed him for having won what for us was a precious breathing space. At once we made our way back to London, soon finding in Muswell Hill a cheap, tiny flat on the seventh and top floor of a high-rise block, and while Dorcas rendered it habitable, I got on with my book.

Although already a qualified and experienced teacher, she was barred as a married woman from employment in London's schools and, since I still remained on a small fixed salary and temporary contract, it was urgently necessary to get on with the book as a means of ensuring if possible the chance of a longer-term contract.

Under the mounting ferocity of Hitler's threats the world wilted, while we stayed closeted and at work in the quiet of the flat, on the rare evening using a cheap 'privilege ticket' to visit the theatre and at weekends walking for exercise on Hampstead Heath. Maintaining this apparently humdrum existence, we in fact enjoyed an *annus mirabilis*, an unforgettably wonderful year in simply being and working together. We tasted 'the fullness of joy'.

No sooner had the typescript been handed to the publishers than the simmering quarrel about Danzig between Germany and Poland boiled over into war. At the time it was midway through the university's summer vacation and, not having heard a word about the school's plans, I went down to Victoria where it was temporarily housed in a run-down former Salvation Army hostel. The building seemed deserted, but wandering around I came on the director, Ralph Turner, sitting beside the school's secretary on a bench in a corridor, ashen and disoriented, staring at the floor, seemingly unable or unwilling to tell me what the school proposed to do. On the following day, therefore, I went again, astounded this time to find the whole place closed and a typed notice on the front door stating that the school had moved to Christ's College, Cambridge. As I walked away the disconcerting thought crossed my mind that the whole place could well fold up and disappear overnight.

Dorcas and I now faced the dilemma that we were still committed to a three-year lease on the London flat, which in its elevated, exposed and relatively inaccessible position would be untenable in the event of bombing. Trying and failing to make contact with the school in Cambridge, we decided to take an early morning train there to look for cheap lodgings, discovering at Cambridge station that bicycles could be hired, and spending the rest of the day peddling round the town's outskirts and local villages.

Eventually, by the late afternoon in what became a hot, sultry day, we found in the village of Milton on the northern edge near the fens a small, semidetached, brown-brick house that was to let for a rent of no more than ten shillings a week, and there and then, locating the landlord in the village, we took it. Two days later, piling our belongings from the London flat into a hired van, we got into the cab alongside the driver and made off to the house in Milton, which for the rest of the war was to remain our home.

Somehow discovering that I was now on the spot and readily available, the school suddenly came to life and asked me to start looking for lodgings for the hundred or so students who were shortly expected to follow from London. For the rest of that first term, in addition to my own teaching and research, I acted as a lodgings and welfare officer. Nearly all the students were from Asia and therefore likely soon to return home, so, in anticipation of an early call-up into the services, I asked the director for a testimonial. I was somewhat dashed to receive in response a one-sentence reply simply attesting that he 'had always found Dr C. H. Philips to be thorough and punctual', which I thought unlikely to get me very far.

Some months previously, in response to a general call from government, I had put my name and qualifications on the central register for war service, so I thought it was timely to send off a reminder, but the winter months slowly passed without reply and in my spare hours I started a diary.

Milton Village,
Cambridgeshire
6 May 1940

Words offer a hostage to fortune and there is no predicting what our fate in this war will be, but since my aim is to become an historian it would be remiss not to leave some trace of what we are going through, some prints in the sands of time. But memory is like an ancient map, here and there exact and clear, yet fuzzy in places with many an empty quarter where 'there be dragons'.

In recent months, while totally absorbed with my book, our convictions about the world outside have been turned upside down, so we need to think again about how it has got into its present mess.

Dorcas is busy digging in her first-ever garden, where wall-flowers, peas, carrots and potatoes are now growing. We have only just got settled in this little house, so were startled today to get a letter from the college, giving no reason, asking whether we wish to return to London. As if in reply, she has just called me to see a blackbird's nest with four spotted blue eggs in the hedge at the bottom of the garden. This small village of Milton of about 300 to 400 people, looks as run-down, cluttered, dusty and decayed as an old attic, presumably given a place on the map by virtue of the local sewage farm, though our house, like most in the village, has no sanitation, not even a cesspit.

✳ ✳ ✳

That the Nazis have just invaded Norway is puzzling unless they mean to attack the Low Countries. The fog of war has descended on the British attempt to forestall them and, not possessing a wireless set, we have already learnt that there is no hard news unless all the newspaper placards carry identical headlines.

Newly married, we personally had blessed Chamberlain and his government for giving us a 'year of peace', though it was scarcely with 'honour', but he has made poor use of it and, along with his close colleagues, Hoare, Simon and Zetland, begins to look like a blinkered timeserver. By comparison, Churchill appears fitted and destined to make war terrible to the enemy, yet appoints a diehard like Amery to the India Office, where he is unlikely to make any gesture, even of dominion status, which would surely be enough to rally India's nationalists to our side.

German attacks on Holland and Belgium have begun. Evidently they have learnt the lessons of their strategic mistakes in 1914, so doubtless this time they will make not for Paris but the Channel.

✳ ✳ ✳

Blue skies and light breezes prevail, and the garden, warmed by the hot sun, is rampant. Life in Cambridge is attractive and comfortable beyond anything we've ever known. The River Cam beguiles, smooth, green and cool, crowded daily with punts in which young women students lazily recline and their young men strive to demonstrate their virility. The war seems far away.

In the mornings I teach at the college or work in the main library, always with an awful, empty feeling of uselessness. Dorcas and I have qualified as first-aiders in St John's Ambulance courses and have offered to join an air-raid precaution group, but perhaps because of our age been politely put off.

15 May 1940
Only now are we beginning to appreciate the scale of the military threat the Germans pose to us and our world. In the 1914–18 war they proved outstanding as soldiers, their weaponry equally so, and, while seemingly losing none of their strategic sense, military skill and power, have acquired a new ferocity. In Poland they have used their air force to blast holes in the enemy's defences and deeply infiltrate through the gaps, causing the Poles to retreat along all fronts and so get mopped up. Britain's survival now seems to depend on the morale and tenacity of the French army.

16 May 1940
As one French military disaster after another is reported, thousands of soldiers and civilians, their morale destroyed, take flight across France in panic and disorder. Mere onlookers, we feel guilty and conscience-stricken, but Dorcas reminds me that when Jane Austen was told that thousands had been killed and wounded in the Battle of Waterloo in 1815, she shrugged it off, saying, 'Thank God I don't know any of them.'

21 May 1940
In the past 12 months our fanciful dreams of conscientious objection have faded. In this massive clash of nations and moralities, in total war we have to rebel or conform totally. There is no escape and, in the face of the barbaric beliefs and actions of the Nazis, how can we stand aside? The German army has taken Brussels but it is the drive on Paris and the Channel which directly threatens us. Will they now swing from Sedan to the coast? Brilliant sunshine foments our agony. The French seem unlikely to recover from the loss of their Maginot line and the British army today stands back to the Channel. Digging last night after dark in the back garden, my neighbour, a bricklayer, called out, 'We must

make the best of a bad job. But it'll be all right in the end, you'll see!' But what on earth is that except an irrational conviction that staunch optimism will take us through to victory? Even if Britain survives, the British empire, lacking moral legitimacy, will never withstand the shock of this war. Britain can never be the same again.

Paradoxically, in this crisis Parliament has just passed a Development and Welfare Act to promote economic and social welfare in the British colonies, even following the Russians in envisaging five-year development plans. Magnificent no doubt as a gesture of intent, but perfectly reflecting its muddled way of carrying on, for, despite our long experience in India, we have never yet created a training and study centre to establish how development is to be brought about in poor countries whose resources are scarce.

22 May 1940

In the senior common room it has taken these military disasters to bring old enemies together, all talking in hushed tones, looking at each other for reassurance. Today, I tried to comfort Wartski, the gentle, desolated Jewish lecturer in Hebrew, who is visibly trembling at the victorious approach of the Nazis. On the battle map in *The Times* newspaper, we took comfort in boldly moving armies about and reversing the threatening, dreadful black arrows, gradually gaining courage, becoming ebullient, planning successful counter-offensives, smiling and nodding to each other.

24 May 1940

The Germans have reached the Channel, marking the end of an epoch for Britain. George Eliot was right in thinking that the happiest nations have no history. What would defeat really mean? The loss of the fleet; an army of occupation; persecution of the Jews; closure of the universities; young men, including me, transported to labour camps?

26 May 1940

Britain is too small an area to allow sustained guerrilla warfare, which may be the only ultimate response left to us. With uncannily apt timing, I was today called to register under the

Military Service Act, happening there to fall in with a former fellow student at Liverpool, one Cockroft who, round-shouldered and pale-faced, peering through thick spectacles, was shuffling along splayfooted, no more promising a soldier than I.

27 May 1940

So my first book is about to be published! If we do not survive this war perhaps this book will. In fine weather I'm finding it a struggle to go on working, especially while the students, ignoring the war, are out on the river hell bent on enjoyment.

Facing the threat of defeat, the government has at long last announced measures to increase war production, and fully to mobilize the country. Britain's immediate future no doubt now depends on the number of planes we can keep in the air and on the pilots we can train in the next few months. Today, frantically hanging on the news, we have finally bought a small wireless set.

2 June 1940

At all crossroads around Cambridge, soldiers are digging trenches and stringing lines of barbed wire, and overnight some innocuous-looking buildings have acquired military guards. However, the university authorities' cancellation of May week appears to be causing much more of a local stir!

5 June 1940

My book arrived this morning, resplendent in a shining cover of black and gold, representing five strenuous years of effort, and neither Dorcas, who typed and retyped, worked at the index and strengthened the argument, nor myself, have spared ourselves. As I turn the pages it all seems irrelevant against the background of war. But perhaps as an honest attempt simply to find out and to describe what happened in the past, and doing so in a spirit of objective tolerance, it can stand as our modest symbol of intent, our tiny gesture of defiance. As a contribution to history proper I have shown how through the East India Company in London and Asia the City of London's moneyed interests consolidated their role as an international financial centre in supporting the growth of empire.

6 June 1940

First thing this morning, on entering Christ's College, I was staggered to see the grassy, normally inviolate quadrangle covered with sprawling, sleeping bodies of soldiers in various states of undress, many without boots, their equipment lying scattered. Here and there some were sitting, unshaven, filthy, their eyes empty and staring. Ominously there was hardly a weapon to be seen. This is without doubt a defeated army; and at the sight I went cold, shivering with pity and fear, certain we had lost the war. I wonder whether, in due course, they will get a Dunkirk medal; or, like those who fought in the Dardanelles in the First World War, be denied on the veto of King George V who reportedly said, 'We do not issue medals for retreats'?

26 June 1940

France has been conquered and an ominous silence hangs over the fate of its fleet. Here all militarily untrained men, including me at present, enter the services in the ranks, except resident students under the age of 25, who may directly enter officers' training units. After registering for military service the other day I was for some reason called back for a second interview before a board of two complacent gentlemen — one a bland, cherubic, chortling, middle-aged clergyman, bald-pated with a wispy fringe of white hair and a shining gold cross on his chest, who kept looking upwards as if calling in aid the Lord God; the other, much older, a don, peering through thick spectacles, puffing clouds of cigar smoke at me, once only exploding into incomprehensible speech before subsiding into a mumble. Scarcely asking me a question, and that only to check my name, the parson said they had recalled me to say they would recommend me for a commission. I can't imagine anyone taking any serious notice of them.

30 July 1940

As if in reaction to our overwhelming defeat in France, our newspapers seek refuge in and are much put about by minor domestic scandals and abuses at home. There are to be special war bonuses for miners, civil servants and teachers, implying that the wages of workers in industries are always to be raised *pari passu* with inflation. Are sacrifices not to be shared? Are the troops and their dependants also to get similar treatment, or are they, as in the First World War, to be the donkeys? How far does the implication of 'total' war extend? Surely, the freedom of all, troops and home front alike, is at stake?

31 July 1940

Siegfried Sassoon and C. E. Montague some time ago told us how the hopes and idealism of the citizen army of 1915 gave way in trench warfare to tedium, disillusion and despair. And this time? If we do manage to hold firm in the breach and save ourselves, if the great majority engage in war fully, sacrificing equally, sharing equally in any gains, we might emerge as a more homogeneous society, making perhaps not a Utopia but a country in which most of us will be conscious of seeking and hoping to achieve a better national life. If only the government would define some priorities for a fairer, better society and seek to create a more acceptable economic equilibrium between rich and poor, employers and employees. Such attempts are always likely to be precarious; but at least we might aim at some 'golden mean', to be achieved pragmatically and not through ideology or inflexible conviction, or by accepting 'isms' or extremes of religion.

> Distant alike from each to neither lean,
> But ever keep the happy Golden Mean.

13 August 1940

Big air battles are developing over the Channel, no doubt marking Germany's attempt in daytime to destroy our forward fighter aerodromes and communications. If it succeeds, invasion will surely follow. Our coalition government still seems hesitant to use the comprehensive powers it has taken, the Ministry of Supply, for instance, resting content with appeals for employers to sell their machine tools to the nation. A government minister used the phrase 'democratic compulsion' the other day in Parliament, which we interpret as meaning 'Do as you please!' The newspapers have reported that small savers in current national savings certificates have contributed some £139 million, but the 'better off' are evidently not much attracted by war loans at a mere 2.5 per cent interest, and have produced no more than £143 million since the war began.

20 August 1940
When registering yesterday for military service the clerk's first question to me was 'Standard of education?', to which I answered 'University'. 'No, no,' he interrupted crossly, 'Elementary, secondary or public?' He then passed me to 'The Major', whose first question was 'Are you a public school man?' When I said 'No', he again scanned my registration form, frowning and murmuring 'University lecturer'; and thereafter, throughout the short interview, kept on asserting, 'You're a difficult case,' several times asking, 'A university man, you say?' I replied, 'Liverpool and London', which caused his frown to deepen. London he could just about accept, but Liverpool seemed beyond his ken. At last, as if plucking up courage, he challenged me, 'Why haven't you volunteered for any service?' and when I said that I had applied to RAF intelligence, his face cleared and he immediately dispatched me to see his RAF counterpart. But the latter, just as promptly, sent me back saying that my volunteering lay outside his remit. On returning I found the army office deserted, everyone having departed for tea, leaving on the table the file containing all my papers; and for 15 minutes I stood contemplating it, much tempted to take it and walk off.

When the major got back, swallowing his obvious irritation at my return, he said he could recommend me for 'clerical staff, special duties', but when I asked what 'special duties' meant, he seemed baffled, and repeated 'You're a difficult case,' then brightening up, as if with a stroke of inspiration, added 'Of course, there's always the military police.' It was obviously my cue to depart and as I was leaving he called encouragingly, 'You wouldn't have to handle men or even a rifle!' If I'd had a rifle I'd cheerfully have shot him.

24 August 1940
Dover is being shelled from across the Channel and air raids have

begun to reach London, though whether these early attacks have succeeded in putting our forward aerodromes out of action is not yet clear.

29 August 1940

Our personal lethargy and obsession with the war have been dispersed in a bicycle outing with Professor Harold Bailey, a former colleague at the school and now a fellow of Queens' College here, and specialist in the little-known languages of central Asia. He rarely talks, hardly says a word, but has a devouring passion for work and for riding his bicycle. He seems to ignore the war.

When I began to organize the History Society at the school before the war I invited him to give a lecture on central Asia, fully expecting some contemporary insight into Russian policy there. The students eagerly packed the lecture room to hear him. Happening in the first minute to refer to the region of 'Khorassan', he promptly turned to write the word down in the top left-hand corner of the large blackboard, and for the next 20 minutes or so, quite oblivious of his audience, absorbedly and remorselessly covered the whole board with line after line of etymologies, quite incomprehensible to everyone except himself. When he had used up all available space he paused as if frustrated then turned round, smiling, completely unselfconscious, optimistically asking, 'Now where was I?' Then he stunned us with another 40 minutes of etymologies, after which no one had the courage or strength to ask a single question.

Dinner at Queens' after the bicycle ride provided a new experience. Seven of us sat at table, smoothly served with a plentiful, not very well cooked meal, everyone seemingly at ease with much small talk and feeble attempts at light humour. Bailey made not the slightest effort to join in, nor did he do so when we adjourned for coffee and port. Conversation among the rest was kept going artificially, not at all intellectual in character, dominated by apprehension about looming food and staff scarcities and bombing and machine-gunning. I played my part, but felt uneasy and claustrophobic to be among so introverted, self-satisfied a gathering, and was glad to get away. It was not my milieu.

30 August 1940
Air raid alarms sound in Cambridge and no bombs drop; bombs drop very near us but no alarm sounds.

2 September 1940
Last spring, as part of my study of British experience in India, I started some research into the extraordinary life of David Scott who, as a young man and free trader at the end of the eighteenth century, made and lost several fortunes in Bombay before returning to London and becoming chairman of the greatest monopoly in the world, the East India Company. He entered parliament and became chief adviser on India to Henry Dundas and the prime minister, William Pitt. Discovering that many of his letters were preserved in the John Rylands Library at Manchester, I applied to the university for a small grant to pay a visit.

To my surprise, this produced a gift of £30, so I asked the War Office for a short postponement of perhaps three or four weeks in my call-up, on which I was promptly summoned to put my case to a board meeting in Trinity College.

Gathered in the anteroom were a dozen others, several accompanied by legal representatives. I was the first to be called before the board, which consisted of three elderly gentlemen, the chairman in the middle, broad-shouldered, wearing a rough brown tweed suit and purple shirt with, oddly enough, a polka dot bow tie, revelling in his role. On one side sat a plump, pink-faced member, fiddling endlessly with a pair of spectacles, and on the other side a shrimp of a man apparently fast asleep. As soon as my appeal statement was read out, the chairman in a loud voice, no doubt intended to wake up his neighbour, waved me out declaring that my case was outside their remit. The sleeping member awoke with a start. As I rose to leave, picking up from the table the copy of my book on the East India Company, which I had brought with me, the chairman, perhaps regretting his abruptness, put out his hand for the book and, on seeing the title, beamed with pleasure, saying, 'I went to school at their old college, Hertford, now Haileybury.' At this we all smiled and the chairman for the next several minutes got absorbed in leafing his way through the volume. Without another question or comment I was asked to retire and a few minutes later the clerk came out to say the post-ponement had been granted.

4 September 1940
Reviews of my *East India Company* begin to appear, those in the *English Historical Review* and the *Times Literary Supplement* being especially fulsome, the latter in bold headlines and double column praising it as a definitive, final study, which would never need to be done again. This morning, too, personal notes of congratulation arrive from the director of the school and from Professor Dodwell.

11 September 1940
In daytime air battles are taking place over London. Does this mean that the Germans have changed their evident strategy of seeking control of the Channel and our forward aerodromes, and if so have we won the first battle of Britain?

Last night there was heavy bombing accompanied by wide-spread fires in London. German barges are gathering in the French Channel ports, so we move to a crisis in our fortunes, especially with our fighter forces nearing exhaustion. Belated attempts round Cambridge are being made to cover all open fields with concrete blocks to deter paratroop landings, but, alas, the supply has run out. It is reported that the St Mellons Golf Club has adapted its rules to suit the circumstances: 'A ball moved by enemy action may be replaced ... a ball lying in a crater may be dropped ... a player whose stroke is affected by the simultaneous explosion of a bomb, or by machine-gun fire, may play another ball ... penalty, one stroke.'

14 September 1940
The German bombing of Buckingham Palace is condemned by the press as a 'deliberate, dastardly act'. Fortunately around here the German bombers seem to be less accurate.

17 September 1940
Hourly we await invasion. Everyone we meet asserts that the Germans will be annihilated if they attempt to land, but oddly,

Churchill's advice that 'each one should take one' doesn't seem to have much appeal or carry conviction. The garden fork, my only weapon, scarcely encourages me to give effect to Warren Hastings's precept that 'The only way to wage war is to make it terrible to the enemy.'

Our spirits are temporarily lifted by congratulatory letters on my book from Professor Lewis Namier and P. E. Roberts, senior tutor of Worcester College, Oxford, who, seemingly dismissing the war, asks about my next book.

20 September 1940
Future generations will marvel at Britain's loss of nerve between these two great wars and the precipitate nature of her political and economic decline. The appalling extent of losses during the First World War took more out of us than anyone realized, not least in spirit and confidence. The sort of political leadership implicit in Chamberlain's 'Peace in our time', 'Peace with honour' and 'Hitler missed the bus' is mirrored in the Labour opposition's retreat into its own cloud-cuckoo-land. As for the mass of people, perhaps Trotsky is right in asserting that 'they are but the packhorse of history'. Will this British packhorse, if it survives the war, be blessed with worthier leaders in peace?

21 September 1940
Tonight our Milky Way glows in the heavens, apparently forming only one of ten billion galaxies in the universe, and our sun just one of 300 billion stars. James Jeans in *The Mysterious Universe* says that more celestial bodies exist than there are grains of sand on the seashores of the world. And the biologists tell us that when mankind has had its day, the ants will inherit the earth!

25 September 1940
Bombs on Cambridge last night but little damage. Our air force seems to be holding its own, both over the Channel and the south.

26 September 1940
Arising from another application six weeks ago I was summoned for interview by the Air Ministry at Adastral House in Kingsway,

so Dorcas and I went to London by cycle and train, daunted on the way by the many signs of bomb damage. Nearing King's Cross we heard an air-raid warning, but all was clear by the time we arrived. Everywhere uniforms abounded. Failing to find a place for lunch we wandered around Holborn and down Kingsway, suddenly startled by an air-raid warning and the speed at which the streets emptied. On the roofs air-raid wardens, little Jim Crows, blew whistles and shouted. An enormous racket of anti-aircraft fire deafened us as, in the sky immediately above, two flights of enemy bombers in formation roared across, shells bursting around them. Abruptly the firing ceased and three British fighters streaked over. Finding we were outside Adastral House, I showed the guard my interview letter and we were allowed inside, at once caught in a confused rush downstairs and carried into the basement shelter. We settled on a wooden bench, soon being joined by an elderly man in an outsize RAF uniform who was mulling over a file labelled 'secret and confidential', which, by craning my neck, I could see contained a list of British aerodromes.

After half an hour the all-clear sounded and I found my own way up several flights of stairs and along a corridor to the interview. Two officers in RAF uniform awaited me, one puffing clouds of smoke from a pipe, the other immediately shouting 'What are you doing here?' A confused conversation followed, brought to an abrupt end with a blunt, 'You are too young for us!' Nonplussed because I was there at their invitation and had no idea what job, if any, we were talking about or whether there were any age limits, I gave some details of my qualifications, on which they showed renewed interest, opening a discussion which lasted for some 20 minutes, at the close of which they said that after all they might 'find a niche' for me, and promised to let me know the outcome, 'without fail', within ten days.

9 October 1940
Well past the ten days and not having heard a word from the Air Ministry, we decided to set off to search for David Scott's letters in the John Rylands Library at Manchester, going first by bicycle to Dorcas's home on Merseyside, a journey of 200 miles, which we had reckoned we could manage in two days.

Our journey proved worthwhile for we found a rich store of Scott materials. The library itself, a converted church, Gothic in style and atmosphere, admirably suits the dedicated historian. But we were upset by the sordid, run-down character of that part of the Liverpool–Manchester conurbation, which backs on to the railway, doubtless some of the worst surroundings created by man. How can people living in such conditions feel that they have anything worth fighting for or defending? To what can they be loyal? Across the whole area, which includes Farnworth, Warrington, Runcorn and Widnes, the factories create a thick pall of smoke polluting a wasteland.

People on Merseyside are much agitated and resentful at the apparent absence of defence against prolonged air raids. They claim that German bombers flew over Liverpool in daytime with not a British fighter in sight. The people of the Scotland Road area, who have suffered severely, marched in procession to the town hall carrying banners demanding 'PEACE OR PROTECTION', and persuaded Lord Derby to take their appeal to the air minister. They have been given promises: but meanwhile the bombers have turned their attention elsewhere.

On our return we found a letter from the Air Ministry saying that if I had been 32 years of age they could have employed me. Dorcas had begun to admire the RAF in their blue-grey uniforms, but now thinks they look like peacocks!

16 October 1940

Yesterday evening in the middle of a quiet game of draughts in front of the fire, a terrific bomb thump flung the counters across the room and sent us cowering and shivering to the floor. This morning we found a deep crater, about 50 feet across, in the field behind us, only a quarter of a mile away.

The Nazis' blitzkrieg by day over the Channel must have failed because they have switched to night attacks on our larger cities. This may mean that there will be no invasion this autumn; if so, the focus of war will probably switch to the Near East and Africa. We retreat everywhere and, as in 1917, wait to be rescued by the USA, provided meanwhile we do not break altogether.

How long will this war last? At the start many, as in 1914, said it would be quickly over. If so, we will have lost! Three or four years would be as much as we could withstand, but to make sure of surviving, we have to hope for and expect six.

University term has started, the streets of Cambridge again filling with untidy, boisterous young men, the river crowded with punts and boats, the towpaths made hazardous by perspiring, bawling, rowing coaches pounding along on bicycles. Nothing here appears to change!

21 October 1940

Women and children evacuees begin to arrive in the village, and, as if lost, are already wandering up and down our village street. We've offered to have two; but how long will it be before they get bored and begin to trickle back?

24 October 1940

Londoners, subjected to night after night of heavy bombardment, are clamouring for deep shelters. Two years ago when this question was first publicly raised, John Anderson, the home minister, said that if such shelters were provided the people would never leave them in daytime, an argument reminiscent of the debate in 1918 among the generals over the German decision to build deep underground shelters for their troops in the famous Hindenburg line, which in fact did succeed in long thwarting the Allied army. I've no doubt that similar shelters for the public will soon be provided in our big cities.

Understandably, during air raids, especially at night, people prefer to stay in their houses, sheltering under tables or, better still, under the stairs, rather than in Anderson shelters in the garden. The latter are cold, often damp or subject to flooding and, in an emergency, difficult to access. Already in Cambridge, which suffers little bombing, there are many who choose regularly to sleep in the deep, public shelters.

26 October 1940

There is speculation in the press about the import of Hitler's recent meetings with Pétain and Franco, which he must surely have hoped would enable him to intensify the battle in the

Atlantic. But Franco is nourishing Spain's independence. Hitler must still be aiming to control the Near and Middle East, and from his point of view our extended line of communications across the Atlantic and round the Cape must form our weakest link. In the First World War it was customary to refer to the battles of Mons, of the Somme or of Ypres, now we talk of battles for France, Britain and the Atlantic.

14 November 1940

There is no longer any teaching for me here. A fortnight ago I made one more despairing effort to get into the fighting war, writing to the secretary of state for India, L. S. Amery, giving him details of my experience, telling him I had lived in India, spoke some Bengali and Hindustani, and asking for wartime employment in relation to India, perhaps in the Indian army.

24 November 1940

Amery has replied saying to my surprise that he cannot help me, and recommending that I put my name on the central register for war work; which brings a smile, because I first did this in 1938 and repeated the application a year ago without result. I've become like Somerset Maugham's fictional hero, Ashenden, forever seeking to join the good fight, forever suffering rejection, and I'm learning the hard way that to be well educated and willing is not enough without contacts and people in the right places!

11 December 1940

An order has arrived to present myself for interview for direct entry into the Army Educational Corps (AEC), presumably in response to a letter which last August I sent to the civilian director of army education, Mr Bentall, on first reading in the press that the corps was to be reconstituted. However, in the very same post there is also a circular letter from the War Office saying that there are no vacancies in the corps!

19 December 1940

Yesterday I went for interview for the AEC, the only civilian among 40 candidates in uniform, ranging from corporals to major. As individuals came and went everyone else kept jumping up and down to salute, while I sat tight, soon imagining that I had strayed into a Gilbert and Sullivan opera:

> The other night from cares exempt,
> I slept — and what do you think I dreamt?
> I dreamt that somehow I had come
> To dwell in Topsy-Turveydom!

Officers were interviewed first, other ranks next and, very late in the day, I was last man in. There were three interviewers, all in the same room, oddly enough acting quite separately, each at his own desk, one a colonel, the other two half-colonels. First I went before the colonel, a tall slim figure, white-haired and moustached, pink-faced, kindly, full of smiles and infinitely charming. Ominously not asking me a single question, he congratulated me on my qualifications, then stretched credulity by assuring me that it was the right time to enter the corps and that I would be appointed as a subaltern, acting captain no less, and adding the stern warning, 'You musn't become the scholar with the troops.' With a confident pat on the back I was then passed to his younger colleagues, the first of whom virtually repeated the same act. But the second, a grizzled, scowling individual, obviously playing the hard man, rattled out question after question without waiting for answers; 'What, no military training? Not even at the university? Why haven't you been called up? Have you travelled? What, to Bengal? Don't know that side myself! What work does your father do?' No one enquired whether I had any ideas about educating the troops. Immediately warmed by the glowing promises, I later feared it would turn out like my abortive interview for the RAF. Anyway I have been assured that 'without fail' — ominous words — I will hear my fate within three weeks.

Tonight we cycle to Wallasey for Christmas.

30 December 1940
For five successive nights before Christmas, Merseyside has endured terrible, terrifying air raids, the worst on the nights of 20 and 21 December. The first raid began at 6.30 p.m. with scarcely

any warning, continuing until about 4.00 a.m., and was repeated for just as long on the following night. There are nothing like blackouts, blitzes, bomb shelters and, above all, bombs to encourage a collective spirit. We offered shelter in our fortified passage to some neighbours, Mr and Mrs Jenkins and their son, John, making seven of us huddled together along with the terrier dog, Teddy. For the first couple of hours I hardly noticed the bombs and gunfire because of worrying about Mr Jenkins, who suffers from a weak heart and had turned deathly white, agitatedly panting aloud in hoarse gasps. About 9.00 p.m. there was a tremendous roar, the walls and beams shuddered, the lights went out and great lumps of ceiling plaster fell on us. Dorcas's mother, Emily, began to cry, Dorcas kept shouting, 'We're all right' and, reassuringly, a few minutes later the lights came on again. I could not stop trembling as I tried in vain to stop the dog from barking.

The bumping and shaking continued remorselessly, with loud intermittent cracks from an anti-aircraft gun which had moved into the street just outside. Through the early hours we talked and sang songs, slowly drifting into a kind of stupor, only disturbed by crash after crash, accompanied by the falling clatter of broken tiles and glass. At 6.45 a.m. after the 'raiders passed' siren, hesitantly we crept upstairs to bed only to be sent scurrying downstairs again by blasts from delayed time bombs.

At first light I poked my head outside to see what was left of the world and whether there was anything I could do. About 50 yards away in a gaping, smouldering hole in the terraced houses opposite, two policemen and an ARP group were digging. All down the street people were aimlessly salvaging odds and ends, one elderly woman bitterly crying that her Christmas toys for the grandchildren had been spoilt.

By mid-afternoon we were all suffering from nervous reaction, anxiously standing around, aimlessly chattering. I could not concentrate and kept shivering uncontrollably. As we feared, as soon as night fell the air-raid warning sounded, followed within two minutes by the sound of gunfire. Again the seven of us and the dog squeezed ourselves into the strengthened passage. This time the bombing and gunfire went on longer with even greater intensity. In a lull in the early hours I peered outside. Over the river in dockland there was a brilliant orange and purple cauldron of fire from which great flashes of white light kept bursting. Smoke, oily and pungent, drifted everywhere. Down the street, 60 yards away, a house still crackled with flames, glass from its windows showering to the pavement. In the middle of the road a broken gas main flared, and a tangle of firemen's hoses lay useless, the hydrants destroyed. On an exposed end wall a saw-toothed impression of a staircase zigzagged nowhere.

With daylight we looked out on a changed landscape, a wasteland of rubble surmounted by the shell of the local, brick-built chapel, both ends blown clean out. Curiously, immediately around us not a window had been broken.

Apparently some 200 civilians were killed in Wallasey in these two nights. Later that morning I tried to go for a walk, but could not get far in any direction, the roads being closed by great holes and piles of rubble. At one point, numb and almost indifferent, I came on a pathetic wooden cross with a white pillow case caught on a nail fluttering in the breeze.

When bombed out you temporarily lose all interest in the progress of the war. Like soldiers in trench warfare, the mind is wholly fixed on one's own sector; and the bombing creates hate for the bombers and stiffens resistance, and does not, as I used to think, weaken the will to fight on.

22 January 1941
A fortnight ago we travelled home to Milton, having to stand the whole way in the crowded train, although the first-class compartments remained comparatively empty. At home, not finding the promised answer from the War Office was disappointing, although not surprising, so after waiting another week I wrote asking for a decision, and within a couple of days received the answer, which by now I half expected, that the Army Educational Corps could not find a place for me.

My depression is deepened by the awful news that one of my senior colleagues in the college has gone raving mad and murdered his wife with a fork and, on being consigned to Broadmoor, has hanged himself with his tie. I last saw them when invited to a musical evening in their then luxurious home in Highgate, he singing in a light baritone voice to her piano accompaniment; an elegant, civilized couple whom I envied. Thank God, Dorcas and I still have each other! In the face of fate, and among the wreckage and turbulence of total war, Dorcas and I have resolved to cling together for as long as possible. And if separated by some catastrophe of war to try to meet again in Trafalgar Square on her birthday, 31 January.

There is a local shortage of meat, eggs, cheese, butter and fruit; and clothes have risen in price by 100 per cent in the shops. We pine for an apple, orange or banana; and are glad to get fish even at double the prewar price.

Our armies have started to win unexpected victories in North Africa, so presumably the Cape route for supplies is still being maintained. Here in Cambridge concern about possible invasion has virtually disappeared and the local Home Guard has happily turned its attention to the nightly darts competitions in the pubs. One cheering piece of news is that at long last indoor air-raid shelters, in the form of massive steel tables, are to be made available to households in towns. We crawled into one at a friend's house in Cambridge and, looking out through the wire-meshed sides, felt like caged monkeys. But being warm and dry, and easily accessible in emergency, I would much rather use one in preference to a cold, damp Anderson shelter at the bottom of the garden.

12 February 1941

We went by train to London today, first having to cycle to Cambridge station through a blizzard. Indignant over the wholly misleading impression given me at the interview for the Army Educational Corps, I had written expostulating to the civilian director, Mr Bentall, at the War Office and, much to my surprise, had been asked in reply to go and see him. A tall, bald-headed, sharp-faced man with warm, brown, expressive eyes, he gave me a friendly welcome, at once saying that the interviewing committee had gone well beyond its brief, that only 54 places were available, mostly for men over 33, and regretting that he could not include me among the number. Grateful for his frankness, I sat silent, which appeared to unnerve him, for he seemed to grow uncertain, and, after much beating about the bush, finally, almost in desperation, suddenly made up his mind; 'I tell you what,' he said, 'I will consider an application from you when you are in the army'; and, smiling broadly, visibly relieved and confident that he had settled the matter, he saw me out.

28 February 1941

Occasionally one or other politician makes mention of the postwar world. Some Labour Party members, while writing off our empiré, have been gleefully condemning our imperial past. Those who condemn it, the work for example of the British in India, seem to be protesting that it should never have occurred, and seek as it were to remake history on a more elevated model; absurdly they try to reconstruct the past. But meanwhile surely, while asking questions about the motives, we can at least admire the performers and the scale of their performance, often in the face of apparently overwhelming odds. Some Tories and Labour members talk with confidence of reforming Germany after the war, but say nothing about Britain.

A lone German raider made a machine-gun attack on Cambridge today but no one was hurt. A similar attack last week on Newmarket, on market day, caused many casualties.

Monday 14 March 1941

With deep misgiving we heard that on 12 and 13 March Wallasey and Merseyside had once again been heavily raided, and feared for the safety of Dorcas's parents. On the following morning a cryptic telegram arrived saying that they had been bombed out and were leaving Wallasey on their way to us. When we met them at the station, each carrying a case, they both broke down, overwhelmed to be safe but obviously badly shaken, their house and belongings blown inside out, their clothes and faces cut by glass splinters. What sour misfortune piled on misfortune — for Emily's husband, Jack, in the First World War had lost the use of his left arm and endured 18 months and seven operations in hospital and now, in this war, has seen both home and livelihood destroyed.

As soon as he was feeling more himself, I went back by train with him to Wallasey to rescue their remaining belongings and to board up what remained of their home. Wallasey and its people looked devastated, as if struck by both earthquake and hurricane. Remarkably, their house still had its roof intact, but all window frames and doors had gone; and inside, most of the movables had been looted, including the telephone and even the taps in the kitchen and bathroom. With hundreds of others I spent the first day queuing to get some screws and nails at the town hall, then set to work patching up walls and ceilings, and, with old wooden doors and beams rescued from neighbouring bomb sites, boarded up the window frames and doorways. Finally, still without water, cleaning materials or electricity, we swept up the mess of soot, dust, glass and plaster. Working in the cold and in clouds of fine dust filled and irritated my lungs and gave me a sore chest, and by the third day I could hardly breathe. I felt ill, mentally and physically exhausted, ready to drop.

We had just about finished when there was a loud bang on the boarded front door where a policeman stood holding out a telegram, sent on by Dorcas from Milton. In it I was ordered to report for military service with the Suffolk Regiment at Bury St Edmunds on Thursday 27 March.

By that Thursday I was back, not however with the army at Bury St Edmunds, but at Milton and in bed with congestion of the lungs and a high fever, at long last formally a soldier, but anxiously wondering whether my urgent request for sick leave would be granted.

4

Roll on Duration

My long anticipated, first day as a soldier was ruined by the manufacturer's label in my new khaki battledress uniform. Still shaky from the ordeal by bombing on Merseyside, I had duly reported on 14 March to the headquarters of the Suffolk Regiment at Gibraltar Barracks, Bury St Edmunds, over a week late, making a less than auspicious start to my army career. When quitting our London flat at the outbreak of war it had not proved possible to cancel the original three-year lease, so, although we could ill afford it, we had to continue to pay the full quarterly account to the landlord, Sydney Bowra & Company, but, about a year later, the local authority went out of its way to advise me that this payment still included a substantial portion for rates, which evidently the landlord had promptly ceased paying, although illegally continuing to charge me. With difficulty and some show of unpleasantness, I had finally got the money back, but it did my morale no good at all when the first thing I saw prominently displayed on the maker's label inside the new battledress was the name of that landlord. At my disbelieving 'Bloody capitalist! I'm not wearing that!' the stores corporal looked astonished, but, after I explained, grabbed the battledress and promptly tore out the offending label. 'Roll on Duration', he said, a phrase that was to epitomize my army service.

The platoon I joined was made up of a motley lot, 22 in number, looking rather like the scrapings of the East Anglian barrel with a few bad apples thrown in, including several mentally backward farm labourers, three illiterates, of whom two, Charley and Joe, were twins and, sticking out like a sore thumb, a couple of middle-aged, former regular army 'old sweats' who had served in India and bitterly resented their recall to the ranks. No one seemed to have the slightest interest in the world outside, not even in the sensational arrival in Scotland of Rudolf Hess, Hitler's deputy, or the Nazi paratroopers' dramatic conquest of Crete. Soon, for me too, it was the little things that began to loom large, polishing buttons, 'boning' the toecaps of my boots and not being able, like everyone else, easily to flick open the clip on the rifle butt or to manage a trot while carrying the Bren gun's heavy steel ammunition box, or to command any adequate, convincing response to the monotonous, mind-blowing repetition of the same six or seven expletives to which all conversation in the platoon was reduced.

On the second day the whole platoon underwent a written intelligence test, which was easy enough though the twins sat nonplussed, twiddling their thumbs. But all were puzzled when several days later, only the twins and I were summoned to repeat exactly the same test in the presence of an officer of the Army Educational Corps, Captain Congreve, who incidentally, many years later, turned up as one of my administrative officers in the University of London. What the test was for and what he made of the results we never discovered.

At meal times we fed like pigs at the trough, grabbing, tearing and stuffing. The twins, Charley and Joe, after meals invariably scoured the tables and floors for leftover scraps. Lights out and morning reveille always precipitated a cats' concert of coughing — smokers' coughs, soft, rumbling, phlegmatic coughs, hacking and whooping coughs all swelled the mammoth chorus. We awoke to the mixed stench of stale tobacco smoke, sweaty khaki woollen shirts worn night and day, and blankets full of dust. As a pestilential irritant, especially during the night, a plague of earwigs kept me awake, crawling everywhere and getting into everything.

By the time I joined, the prevailing tone in my hut had been set by the two old 'sweats', who had lost no time in recreating their Indian army lifestyle. As soon as parades were over they promptly got out the bed boards, 'biscuits', and blankets and hopped into bed where they lay, scrounging cigarettes and cups of 'char', for-ever boasting about their sexual prowess. While for them our hut was 'a fuckin' good mob', all the others were apparently beyond contempt, containing nothing but 'fuckin' cunts and buggers'; and I too soon found myself dubbed 'a funny fucker'. Getting ready to go out on the town formed the high spot of their day. Their meticulous preparations — polishing buttons and boots, creasing trousers and creaming their hair, while the rest of us watched with awe — were a scene matched only when they later predictably described their exploits, so lurid and bizarre as to strain credulity. Alas, we never got to see the fabulous Madge and Sheila, who apparently provided such sexual heroics.

A young officer scarcely out of his teens gave us a lecture on the history of the regiment and the importance of taking pride in it, for henceforward, he declared, it was to form the centre of our lives. But the message went clean over our heads, unlike the prac-tical advice given on the same day by the MO on how to get a free supply of 'French letters' and protective ointment against VD, which did command avid attention.

In the town centre I discovered a small regimental museum and library where I could enjoy some quiet in the evenings and where I was able to put the finishing touches to an article I was preparing at the time of call-up on the initial emergence at the end of the First World War of the Army Educational Corps. That episode, started by Lord Gorell, had marked a noble effort to rescue something from the disasters of war, a glimmer of hope for a better world. Now that we were committed to total war, could something similar, I wondered, be conjured up or attempted?

Based on papers I had earlier come across by chance in the Cam-bridge University library, I thought that the subject would repay study and, happening to see in the daily paper that a director of army education had just been appointed at the War Office, decided on the spur of the moment to send my article to him. Earlier the same day on which I dropped it in the postbox I had surprisingly found myself promoted to the rank of acting, unpaid lance-corporal and, flushed with this unexpected elevation, signed my name on the accompanying letter with a flourish, adding the bold, magic capital letters, L/C. It nearly proved my undoing!

Some three weeks later my name went up on camp orders to report at once to the commandant. Standing before him I could see from his thunderous looks and the way he was tugging at his bristling ginger moustache that I was in for trouble. Not choosing to stand me at ease he flung a brown manila envelope on to the table, bellowing, 'What's the meaning of this?' Tentatively I picked it up, immediately recognizing that it contained my article; presumably returned from the War Office, but, as I soon saw with alarm, the really offensive item was on the label, which was addressed to 'Lieut. Col. C. H. Philips'. But ignoring altogether this meteoric promotion, he simply reprimanded me for what evidently in his eyes was the much more serious matter of having directly addressed the War Office. As I was marched out, the sergeant major, more in sorrow than anger, murmured 'And I thought you were a likely lad!'

Never a day passed in the huts or on parade without frequent reference to two big forthcoming events, the TOET (test of elementary training) and a field 'scheme', both of which were ceaselessly invoked by our instructors to spur us to greater effort. But when the TOET came, it proved a sad disappointment, for, irrespective of our performance, we all passed, even the 'Terrible Twins'. Few of us in fact had been able to reassemble the Bren gun in the required time and, on the rifle range, the majority missed the targets altogether. Curiously, at 100 yards' distance I did not register a single hit, but at 200 yards, wearing both my 'tin hat' and respirator and with fixed bayonet on my rifle, every shot registered! If proof were needed, this confirmed the view in the platoon that I was a 'funny fucker', or alternatively a 'barmy bastard', or better, a 'busty little bugger'!

From start to finish mystery and rumour shrouded the 'scheme' and we never succeeded in discovering what it was all about. So far as my platoon was concerned, it started with a parade in full kit and the issue of an extra blanket, then for three days in sweltering heat kept us in barracks awaiting an urgent summons which never came, after which we boarded trucks to the local football ground to spend the night. On the next day we kicked our heels before being carted to the headquarters of the general in charge of the scheme and, as ill-luck had it, our platoon was ordered to guard the main entrance. My own section, which numbered six, including the twins, was given the night watch and, as the only one with a torch, I went off to locate the general's headquarters. On returning I could hear a tremendous hubbub rising from a long line of cars and motorbikes held up at the gate. In the middle of the gateway, just visible in the dark, stood one of the twins, Charley, questioning a dispatch rider about his identity card and repeatedly shouting, 'No, no, wrong number', and then, 'No, your number is 15541', which, using my torch, I soon discovered was not the identity number at all but the date of issue. Behind him, his twin brother, who stammered slightly, stood with rifle levelled, shouting, 'Rec-rec-recognize to be advanced. Stand or I f-f-fire.' Nothing in fact would have persuaded that dispatch rider, or anyone else in the vicinity, to move one inch.

Early the following morning we were returned to barracks, ordered to put on our 'denims' and taken by coach some 60 miles to a large warehouse on the outskirts of London where, in the hot sun, we spent the rest of the day loading lorries with sacks of sugar, which leaked, and melting cases of margarine, which together congealed into a glutinous mass on our hair and shoulders, attracting pestiferous swarms of flies.

In the continuing heat wave during the following three days we marched and counter-marched, no doubt for the exercise, through the lush wheat and barley fields around Stowmarket, at one point, doubtless to keep us on our toes, being ordered to charge the unoccupied banks of a canal, into which our young over-enthusiastic officer obligingly fell, after which we all felt free to join him.

But in the blazing sunshine, with the wind just steady and strong enough to disturb the grass pollens, I began to suffer the cumulative effects of hay fever. Unable to stop sneezing and coughing, by the time we got back to barracks I had developed such a high temperature that I was at once packed off to the sick room. There, the following morning, the medical officer said I would have to undergo a medical examination and, a fortnight later, I was reclassified from A1 to B and declared 'not fit for operational duties in the field', a verdict on which the platoon unanimously congratulated me, but which I feared was more likely to lead to an army career devoted permanently to cleaning up the cookhouse and painting the company's lines. But the immediate, fortuitous outcome was that my name was removed from the next draft, which I later learnt went straight from England to Singapore, there to walk into the hands of the Japanese.

Back in the barracks, I was shortly afterwards ordered to take on the duties of the regimental army schoolmaster who had just been posted. His job was to look after the band-boys, a group of 16 orphans of former regular soldiers who had volunteered to become cadets, each learning to play an instrument and in due course taking his place in the regimental band. Their ages ranged from 9 to 17 and, for three blissful weeks, I ran my own little army, spending all day with them, taking all subjects. Whatever my predecessor had tried to teach them, one and all certainly knew how to calculate the horse-racing odds and there was bewilderment when I told them I did not know how to start a 'book'. But it was far too cushy a billet to last long and, without explanation, I was surprised, though not sorry, to be posted to a pre-entry course of two weeks at Wakefield for the Army Educational Corps. Evidently my medical downgrading had provided the magic key. There, with 70 others, I listened patiently to lectures by world-weary, long service 'regulars' on how to inspire the troops; but my clearest recollection is that of a fellow sufferer, Eric Hobsbawm, possibly rivalling me for the role of the least likely soldier in the army, who was later to become a professorial colleague in the History School in the University of London. His clearest memory, he later told me, was that I had with me *two* clean, snow-white handkerchiefs!

Promoted as sergeant-instructors we were duly sent on our way 'to educate and inspire the troops', my own posting taking me to a company of young soldiers at Methwold in the depths of the Fens, not far from King's Lynn, where they were guarding an operational aerodrome. On a grey, wet afternoon I was collected at Brandon station by my new boss, Lieutenant Tanner, in a motorbike and sidecar, and driven through dark coniferous forests, past heaps of sugar beet alongside overflowing ditches, to reach the camp just as darkness was falling. The company, which had only recently been formed, was settling into several newly erected huts, buried in a small wood, still lacking light, heat and water, and with paths already knee deep in mud. No one expected me and, needless to say, the quartermaster's office was closed and there was nowhere to sleep. Lieutenant Tanner made a discreet departure, leaving me to find some space and to borrow a couple of hard, flat biscuit cushions on which to sleep. Told that there would be supper in the sergeants' mess, I finally discovered it in a small section of one of the huts, where nine sergeants were already gathered, mostly 'old sweats' in early middle life, who, judging by the vehemence of their language, deeply resented their recall, apparently to mind 'the kids!'

In a fug of tobacco smoke we sat around a hurricane lamp, eventually rewarded by the arrival of two large, steaming bowls, one full of brown stew and vegetables, the other of rhubarb and custard. Without a table, everyone had mess tins, but since mine were still packed, I was invited to eat directly from the communal bowls, which I did, fascinated to see that several of the sergeants took their stew and pudding mixed together, convenient in that you needed only a spoon for the lot.

Next morning early I was awakened by a lot of confused shouting, from which I gathered that one of the American bombers returning from a raid had crash-landed on a slit trench manned by some of the boys, killing three of them and badly injuring others. During the day there was a lot of angry argument, and that night a small group went on the rampage against the planes, which they were supposed to be guarding, plugging the gun muzzles with mud and slashing the fuselages with their bayonets. Some of the culprits were soon identified, forthwith tried, convicted and dispatched to the nearest 'army glasshouse' at Gamblingay, predictably, on their return to be treated by their comrades as heroes. A few weeks later on Christmas Eve, in a renewed gesture of defiance, about half the company took off on unofficial leave, setting the military police throughout East Anglia a pretty unseasonable problem.

Most of our daylight hours were taken up in drill and marches, so any instruction had to be given in the gloom of late afternoon, my talks on the progress of the war commanding no more attention than my farcical attempts to teach map reading by candlelight.

But in the process I realized that a sizeable proportion of the lads, as many as 70, could neither read nor write, and in discussing this with my fellow sergeants, found one, Joe Tremayne, who was keen to join in doing something to help them. A little older than myself, Joe had some experience as an assistant producer in the BBC's education branch and passionately believed in the power of education to change people.

Between us, we persuaded the young company commander to rearrange the training programme to enable us to mount a ten-week course to explain the basic elements of reading and writing. Starting by preparing a simple grammar essentially providing no more than a sentence structure of 'subject, verb and object', along with rudimentary exercises, I soon realized that all our efforts would be futile unless we simultaneously provided a regular, preferably daily, supply of similarly graded, simple reading matter. So while Joe put the grammar together and gathered a team of volunteer teachers, mainly from a group of former public school boys, I produced an illustrated daily broadsheet on the course of the war, the text of which the boys on the course used to chant aloud in unison.

Through his former colleagues in the BBC, Joe was able to enrich this with a popular supply of coloured comics. By a fortunate coincidence, heating and lighting was at long last installed in the huts, so morale shot up, further boosting our programme. After six weeks, a majority of the boys were able to write and read a very simple letter, and even more strikingly, showed a simultaneous, dramatic improvement in dress and bearing, both as soldiers and individuals, which their achievement of literacy appeared to bring about. Sensibly, the young company commander promptly capped success by promising those who made the grade what they most wanted, which was expedited transfer to fighting units.

With the onset of winter a series of numbing north-easters hurled sleet and snow deep into our wood, and the sharp frosts that followed laid bare the fields and reduced the trees to skeletons. The winterscape became a desolation confining us to barracks for prolonged periods, so the literacy programme came as something of a godsend to the company commander and enabled us not only to go on with the intensive course, but also as a useful relief to get together some tools and materials for woodworking classes. But over-much rushing around and too enthusiastic teaching in such awful conditions, mostly at night, took their toll of my health, leaving me with a persistent cough, which for weeks I failed to shake off; finally I went down with pneumonia, being then carted off in a windowless, freezingly cold ambulance to a hospital just outside Cambridge.

Some weeks later, back on my feet, I found, on returning to Methwold, that Joe Tremayne had been posted and I had been promoted to the rank of sergeant-major with orders to transfer and support Captain Pitcher, AEC at division headquarters in Thornham Magna in the heart of rural Suffolk. It was rumoured, too, that the War Office, disenchanted with what it regarded in general as a failed experiment, had decided to disband the young soldiers' battalions.

As I made the short journey under the bright sky of spring through Suffolk's lush, green fields, I began to thank my lucky stars for an escape from the darkest Fens, but within a few days I realized that I had been sent not so much to assist Captain Pitcher as to cover up and make good his undoubted deficiencies.

A tobacco salesman before the war and now a Conservative parliamentary candidate, he had apparently made use of some political association with Anthony Eden, the government minister, to wangle his way into the army with a direct commission, in the education corps, though he lacked qualifications of any kind. Pickwickian in face and figure, he shuffled around the office, always mumbling and gesticulating, his thick pendulous and petulant underlip flapping and quivering as he talked. In announcing himself on the telephone he had the memorably endearing habit of shouting 'Pitcher, I'm Pitcher, P for Pig', but throughout the division, where he was already regarded with a mixture of contempt and amusement, he was more often than not referred to as 'The Old Mug'. Each morning he remained in the office, mostly on the telephone, more often than not pursuing his own private and political business, and never returning in the afternoon until after tea, then sitting despondently, hunched on a chair, calculating his claimable expenses, alternately twiddling his fingers and scratching his head, sighing and talking to himself until it was time for dinner. In no uncertain terms he made it plain that my job was solely to run the office and every evening to man the telephone.

The only thing that Pitcher himself attempted to do, which by any stretch of the imagination could be described as educational, was to try to arrange visits by civilian lecturers to the units in the division, but because they were scattered round the broken East Anglia coastline and therefore accessible only through a complicated system of road and rail communications, the programming and timetabling of the lectures had proved quite beyond him. My job to start with, therefore, was to make good this failure and, although straightforward, I found that it had its ups and downs. One stroke of luck was to recruit as a civilian lecturer a beautiful, intelligent, shapely young woman with an attractive Hungarian accent, who proved immensely popular in the officers' messes throughout the division, especially in the isolated coastal batteries, and with the added advantage to me of getting rid of Pitcher from the office, for he made a point of accompanying her everywhere. However, with a sure sense of survival, he took care to distance himself from another lecturer on the circuit, a deep-sea diver, whose *pièce de résistance* was to descend fully garbed into a vast four-ton tank of sea water. When inviting the diver I had quite failed to appreciate the scale and complexity of his impedimenta, especially the enormous tank for diving in, or that getting him and his gear to the coastal batteries would tie up the greater part of the division's reserve of motor transport for days on end. It was little consolation that of all my activities these were the only two to come to the divisional commander's personal attention!

To make sure I stayed in the office, Pitcher by turn tried bullying and pulling rank, but he was too obviously a preposterous charlatan for me to take seriously, though he did cause trouble by fruitlessly trying to postpone an order which arrived for me to present myself to be tested for a commission on a three-day War Office selection board at Colchester. Duly passing this, I was delighted to leave Pitcher to his own futile devices.

My orders were to proceed to an OCTU at Dunbar on the Lothian coast near Edinburgh. While waiting, I was taken to what was obviously a hastily improvised camp near Wrotham in Kent on a ten-day intensive course in motor driving and maintenance.

Unfortunately it turned out to be a very wet period. There I joined several hundred fellow sufferers, each allowed to keep only one kitbag, and forced to bed down in the open on the bracken under canvas awnings slung between the trees. Within hours this whole wooded area was reduced to a quagmire of clinging mud and running water. After breakfast we got cold tea and bread green with mould, after which we queued in the rain for mail and then for our turn in the latrines.

In the half light of early morning we took to the road in open, four-ton lorries, the driver perched high on an exposed, precarious seat without windscreen or cover, gradually acquiring a lordly, statuesque style of driving, particularly generous in rounding corners, from which my friends maintain I have never wholly recovered. More enjoyable was the day allotted for training on faulty, ancient AJS motorbikes; mine lacked footrests, so I had to make use of the exhaust pipe, which, while it certainly kept my right foot warm, ultimately burnt a hole through the sole of my boot, for which our corporal instructor promptly put me on a charge.

By the time we had washed our vehicles at the end of each day it was pitch dark, so much of the evening was spent hunting for our kitbags, which had invariably been moved during the day. It was such an appallingly bad and so inefficiently run camp that, on discovering that one of our number was related to a local MP, a group of us got together to send him a round robin complaining about the unique combination of 'bull and bumbledom'; and, several weeks after we had left, we were gratified to learn that the camp commandant had been sacked. With this course safely behind me I left for Edinburgh and the OCTU at Dunbar.

To be going north to Edinburgh gave me a welcome sense of expectancy, for I knew that the Scottish National Archives housed a collection of letters of David Scott, whose career in India and in London I had begun to investigate in the weeks just before being called up. It was an opportunity not to be missed, so, before reporting to the OCTU, I sought out Mr Meikle, the curator, and arranged to be given access on the occasional free day, even if a Sunday and I could get into Edinburgh. So, on free days throughout the six-week course, accompanied and helped by Dorcas who had rushed north to find 'digs' for this period in Dunbar, I was able to trace David Scott's early life, both in Forfar and at the University of St Andrews, before he went off to seek his fortune in India, and later fame and power in London.

Much later, early in 1945, while moving about the Middle Eastern theatre of war, I used the occasional free day to put what I hoped were the finishing touches to my study of Scott's career. But there was still one gap, for in reading his correspondence I had not come across a physical description of him; I was therefore delighted when I discovered that there existed a portrait painted by the famous George Romney, which was hanging in the town hall of Scott's home town, Forfar, but I had not a hope of going to see it. However, a letter to the town clerk duly produced a photograph which finally reached me in Cairo.

In my mind I had long since built up a picture of Scott as of middle height, sturdy in build, fresh in complexion, every inch a 'hale fellow, well met' outgoing character, but to my astonishment the photograph of the portrait showed a tall, thin, almost emaciated figure, with a pale-faced, dyspeptic, withdrawn look. Quite unable to double-check, but still with deep reservation, I allowed it to appear as the published book's frontispiece. Twenty years later, happening for the first time to be passing through Forfar, I took the opportunity to visit the town hall, where sure enough I found Romney's portrait hanging in the main hall and, to my surprise, hanging high on a wall some 20 feet above floor level. Presumably the photographer, ignoring perspective, had simply taken his black and white shot from ground level, in the process completely distorting the portrait in oils, which itself did show the hale and hearty Scott to be the spitting image of what I had envisaged.

To be able to enjoy this occasional escape into academic life in Edinburgh was a godsend, for at the OCTU my platoon came under the mesmeric, tyrannical control of an officer who, having recently returned from an overlong spell in the North African desert, was said to be both 'sand and bomb happy'.

In staccato, inconsequential terms he spouted an unbroken stream of gibberish. 'Bang on, go for a shooter. Never miss the breach. Never spake a man like this! Out, hyperbolical fiend.' Every now and again, he would glare, this mishmash of the Bible and Shakespeare giving way to a hiatus of normal speech. In a fight I had no doubt of his ferocity and I had not the slightest wish to be with him or against him.

Six feet tall, gaunt and rangy, his black eyes staring from a face deeply lined and crosshatched, with a luxuriant moustache flourishing on his upper lip, as surprising on those craggy features as a clump of wild flowers on a Scottish rock face, he put the fear of God into me. Dubbed 'the Mad Mullah', he drove us mercilessly. On night guard on the cliff top overlooking the North Sea in that bitterly cold January, he never failed to turn us out for minute inspection in the early morning hours and again an hour or so later to try to catch us out.

One freezing January morning he paraded the platoon in full kit. 'Today', he said, 'it's introduction to water!', promptly jogging us several miles through the snow into the neighbouring Lammermuir hills, whose red soil in the crisp morning air was sparkling with hoar frost. Reaching a small stream about 30 feet across and a couple of feet deep, we were lined up along the bank. 'On that hillock yonder', he said, pointing a finger, 'I've got a sniper firing live ammunition'. Thus prompted, the sniper obligingly got off a couple of shots, which, with uncomfortable proximity, thudded into a neighbouring bank. 'He's a good shot', added the Mad Mullah, at which my neighbour murmured, 'Thank God for that!' The Mullah went on, 'You've got to get to that small tree', pointing two hundred yards or so downstream, 'and if you don't want to get shot, you'll have to go down to water. Now, get in!' A look of disbelief flashed across our faces and instinctively, with unusual precision, every man took a step back, as if to give further thought to the matter. 'Go!' he roared, 'Get in!' Incredibly he meant it and in twos and threes, several of us with a push, we jumped in, falling over each other, and after a moment's anguish began to crawl through the reeds, holding our rifles aloft, encouraged to keep our heads down by an occasional shot from the sniper. Coloured by the soil, the icy-cold river ran red, staining our uniforms and leaving us shivering, but mercifully the wind was light and, jogging back to camp, we soon dried out. But for weeks afterwards my delicately tinted pink underpants never failed to evoke ribald comments.

At the close of the course in March, I was posted as education officer, with the rank of second lieutenant, to Dover Garrison, described by the press at the time as 'Hellfire Corner', where, in preparation for the Allied assault across the Channel, the area along the coast and some 10 miles inland was gradually filling with men and women of all services, reaching before D-day something like 60,000 in number. Much later we learnt that they were to form General Patton's decoy army to deceive Hitler.

En route to Maidstone I reported to the command education officer, Colonel Joseph, a portly little man, fussy with his own importance yet withal one of the more pleasant of the peacetime regulars who, on the reconstitution of the education corps, had floated like froth to the top where, for the rest of the war, they contentedly effervesced. He instructed me to go straight to Dover to mount a crash programme capable of meeting the educational needs and requests of as many of the thousands of service people as possible, and promised me the support of four or five army education sergeants.

Garrison headquarters were sited high up in Dover Castle itself, where on first arrival I was given a taste of the front line, being penned in by German shelling across the Channel, ducking at the sharp crack of each exploding shell, so very different in sound from the more familiar heavy thump of bombs.

Later that evening in a pub in the town I met two of my promised assistants, WO John Pashley and Sergeant 'Doc' Findlay, finding that they had already made themselves comfortable in one of the empty, evacuated large houses of Dover College on the other side of the valley.

A tall, melancholy streak of a man with a pale, long drawn face and a nice, surprising turn in throwaway humour, Pashley was an engaging northerner who quickly made himself popular with local civilians. Already spotting the potential for our purposes of the vacated houses of Dover College, he had at once set in train the process of commandeering them. Doc Findlay, who like myself had a university doctorate, resembled Chesterton's character, Father Brown, short, plump and sanguine, out to enjoy the good things of life, yet down to earth and shrewd in mobilizing local volunteers. Working under pressure, we never made the time to become close friends, but found an easy rapport and quickly shook down into a good team.

Together we roughed out a scheme using Dover College as a base to create an education centre big enough to attract and accommodate hundreds of service men and women. In comparison with their conditions in the field it was essential that it should be warm, well-lit and pleasingly decorated, with comfortably furnished canteens, rest and reading rooms, and, most important, bathrooms with hot water, offering a quiet, restorative retreat to the troops returning from arduous, often dirty, field operations. We kept it open day and night, and around this nucleus saw virtually no limit to the potential in providing a rich, varied educational and recreational fare both for individuals and groups, small and large.

To our appeal for support, the national YMCA in London responded generously with money, materials, furnishings and domestic management, so that within a few weeks and with the ready help of local civilian and service volunteers we became fully operational.

With a virtually captive constituency and a rich supply of teachers and lecturers from the local units, we were able to create a core of regular daytime and evening courses in drama, music and films, around which we sought to respond to every individual educational request, soon offering classes and personal tutoring in languages, the sciences, mathematics, art, sculpture, pottery, and wood and metal work. For materials, especially wood, we ransacked the local buildings already destroyed by shellfire and bombing.

By the following autumn and through the winter, despite frequent shelling, the centre was attracting well over 1500 regular users, the whole operation soon catching the attention of local and then national newspapers and radio, which, sensing a dramatic success story, puffed up the drama of 'army education in Hellfire Corner', conferring on us the sobriquet of 'The Front-Line University'.*

---

* For a fuller account see my article in Rewley House Papers, Oxford.

To my delight this fast and furious life was enhanced by the unannounced arrival of Dorcas, who, discovering that because of the regular shelling there was a shortage of local teachers, had contrived to get herself appointed to a Dover primary school. This was the latest in a series of jobs she found for herself in order that we might keep within easy reach for as long as possible, becoming in turn a tax inspector in Bury St Edmunds, a shop assistant in Methwold, a farm girl in Suffolk and what in fact amounted to a childminder in Dover, for, to avoid the shelling, she found herself having to shepherd the children several times a day in and out of air-raid shelters. In the evenings she lent a hand in the canteen at the education centre, and tutored in French and German, and on our occasional day off we roamed the high downs around Dover.

With so large a number of service and civilian users packed together both by day and night the centre obviously ran enormous risks from the shelling, yet I found no difficulty in arranging periodic visits by the famous London orchestras, and weekly visits of distinguished lecturers, including Archbishop William Temple and his *alter ego* Dr Hewlett Johnson, 'the Red Dean', also the novelists J. B. Priestley, John Brophy and Pamela Frankau, and the scientists John Blackett, J. D. Bernal and Peter Medawar, the last of whom many years later became a colleague on the University Grants Committee.

'Big wigs' in plenty from the War Office, including Sir Ronald Adam, the adjutant general, and Philip Morris, soon to become the director general of army education, descended on us and, in the light of our popularity and success, advice soon went out from the War Office to the home commands that army education centres on Dover lines were to be opened wherever possible. Within a few months centres were started at Canterbury, Cambridge, Liverpool, Salisbury and Glasgow, later followed by others in the Middle East and Italian theatres of war. In southeast England also, largely through the enthusiasm of Frank Jessup, who later became director of the Oxford Extra-Mural Delegacy after the war, similar civilian centres enjoyed some popularity well into the postwar period. But the Dover centre itself did not long survive intact, for, within a week of my being posted from Dover in the autumn of 1944, a German shell hit and largely destroyed the main building, including the office in which, until then, I had been working every day and night.

Presumably largely because of the popularity and success of the Dover centre, I had been promoted to the rank of captain and was then sent north to Cuerden Hall near Preston to serve under the chief instructor, Major John Haynes (later director of education for Kent), who was put in charge of a large group of instructors to open a brand-new army education college. As soon as the Allied forces had established themselves on the European mainland, the need to create for the troops behind the lines a framework for adult education and to make ready for anticipated demobilization became evident and urgent. The role assigned for Cuerden Hall therefore was, on short six-week courses, to train or refresh large numbers of men and women, mostly former teachers, as instructors in subjects ranging from the academic to the practical, which it was envisaged the troops in their units with time on their hands would increasingly be demanding.

Following my mixed and on the whole sobering experiences thus far in the education corps, I found it reassuring and exhilarating to work with John Haynes, who combined a steady vision of what adult education was about with the organizing ability to create a rumbustious team spirit.

Endowed in this way with a strong sense of the value of serious study, and infused with a bubbling sense of *joie de vivre* and a will to involve the students, places on the Cuerden courses soon became widely sought after throughout the army home commands. To the prescription that presentation and content belonged together — hilariously illustrated for example in the Dobson and Young lessons in music, which soon afterwards became famous on radio and later television — the students responded with great enthusiasm. This philosophy in teaching adults cohered so closely with what I had myself been attempting to achieve at Dover that it confirmed what became a lifelong practice; thus 30 years on, as vice chancellor of the University of London, even in what purported to be austere, scholarly graduation addresses, I was still seeking, in Dr Sam Johnson's words, *docere et delectare*, both to teach and delight.

With the Nazi armies now in full retreat on the eastern and

western fronts and the war in Europe moving to a climax, I was looking forward to serving out my time at Cuerden Hall, but no sooner had the courses settled down than I was promoted to the rank of major and ordered to join Lieutenant Colonel Norman Fisher, who was commanding the army education college at Harlech, on a War Office mission to the British forces in the Italian and Middle Eastern theatres of war.

Among the service men and women of all ranks passing in large numbers through Cuerden Hall, it was impossible not to be impressed by the spirit of energetic optimism which, with victory in sight, was arising in Britain. Looking ahead to peacetime, the thoughts of most were turning to postwar problems and prospects. In accepting the need and duty to fight and defeat Hitlerism, many had looked also to a better future for the British people, and those of us in the services had been especially encouraged when the Army Bureau of Current Affairs (ABCA) started to circulate weekly pamphlets describing and discussing the progress of the war, and later the forward-looking, home structured *British Way and Purpose* booklets detailing the social and economic reforms which peace might bring. This appeared to reflect a belief that out of the mess of world war some good might emerge, that mankind could make a better world, that governments, if so minded, could successfully plan for economic growth, for good health care and education for all, and for the elimination of grinding poverty. Many, like myself, gained courage and hope in believing that the doctrines of violence and evil which the Nazis exemplified were in imminent retreat before a renewed confidence in the Western world in moral progress and the creation of a more equal and more caring society.

Early in 1944, when Bill Williams, the director of ABCA, paid a first visit to Cuerden Hall, I took the opportunity to raise the question of whether a series of pamphlets specifically on postwar reconstruction was being prepared, and, on his invitation, submitted a draft proposal. Later that year the War Office arranged a conference on the proposed army educational programme during demobilization at which I was invited to give two keynote lectures, one on the philosophy underlying the programme, the other on its educational content. Casting back to the work I had done while awaiting call-up on the origins of army education in 1917 and the failure to meet the identical challenge at the close of the First World War, I pointed to the opportunity now offered and to the moral. It was a subject on which I felt strongly and therefore spoke with warmth. Among the top brass present was the director general, Philip Morris, whom I had first met at Dover, said to be 'a very cool customer', who to my surprise offered his compliments both on what I had said and on 'the fire in my belly'. Two months later I was again summoned to see him at the War Office and told that I was at once to accompany Lieutenant Colonel Norman Fisher on a mission to Italy and the Middle East to explain to units in the field and to AEC personnel there what role education was to play in the period of demobilization and also how the 'release' of service men and women was to be arranged.

In leaving immediately after Christmas we could not have got off to a more miserable start. A thick fog prevented takeoff from Northolt aerodrome, so we had to be rushed to Swindon where, with little or no visibility and amidst two lines of blazing tar drums to clear the runway, we finally got away in a Wellington bomber that had been converted into a cargo carrier. With a couple of blankets each we curled up in the cargo hold for what turned out to be a numbingly cold journey, and 24 hours later, after two unscheduled stops in the south of France, landed at the Allied Force Headquarters at Caserta, near Naples in Italy.

En route I started sending to Dorcas a daily account of the mission, which lasted for nearly four months.

5

At War with Michelangelo

c/o Chief Education Officer
AFHQ, Caserta
31 December 1944

S afely here after a foggy start from Swindon and a sunny,
though extremely cold journey, stopping twice in the newly
liberated south of France before flying to this sprawling
Allied headquarters, an overblown city of huts and tents, now
housing thousands with separate messes for every rank —
generals, brigadiers, colonels, majors and so on *ad infinitum.*
What a bureaucratic nightmare General Alexander, the C-in-C,
has created for himself! I recall that the Duke of Wellington's staff
for an army of 40,000 in India consisted of seven! At no more
than 200 miles per hour we had a rough flight leaving me dazed,
my head buzzing, but not sick like poor Norman Fisher.

Installed in a splendid hut with all mod cons, we now prepare
for the fray starting within a few days. I've actually seen oranges
on sale on street stalls and find the southern Italians rather like the
Arabs, all Mediterranean people! Gin and whisky galore here!
And plenty of 'ladies of the night'!

1 January 1945
My quota of air letters is two per week, but no doubt as a
seasoned soldier I'll scrounge more. You are uppermost in my loving thoughts as I wish us both, or I should say, all three of us, a

good New Year. I've already given several ABCA lecture discussion demonstrations, and am beginning to look forward to our proposed travels, though I cannot share Sam Johnson's view that 'the grand object of travelling is to see the shores of the Mediterranean', and that 'until a man has been in Italy he is always conscious of an inferiority'. I may change my mind if I get to see Pompeii or Michelangelo's ceiling in the Sistine Chapel. To strike a more earthy note the MO here has insisted on giving me injections against typhus.

From the air, coastal Italy looks attractive and well tended, a colourful patchwork, more so than southern France; but on closer view the towns are filthy. For our trip we have been provided by AEC HQ with a large, camouflaged touring car with bullet-proof steel sheeting, along with Sergeant Keats, a tough-looking ex-paratrooper sergeant fresh from the desert war zone, as driver and protector. We were told that we shall have need of him because we are going north right up to the front line in mountainous areas and then south along the shattered Adriatic coast before we return. We are advised to take weapons with us and I am surprised to find that Norman Fisher has brought a revolver. Given the choice, today I have opted for an old Lee-Enfield rifle with 20 rounds as per regulations, which I know how to use, not trusting myself with anything else. More to the point, we've laid in a stock of candles for the trip at 40 lire, about 18d, each!

4 January 1945

I've visited what here passes for an army education centre, no more than a converted set of horse stables, and have given some talks. I am much impressed by Norman Fisher's skill as a lecturer, though I find that I am to be responsible for preparing and giving all new lecture subjects that arise, so am starting to organize my material on postwar reconstruction. We're setting out to inform and, I hope, entertain troops who at first sight at these headquarters strike me as bored out of their minds, except on the one subject of demobilization. Perhaps, to be fair, I ought to add wine and women!

Yesterday afternoon we visited Pompeii, the large size of which surprised me. I had expected to see a few broken columns and shells of buildings, but except for the absence of roofs, destroyed by the rain of ash from the eruption of Vesuvius in AD 79, there still stands a complete town, which must have housed some 20,000 Romans. Besides a large forum and amphitheatre, there are two theatres — one for the tragic, one for the comic muse — heated swimming baths and shops, one of which is fronted by an ice-cream stall made of slate (alas, no ice cream) and still intact; and even the ruts from cartwheels remain in the roads. My painful hours as a schoolboy with Caesar and Livy at last begin to come to life! Excavation there is still uninterruptedly proceeding, which no doubt is one way, the Italians' way, of putting this unwanted war in its place. They have taken to peace like ducks to water! But what an unsavoury lot they are!

Rome, 9 January 1945
On the way here we managed to visit the Anzio beachhead, making me wonder why the Allies when they landed in such easy terrain took so long to get inland; also to the Cassino mountain area dominated by the monastery on top. The town itself is virtually destroyed. We dared not leave the narrow road because of extensive minefields, still uncleared, and miles of broken barbed-wire entanglements surmounting great craters made by the Allies' air bombardment, testimony to the ferocity of the fighting. Mount Cassino must form one of the strongest defence positions against attack in Italy, as the Germans well appreciated, and it could only be frontally forced by destroying it.

In contrast, we are now staying in a luxury hotel in Rome, which we reached yesterday; a bedroom with a bathroom, luxurious curtains and carpets in Chinese gold and celadon green, telephone to hand, a bell for both the waiter and chambermaid (though no precise instructions to make sure of getting the one you want!). I've tried them both but in fact no one appears. It's a bit like Italy in general, first appearance often dazzling, later performance poor! We arrived soaking wet and have been drying out.

Tomorrow's course takes place in the university city, so I've been to check the lecture hall. The university campus as a whole, although only half completed, already reveals what a genius for design the Italians enjoy, putting in its place our stolid, crude, monolithic Senate House in Bloomsbury. Last night we went to the opera to hear the famous tenor, Gigli. Like the campus, the stage setting was magnificent, easily accommodating hundreds of players, glorious in brightly coloured costumes, better and more luxurious by far than anything I've ever seen. Where has the war gone? A few months ago all this, including the tenor Gigli, who is obviously at home in both camps, was presented just as cordially to the Germans. The Italians do not see themselves as a defeated nation, simply 'liberated', and are determined to exploit every opportunity of pretending we are now all friends so that 'business as usual' can return at once.

Perugia, 12 January 1945
After a snowy, cold and windy car journey lasting seven hours, thanks to our snow chains we safely made our way to this hilltop town, leaving behind our temporary luxury and plunging into a morass of slush and dirt. I'm told the people are poorly fed, but they look wonderfully plump and cheerful to me and, considering it is wartime, remarkably well-dressed too. Just as well you bombed-out Londoners, especially those short of clothing coupons, can't see them! In the distance the Apennine mountains, which we shall soon be crossing and recrossing, look heavily snow-covered. Cheek by jowl with the many splendours of Perugino's and Raphael's renaissance wood carvings, paintings and architecture, the utmost squalor prevails here, with stinking piles of garbage in the back streets and alleys, which the populace appear not to notice. Everywhere the priests are stalking around like crows, but are treated with exaggerated respect. Many of the churches appear to be converted ancient temples, often with Roman and Greek pillars still in place, so Christianity here appears half pagan, all part of the prevailing urban sense of continuity. There may be plenty of priests but little soul, I fear.

Florence, 16 January 1945
It is impossible not to be overwhelmed by the rich variety of goods on sale in the shops — wireless sets, typewriters and quite superb, well-designed perambulators (and to think at home you and I can't even order one!), silk underwear for women and for men,

too, all at high prices well beyond my reach. I'm buying you some hair slides and combs, which I know you can't get. I cannot cope with the plethora of baroque architecture, finding it not at all to my taste, and prefer the simplicity of the ancient Romans, as in the splendid rotunda of the gods, the Pantheon in Rome, which must be one of the stateliest buildings in the world.

The people we meet in the streets mostly smile and greet us, but they have undergone too great a political and spiritual collapse, exacerbated by their widespread and degrading superstition, to give us any confidence that they can fight as reliable allies. Outside the towns the countryside looks handsome, being intensively and tidily cultivated in long, dark lines of olives and vines, up hill and down dale, broken here and there by the destruction and debris of recent battles. Hereabouts many farmhouses lie ruined, roads and bridges are disrupted and warnings against mines abound. Always nearby lies a small pathetic graveyard, neat with rows of white crosses, mostly for British and American dead.

Amid the general urban squalor and destruction the fine medieval buildings of Perugia and Assisi, which house so many striking, colourful, world-famous paintings, have been successfully protected.

In its paintings, its buildings and ancient classical sites Italy contains the core of Europe's artistic heritage, but its people offer no model for anyone with self-respect to follow. Fine art is not necessarily produced by a good society and good people have no monopoly of fine art.

The British School of Army Education inhabits a magnificent house on the campus of the Foreign University, but absurdly only after persisting in our requests were we invited to go there, and then we received a chilly reception from the commandant — tall, thin, grey-faced and abrupt — who seems convinced that we have come to Italy to inspect and report on him. What we did manage to see and hear gave me the impression of a second-grade college run on humdrum limited lines, training for formal routine teaching, not education for wartime or for the peace to follow.

Leghorn, 18 January 1945
We scarcely had time to admire Florence, home of the famous

101

Medicis, with its splendid, square-structured palaces and inner courtyards, surrounded now by a flourishing multitude of small, expensive modern shops, before leaving for the next course in Leghorn on the coast, quite near to the front line. We drove through a gale, which has grown overnight into a hurricane, lashing the sea and drowning this poor, desolate, battered town. It reminds me of shell-shattered Dover harbour and seafront, busy with civilians and troops in daytime and apparently deserted at night. But unlike Dover there is no 'front-line university', no education or even leisure centre for the services here. We wonder what the AEC are busy doing!

At Florence, by the way, I lectured in a room Galileo once used, now adorned with his statue, under whose cold, unseeing eyes I duly performed. He, Michelangelo and Machiavelli are buried here; and I visited the church where Girolamo Savonarola, the religious reformer, preached and the square where he was hanged on the pope's orders as a false prophet.

I won't tantalize you with reports of blue skies and sunshine because the weather is diabolical — rain, snow and east winds turning into a gale. Fortunately I've managed to 'liberate' a leather jerkin to add to the pullover and scarf you knitted.

21 January 1945

From my bedroom on the seafront I can just glimpse Elba, where the exiled Napoleon first went. Today we returned to Florence via Pisa, first moving north near to the front line, though fortunately all was quiet and the Allied control of the air is total. I climbed to the top of the Leaning Tower (really a campanile, a bell-tower for the adjacent cathedral) which lists so frighteningly that I was not sorry to get down. The neighbouring white marble cathedral looks stunning; and as I move around, I find the dominance of tradition most impressive, giving a sense of unity to all Italian building, whether of ancient or renaissance times, whether domestic or public.

Florence stands out as the best city, the best place for a holiday visit for us some time or other, but definitely not in the winter. Meanwhile, I start a two-day course here.

En route today we were entertained to a sumptuous lunch by an

Italian *contessa* in her grand château, chattering away in a mixture of French and English, our tongues, too, no doubt loosened by the rapid succession of wines she pressed on us along with lavish plates of food. No shortage here! The countess, her château and lifestyle of plenty have effortlessly survived the war intact. She told us that political parties are beginning to emerge, dominantly the Christian Democrats, from what I could gather an unholy alliance of the Church and 'big business', and, needless to say, passionately supported by our hostess. Politics for her is a simple matter of getting and keeping, and no nonsense about the art of the possible.

Rear HQ, 8th Army, 22 January 1945
I'm worried about you and our baby, having only this evening received your cable, though I believe it reached yesterday. Your news is disconcerting, but you say you are well, which is what matters most. I can't begin to guess what the chances of survival of a premature baby of seven months may be, but assume that the early days are critically important and by now you will know where we stand. I'll be holding my breath for the next few days.

24 January 1945
I'm sending air letters which reach more quickly than cables. Not having heard again from you I'm feeling more confident, though with sudden lapses into anxiety. I'm thinking of you both, and hoping.

Tomorrow we start for Ancona on the Adriatic, with a rough crossing of the Apennine passes and snow in prospect.

Ancona, 25 January 1945, 7.45 p.m.
On arriving here I received another copy of your earlier cable, but no further news, so I feel despondent, but still full of hope for us. By now you will have my air letters. When I receive more detail I can ask sensible questions, but at present all I can rather helplessly keep saying is how much I love and think of you both, and ask how are you and how is the baby?

Last night we stayed at Assisi, the town of St Francis, its ascending levels of buildings neatly tucked into the mountain side. Although it was raining, I walked to the castle on the hilltop, arriving just in time to see the moon in a break of the clouds; I wondered whether you could see it too.

Tonight we reached Ancona after a rough journey through deep snowdrifts of 10 feet or more, and along precipitous narrow tracks above harsh rocky slopes, chillingly littered with wrecks of army lorries that had gone 'overboard'. They say that Polish drivers are the worst, but our Sergeant Keats is not much better!

Startling news awaited us. Norman Fisher has been recalled to London for a War Office conference leaving me to carry on the mission alone, if need be using local AEC assistants, a prospect I do not relish at all. Moreover, it puts me in a personal dilemma because I still await your up-to-date news. It makes me wonder too what importance the War Office gives to his mission and to what we are doing here.

26 January 1945

Another course for over 100 officers well completed — the eighth so far — amid much general appreciation. What has really startled me is the warmth of reception for my two lectures on postwar reconstruction at home, which create tremendous discussion.

I spent this evening with a young Italian couple, the husband a schoolteacher of about our age and with a similar standard of living, though both are much better dressed and, I guess, better fed. They expressed fears about Italy's politicians, having no faith in the Christian Democrats or the Communists. But social life is recovering and the only serious shortage, they say, is of food, but we had a good dinner! Their schools have not yet reopened. Although gloomy about their corrupt political parties, they seem blithely, naïvely optimistic about the future and confident of a more secure, richer life; and I must say, shortages or not, most of them look better fed and healthier than the British.

They live in the midst of beautiful buildings, fine paintings and striking statues, the best that the artist can produce, but they are as likely to be rogues as the next man, and our poet, John Keats, was wide of the mark in thinking that 'beauty is truth'.

Tomorrow I move for a long spell to army units in the region of Pesaro, which I shall largely be covering on my own. The weather has become bitterly cold.

At War with Michelangelo

Forli, 28 January 1945
I remain here for four days, much cheered by your buoyant letters written ten days ago, reassuring me that you are well and that our baby grows stronger; although reading between the lines I guess that it will be some weeks before he is established. What a testing, anxious experience you've suffered, and how long will you have to remain in hospital?

Norman has departed for London, expecting to return soon after the middle of February, during which period I will move from Forli to Rimini, Pesaro and Macerata before returning to Perugia to the School of Education. I reckon that this is the toughest part of the tour, taking in the forgotten, neglected side of Italy; on the narrow terrain between the stark mountains and the Adriatic, recently the scene of fierce fighting, every bridge over the many narrow, precipitous rivers has been destroyed.

Forli, 29 January 1945
On my own it is difficult to maintain a consistently high level of performance; and of course tiring. I'm wishing I was in Norman's place in London; anyway I've asked him to get in touch with you to bring back your up-to-date news and give you both my love.

All in all, the troops here, most of whom have been away from home for a very long time — three years seems to be the average — during which they've endured much stubborn fighting, remain surprisingly cheerful in conditions in which every house, usually windowless and doorless, is surrounded and every road covered by a sea of mud and dirty snow. People here understandably appear completely demoralized.

I'm sleeping and working in a filthy room in a shattered build-ing, with a broken desk and empty bookcase, on the top of which a lonely, intact, handsome Greek vase stands beside an empty picture frame. Forli, which is about the size of Kettering, which you know well, is shrouded in the decay of war and mountain mist, with a few empty shops and groups of miserable, shivering Italians, hands in pockets, standing on the street corners, no doubt hoping to cadge or steal cigarettes, chocolate or gum from the well-supplied, generous American troops.

In these areas few arrangements are made for me in advance by the local AEC, so I myself have to scout round for rooms, seats, blackboard and chalk, and find some form of heating, usually with firewood collected from nearby shattered houses. No one hitherto apparently has attempted this far forward to run any courses, even on current affairs or the strategy of the war, still less on 'the postwar', though the troops are stuck here with a lot of time on their hands. The least I can do is to show that it is worthwhile and feasible to do so; and as you would expect they are responding well, surprising me by their enthusiasm for my talks on postwar reconstruction, especially the hope of full employment.

So far I've coped with the conditions but am now struggling with a cold and cough, though fortunately I had the forethought to buy a bottle of cough mixture when in Florence. Besides my invaluable jerkin and the woolly scarf you sent me, I'm wearing two pullovers and a Balaclava and look a fearsome, bloated sight. Mercifully, plenty of stew and hot tea is provided; my chief lack, absurdly enough, is regular exercise. I have tried going out for a walk but there are no open spaces, just roads deep in mud and snow. Last evening I was staggered by the sight of hundreds of American lorries, headlights blazing brightly, lighting up the sky and the mountains on their way here without a care about possible air attack.

Last night as I lay down, too cold to get off to sleep, I imagined a triangle of forces or relationships within which we have to live: as human beings we have to live with others; also to come to terms with our natural environment within which we have evolved; lastly to make our peace with that which we define as God. For a general resolution of all this the keynote has to be cooperation not conquest, though most people still seem to choose the latter. Satisfied, I dropped off!

Faenza, 30 January 1945
I'm now well forward among our units, though from here there is no sign of the German positions. I'm assured that they are here! The chaps I meet get on with their routine, showing a mixture of resignation and anger, loyal to each other but vehemently asserting that they are being sacrificed for the sake of the second front in France. 'Soon', they say, 'we here will all be wounded or dead.'

Many of the strongest army divisions and air force squadrons were recently transferred before D-Day and more are going; although hereabouts little impression was made by the Allies in last autumn's attacks, they are confident of a spring breakthrough to the River Po. MEF, they claim bitterly, stands for 'Men England Forgot', and CMF, 'Chaps Monty Forgot'.

News soon got around that I knew all about the release scheme, so all day long I've been pursued by men asking me to calculate the number of their release points.

31 January 1945

This morning I gave a short talk on the general progress of the war to a small infantry unit north of Forli, on the outskirts of Faenza, making use of the kitchen in an abandoned farmhouse, lacking windows, doors and furniture. Judging by the number and quality of the questions afterwards, it was much enjoyed.

In the afternoon, while waiting for my return transport (and eating a good hot meal of spam and potatoes), my host, a burly, jovial, red-faced sergeant, who has a small unit of three men with him, doubting that my transport would turn up, got me bedded down with them for the night in a small, shattered farmhouse. Some hours later, probably about midnight, there was an awful hullabaloo outside and not far away some gunfire. Shouting 'Raid, raid', the sergeant shoved me with the others behind a stone wall where we crouched for ages, my legs shaking from strain, cold and, I suppose, fright. But there was no more noise and when snow began to fall the sergeant said, 'Bugger this!', which was exactly my sentiment too, so we all went inside and had a brew-up. Early next morning my transport, a rackety old jeep, just about made it back to Forli; the driver, on my telling him of the night's disturbance, dismissed it airily, 'Oh, that'll be the Yanks. They're always drunk and gun-happy.'

I now move to Rimini, Macerata and Pesaro to give a two-day course at each place. My driver, Sergeant Keats, has rejoined me, but he is so slack and furtive as to be useless.

Rimini, 4 February 1945

I've finished the Rimini course, having given six sessions on the first day and five on the next. The warmer weather is welcome, but has turned the snow into a universal quagmire of mud. Last night, in the army's own cinema, I thoroughly enjoyed the swashbuckling Errol Flynn in *Captain Blood*, which you may remember we saw together in another world in Cambridge. The war news of the Russians nearing Berlin is magnificent, which cheers everyone. I've been surprised by how much information, mainly in the form of ABCA pamphlets, the troops have about plans for postwar reconstruction in Britain, but, despite their obvious interest, no one, not even the AEC, bothers to present a more general understanding through organized discussion. Believe me, postwar reconstruction in Britain and fairer shares for all is a hot potato! There are two army newspapers, the *Union Jack* and *Eighth Army News*, both highly professional, and an army wireless station, so factually the troops are well serviced, and now, for the first time, I'm beginning to come across useful war information boards maintained, I'm glad to see, by the AEC.

Macerata, 7 February 1945

At Ancona, when HQ knew I was going to Macerata, they advised me to travel in convoy because of the guerrilla threat in the hills. Apparently army deserters — Poles, Canadians, Americans and also British — operate in gangs to raid the lorries on the road. My car was third in the convoy behind two trucks, the first and last carrying manned Bren guns. About seven miles into the hills, we were climbing a narrow, slushy road when the truck in front got stuck, but as my car had wheel chains and there was just enough room to pass, waved my driver on. No sooner had we got ahead than there was a terrific bang and our windscreen shattered. The car slid sideways to the left, stopping just on the edge of a snow-filled ditch. What seemed to be a noise of gunshots, with confusing echoes from the hills, broke out behind us. In a flash I grabbed my rifle and tumbled out, but got the wretched rifle barrel caught in the door and, for a few panic-stricken moments, had to wrestle it free before I could find a low profile behind the car. Meanwhile there was cursing from the other side of the car, for Sergeant Keats had fallen into the ditch which, under the snow cover, was full of icy, muddy water. He had left his rifle behind and for some minutes we had a futile argument about getting it. I felt murderous and frightened by turns, but by now, apart from some shouting, the noise had died down and, peering under the car, I saw the young lieutenant, who was in charge of the convoy, walking up the road shouting loudly, waving his arms, nervously ordering us to leave the convoy and go on alone. Calmer by the time he reached us, he said that we had been attacked by deserters who seemed to have cleared off. So, knocking out the broken windscreen, we drove through occasional snow showers to Macerata, arriving late, filthy, frozen and fed up. I don't think I'm cut out for soldiering!

George Washington said that, if not hit, it was exhilarating to be shot at, but then he also said that he could never tell a lie!

9 February 1945

I'm sitting in a tiny room, no bigger than our dining room at home, crouching over an oil stove, which fumes and smells but at least does heat the place. I've found several copies of *Picture Post* which, by the often interrupted dim electric light, I can just about manage to read. One contains an article on how to become a guerrilla fighter! Plenty of the army deserters here must have read it! There is no water supply so I get only one cold-water wash a day and spend most of my spare moments dreaming of a hot bath. I leave the day after tomorrow.

Our car today had a bad smash, the driver, Keats, being hurt, though not badly; fortunately I was not with him. The car, however, is a write-off, so I shall have to rely on local army transport to get to Perugia and then Rome by 14 February, when Colonel Fisher may rejoin me. I'm glad that this did not happen earlier, but no doubt I'll manage.

Macerata, 7.00 p.m., 10 February 1945

As I write I'm sitting in the lounge of the transit hotel waiting to be summoned to a hot bath, though I've been warned by the desk sergeant not to expect much more than buckets of hot water. I've been called so here I go!

I've had my long-prayed-for bath. Towel under my arm, I was collected by a slim, handsome Italian youth with a flashing smile, who promptly led me at a fast pace through a maze of unlit streets and back alleys and down long lines of narrow dark steps, and, when I was just beginning to fear some sort of trap, flung open a door and ushered me straight into a large lamp-lit kitchen where an Italian family, children, parents and grandparents, was just tucking into its evening spaghetti. They all looked up smiling but, completely ignoring them, my guide took me straight through another door into a primitive bathroom. While I undressed he filled the bath from a hot-water tap and then, while I waited for him to leave, just stood there smiling. After fiddling around for a bit, while he went on inanely grinning, I got into the bath, on which he rushed at me, flourishing a piece of soap, and began vigorously scrubbing my back. You know what a shrinking violet I am, so just as vigorously, with some indignation, I pushed him off. Undeterred, he stood aside still smiling, then, holding up a bottle, enquired 'Shampoo?' 'No', I said, very firmly, but without more ado, he poured some into his hand and sloshed it over my head, after which I gave up. The family was still eating as I sidled self-consciously past on the way back to the hotel. Once there the young man smiled again and disappeared before I could give him a tip.

I've been able to pace myself through the last few courses, all attended by groups of commanding officers who seem impressed by what they have heard and certainly do not stint in their praises, though they are more reserved than the rank and file. All are busy 'drinking life to the lees', whatever their rank, so much so that in reaction I've become almost teetotal, fortified in that decision by finding that some rough, local red wine offered to me quickly took the skin off the inside of the cardboard container!

Did I tell you I had the opportunity to make a record of my voice and, on hearing it played back, was quite surprised to find it was much lower-pitched than I had expected? Of course there are strong Welsh and Merseyside traces, and academic overtones.

Macerata is boldly sited on a hilltop, the town surrounded by ancient walls, honeycombed by narrow streets and staircases, peppered with charming, minute, well-stocked shops, all dominated by several noble buildings, not least of course the church.

I've arranged transport to get Keats and myself to Rome.

At War with Michelangelo

I am at ease now in Perugia at the Army School of Education, warm and dry, the more enjoyable after my wretchedly damp and cold room in the transit hotel at Macerata; and the sun has at long last begun to shine. All has been capped by the good cheer of your four letters, which were awaiting me here. You and your parents have laboured mightily and successfully to succour John, our baby, and since he has at last started to suckle he surely must go from strength to strength. I suspect though that it has all been much more of a struggle than you have let on. I have been trying to buy some rubber teats for his bottles, so far without success.

You ask about our relations with the Italian people. With plenty of chocolate, chewing gum and cigarettes, not to mention *vino*, our troops soon make friends, evoking warm enthusiasm from a largely extrovert population, which itself is quite childlike in dismissing all responsibility for the war or the future. 'All Mussolini's fault', they laughingly say, and I fear they really believe that. I think that the Italians, smiling and cordial on first acquaintance, are a hypocritical, self-seeking lot, superstitious beyond belief and rotten at the core. If I did not keep constant watch, I would lose everything.

Perugia, 13 February 1945
What a luxury to be able to spend a day largely on my own after weeks of living cheek by jowl with others, always on tap and constantly being questioned. My tour of the medieval hilltop towns — Spoleto, Loretto, Siena, Perugia and Assisi — is complete, each commanding the intense loyalty of its almost feudal townsfolk, and each run by its own local, greatly feared barons. Italy is not a nation but a collection of chiefdoms well sprinkled with artists and their work. I've come across some apt words of Mark Twain in his *Innocents Abroad*, which express what I've been feeling: 'I wish to say one word about Michelangelo. In Perugia he designed everything; he designed Lake Trasimene; in Florence he painted everything nearly. . . . I never felt so fervently thankful, so soothed, so tranquil, so filled with a blessed peace, as I did yesterday, when I learned that Michelangelo is dead. . . . Lump the whole thing! Say that the Creator made Italy from designs by Michelangelo.'

From my private collection — 'a frustration of pin-ups'; 'a negative of quartermasters'; 'a had-it of soldiers'. And to conclude, some scrawled graffiti on a wall, 'VINO, VENUS, VD'.

Rome, 14 February 1945

Back in Rome where I found Norman awaiting me, with indirect, reassuring news of you and rumours that on my return home I am to be promoted to higher things at Cuerden. However, I'm twice shy by now. Apparently all three army schools of education at home, including Cuerden, will soon be turning on identical 12-day courses to train instructors for the demobilization period.

Naples, 17 February 1945

We have a new driver and a fresh car, having to leave Sergeant Keats in Rome in gaol for a stupid, drunken attack on, of all people, two military policemen. He has proved a dead loss, no doubt 'burnt out', his stock of courage exhausted through over-long service in North Africa, there having become both 'sand and bomb-happy', and as a driver he was a menace. 'These Eyeties', he used to say, 'are worse than the Ayrabs of Africa', all the while putting his foot hard on the accelerator, making straight for any Italian incautious enough to cross his path. Apparently, suspicious of our motives, AEC command headquarters here specifically attached him to us under orders to send back confidential reports on our tour and what we were up to! He was a miserable spy and rotten soldier withal!

Tomorrow we go south via Pomigliano to Foggia and Bari.

I'm disappointed to hear that you have not yet been able to bring John home from hospital with you, vigorous and determined though he appears to be, and anxiously await more reassuring news. Please, there is no possible reason for you to reproach yourself for delivering him early! The stress brought about by war has to carry some responsibility surely; and it sounds as though you and your parents are performing heroically. My love to you all.

19 February 1945

Back, I'm sorry to say, to vile weather, snow and cutting east winds. As I move south I find the people and the countryside increasingly unattractive, money-grabbing and hostile. Naples' narrow streets constitute a maze of open sewers. Mark Twain's response to a complaint that the streets were too narrow was, 'If they were wider, they'd hold more smell.' Much of this rural area is both arid and uncultivated, mostly dull, here and there with line after line of monotonous vines and olives. I yearn for the fresh, bright-green variegated fields of England. Most of the towns we've passed through are filthy, with garbage and debris littering the streets, blocking every alley and drain: here and there old trams clank along, packed full inside and with people hanging precariously to every nook and cranny outside. Pedestrians show an appalling disregard for military traffic, so that nasty, bloody accidents frequently occur, creating unpleasant scenes which immediately release the normally concealed antagonism to the troops.

As we move south, more and more large white oxen are to be seen ploughing the fields, giving me the feeling that I've already entered the Near East. But here the women, who also carry great loads on their heads, look impressively tough and hefty.

By the way, I made an unplanned, quite spectacular first public appearance in the officers' transit hotel in Ancona, which has afforded general amusement at my expense. I arrived very late at night because on the coast route my car had to queue repeatedly to cross the quick succession of rivers, usually having to be drawn over on a raft by ropes because the bridges have not yet been restored. It must have been midnight when I arrived to find the hotel vestibule deserted and the place in darkness, but, using my torch, I found a chalked message on a board giving me my room number for the night and instructing me to report to the adjutant first thing the following morning.

My room was on the top floor with one window, which would not open, so it was stiflingly hot. Dumping my case at the bedside, I threw off my clothes and, absolutely worn out, crawled into bed and straight into sleep. Just after 7.00 the next morning I came to slowly, suddenly realizing that my case and all my clothes had gone. It turned out that they had been stolen; so there was nothing for it but to wrap myself in a sheet and find my way downstairs into the by now busy vestibule. As I descended, treading gingerly into view in my toga, every bit the image of an ancient Roman

senator, a sudden silence fell and, as I stepped across to the desk
sergeant saying 'Major Philips reporting', there was an enormous
roar and prolonged applause. I've managed to buy a new case,
replace my uniform and acquire a lock and chain for use in future.

Taranto, 21 February 1945
Here in the south succeeding civilizations have left their imprint,
Saracen, Norman, Swabian, Greek and Roman, all have had their
day. Most attractive and unusual are the *tulli*, conical-shaped cot-
tages built of stone, which I saw in a town with the lovely name of
Alberobillo — small fairy-tale palaces just the same as in the
pictures in my old copy of Hans Andersen. We spent some time in
a peasant farmer's house where in the middle of the rough, paved
kitchen floor there was an enormous pile of almonds. My long-
thwarted passion for nuts proved my downfall, for our eager host
invited me to help myself, producing also a bottle of home-made,
rough red wine. Norman joined in and both of us since have been
painfully, though temporarily, laid low. Drinking among the
troops is excessively heavy down here and we found the military
hospital full of lads with stomach trouble and, I suppose, head-
aches!

My lectures are still being received well and today I was asked
whether I intend going into politics!

Amalfi, 24 February 1945
After completing our last course we came to this gloriously warm
spot via Avellino and Salerno, over snow-capped hills brilliant in
the sunshine, then along the invasion coast beside the blue sea. As
I sit on the balcony of a small monastery, perched on the sunny
cliffside surrounded by palms, I can reach out and pick lemons
and oranges. In a flash my cough and tribulations of recent weeks
have vanished.

But I've also had some time to reflect on this mission, hardly
possible earlier because since we left England I've had only four
free days. Without question, the troops in general, particularly the
forward units, from commanding officers down to the ranks, have
obviously enjoyed our courses and have provided an enthusiastic,
personal welcome. This to my mind throws into dark relief the

general failure of the education corps here which, despite the presence of several able individuals, has missed a great opportunity, providing very few courses or leisure centres and a meagre presentation of ABCA and BWP topics, and not much teaching or organized discussion, with the result that most of the corps members, many of them trained teachers, have found themselves turned into office information clerks. The all too evident, groundless suspicion in education corps headquarters of the underlying reason for our tour has been scandalous and absurd, and has undermined the energizing influence we might have had on the rank and file of the corps itself. We anticipate a more responsive, welcoming reception in the Middle East.

In the air, 27 February 1945
We are flying via Malta and Benghazi to Cairo, in the company of troops, both Yugoslav and American, all big chaps so I'm pressed for space. I felt a thrill as we landed on tiny, clean, tidy, patchworked Malta; and I was delighted to meet over lunch several of the British administrative staff who organized Malta's defiant civilian defences during the siege and, with the armed services, achieved the apparently impossible in keeping it fed and free.

Cairo, 1 March 1945
Cairo's mean streets are bright and busy with men in white robes and red fezzes, all set in a flashy Western context of luxurious cars superimposed on a noisy, dirty Oriental society. But Egyptians often possess a dignity lacking in the Italians. I dare not describe the plethora of exotic goods and clothes in the shops, all though at excessively high prices. I did manage to get a sponge for John for about the equivalent of 30 shillings! Today I enjoyed a cream meringue for tea. Would you like a brand new gramophone for £12?

We started work on arrival already aware of the superior organization and quality of the education corps here compared with Italy; we were gratified too by an open, warm welcome.

Last night by moonlight I saw the El Gîza pyramids and the poor old battered noseless Sphinx, whose disfigurement was started by Napoleon's French troops releasing their boredom by taking pot shots. Moonlight sharpened all the outlines and made real for me some of the savagery of the Pharaohs. Tomorrow we fly to Haifa in Palestine.

Mount Carmel, 3 March 1945

A letter from you sent eight days ago awaited me. Your news of John's progress is heartening, but I'm alarmed to hear about the efforts over so long a period which you have had to make in expressing milk for him from your breasts. It must be painful. Please take care. I want you both to be strong and well.

Haifa enjoys a magnificent situation, 1200 feet above the sea on a sharp ridge looking down on one side to the harbour, on the other to the Mediterranean. Harmonious modern buildings dominate in pale grey and buff stone, flat-topped, some of them palatial, creating patterns of shadows in the sun, no doubt built by German architects. The School of Education is housed in a former sanatorium where already we've given several lecture-cum-discussion demonstrations. One of the staff, Michael Stewart, impressed me, calm, measured, academic in style, with a charming, winsome smile, no more than 40, yet already grey-headed, who apparently is a Labour Party candidate for East Fulham. At this school the general standard of teaching is high, comparing well with Cuerden.

You would love the profusion of spring flowers — brilliant red and blue anemones, pale cyclamen, luxurious yellow gorse and broom, blood red tulips and white daisies — all growing wild alongside snowdrops, and groves of narcissi, blue pimpernel and irises, too, sprouting from pockets in the prevailing buff-coloured limestone. As if this is not enough, the snow-capped mountains of the Lebanon rise majestically in the background. Imagine a flower-strewn roof of the world!

4 March 1945

Did you laugh when hearing that Syria had retrospectively declared war on Germany 'with effect from 1 March?'

More of our lecture demonstrations early this morning, then a sharpish visit down the coast to a ruined former crusader castle, Athlit, with remnants too of the Phoenicians and Romans. That old rogue, Richard the Lionheart, came here and Saladin also captured it. Not far away stands Acre, where Sydney Smith thwarted Napoleon and destroyed his thrust for India in 1800. I'm alternately dazzled by flashes of history and the multicoloured flowers which flourish everywhere.

Sunshine has given way, alas, to frequent showers of hail, and reading Freya Stark's *Letters from Syria* I see that the weather in winter here can be as unpleasant as in Italy, which is saying something! Army folk in this former war zone show a sense of security, serenity and even resignation, very different from the fretful, unhappy troops in Italy, which may well simply reflect the difference between feeling safe behind the war lines and being in the war zone, where survival is all.

I've added a third to my lectures on postwar reconstruction in Britain, being especially seized by the potential for producing a better society if only our governments will moderate old convictions and adopt a scientific, questioning outlook, using pilot experiments to test hunches and hypotheses as a means of assessing feasibility and public understanding and wishes, and cautiously feeling a way forward before attempting major, untried policies. I have illustrated this by reference to the White Papers on postwar reform, including the one on full employment, evidently quite *new* to the troops! But will governments, politicians and even businessmen ever be prepared to take the necessary long views instead of always looking for instant success?

6 March 1945

I still feel I'm in paradise, walking on carpets of tulips and brilliant wild blue irises, looking to far-flung azure horizons and being warmed by the sun before having to turn to the job in hand. With the teaching staff here we have usefully exchanged views on the philosophies underlying our respective teaching, giving me the chance to repeat the Dover and Cuerden philosophy that everything we see around us, everything in life, can be educational if we choose to see it so. I've also urged that the question of how to create a fair, tolerant society in a fully employed developing economy in peacetime Britain should form the core subject matter in training army instructors for the postwar period of demobilization. Add a spice of fun and deliberate entertainment and Jack cannot remain bored or dull. One strong difference between Haifa and Cuerden emerged: here the instructors work as individuals, at Cuerden we work in teams.

Following my lectures, Michael Stewart came up and said 'You're a natural for politics!' and urged me when I get back to join the Labour Party. He asked if I had been giving the same lectures in Italy because 'they must be worth thousands of votes to Labour!' Personally I do not mind which party is in power provided it takes note and acts.

We are to meet Philip Morris, the director general of army education, who is here on tour, in about a week's time.

Meanwhile, in the evenings, both in Cairo and here, I've been taken to watch much Arab belly-dancing and jig-jigging — alas, very poor, boring stuff — and it was a relief as a change to watch some real acrobats.

You would be amused and pained to see how the Arab treats a motorcar or van, just as though it's his donkey or camel. Load it until its springs groan and grate, and its tyres flatten! Then if it can't, or won't, go, kick it and keep kicking!

10 March 1945
Away soon to Beirut and Damascus, 'the jewel of the earth'. Drawing my head from the clouds, my recent state of euphoria recedes as I begin to perceive the rivalries and serious political problems emerging here. Yesterday I passed a squad of husky, bronzed young Jews who apparently form part of a big labour corps. They carried shovels on their shoulders and it did not require much imagination to see them making a ready exchange for rifles. A struggle for power and land here between the Jews and Arabs obviously looms.

Judaism, Christianity and Islam have spread outwards from this region and, in moving around, you become aware that the edge of civilized living is never far away, that the town, the sown areas and the desert have been and are interacting all the time.

Beirut, 11 March 1945
Seating in the slow train, which brought us to Beirut, was rough

and hard on the bottom as we dawdled north along the coast; *en route* I could not help recalling T. E. Lawrence's comments on the relative ease of destroying, by raids from the desert, these long stretches of railway track. Tyre and Sidon are no better than wretched little hovels; but Beirut, like Haifa, has many handsome buildings, including the American University, though the prevailing general influence is French.

It is a busy, boisterous place, with Christians cheek by jowl with Muslims seemingly, and surprisingly, held together by the search for profit. Silks, tapestries, rich carpets and everything exotic are to be had for astronomic prices.

Haifa, 14 March 1945
In the last few days we've made the journey by car to Damascus and back, first failing to get across the direct, snow-capped pass at 6000 feet and having to circle round through the Orontes valley, down miles of deep gorges cut through limestone and sandstone with former crusader castles on the hilltops above. A harsh landscape is occasionally relieved by patches of vivid green grass, though the eye is always caught by the towering summit of Mount Hermon. Suddenly, in the foothills, we came on Damascus, which surprised me for I had expected to find it in the middle of the plain. From every side the rivers flow and the music of water from springs and fountains fills the air. And the domes of mosques cover the city. In the *souk* (market) I was tempted to buy you some silk for a dress at £9 a yard, but, needless to say, had to resist!

We rushed back to Haifa to fulfil our commitments, descending into the green fertile valley and Sea of Galilee, through Capernaum and Tiberias and Nazareth, haunted by scenes I first saw in pictures in my boyhood Bible. Along every road and stream life imitates art.

At the Orient Palace Hotel in Damascus in the foyer I could not but admire two sheikhs, resplendent in white robes and gold and red head-dresses. Outside stood a Rolls-Royce and a new, swish yellow sports car. I was told that they were both chiefs of bedouin tribes, that is desert nomads who move with their herds of camels and sheep in the spring and autumn. These chiefs, making use of cars not camels, still keep company with their tribes, yet from the comfort of nearby hotels. One was Fawwaz, head of the Ruwalla, successor of Nuri, a one-time colleague of T. E. Lawrence, though in facial appearance not to be compared with his heroic forbears as drawn by Eric Kennington for *The Seven Pillars*.

After a morning's work in Haifa, I was taken to see a Jewish agricultural settlement in which the settlers own the land in common, sharing the toil and the profits. I also visited the local school, which itself runs a farm, so the keynote of its curriculum is agricultural activity. Commitment and conviction to this degree and in this style are awesome and daunting because they denote a ruthless desire at all costs to succeed and, if need be, fight, conquer and acquire. Poor Arabs!

Jerusalem, 16 March 1945
Calm, warm weather makes our travels enjoyable. We've reached Jerusalem, cool at 2000 feet, and taken a brief look at the old, dirty town and walked round the city walls, at one point looking up to Government House, home of the governor, Lord Gort. How these played-out generals keep on bobbing up! Apparently the Arabic name for the hill on which the house is built means 'Hill of Evil Counsel!'

Yesterday, being Friday, the Muslim shops closed, today the Jewish shops close and tomorrow, being Sunday, of course the Christian shops close. But they all agree to close for Easter! There must be a moral somewhere! Every church, synagogue and mosque seems at some time in history to have interchanged roles. Here true religion and the organized churches have long since parted company. No, don't come looking for true faith here!

19 March 1945
We interlard lectures and demonstrations with quick sightseeing visits, this afternoon to the famous Dome of the Rock mosque, formerly (and inevitably) the site of Solomon's Temple. The rock is accordingly sacred to the Jews; and is so also to the Muslims because Muhammad took off from it for Heaven, and also to the Christians because Christ trod the same ground. Like Jerusalem itself, it forms a farrago of religious superstitions and vested, com-

peting interests. One begins to see how Christianity emerged from Judaism and Islam grew in reaction to both. If any sort of peace after the war is to be found here, Britain will be sensible to get out quickly and turn over the area to international control.

Sarafand, 20 March 1945
While I write I'm half listening to the command AEC officer introducing the director general of army education, Philip Morris. He started by saying how much he dislikes lecturing, but here we are, 20 minutes later, and he's still going strong!

Otherwise, I am still working hard, lecturing virtually every day with little spare time. I'm also agog with what I see, but Norman is plainly bored, aching to get back home. Meanwhile on to Tel Aviv and not long now before our return. I've acquired two useful Arabic words — *maalesh*, 'what does it matter?', and *bukra*, 'tomorrow' — and, like the Arabs, hope to last out on them.

Some of the Arab states have joined to form an Arab League, but I fear that the Arabs, their rulers and their states are too quarrelsome to make a success of it. Though naturally proud to be Muslim and apparently united in antagonism to the Jews, they are still tribal, only too ready to fall out among themselves.

Port Said, 21 March 1945
From the first floor of this hotel I look over miles of sand beyond the waterway which leads to the Suez Canal, not all that different from what I first saw as a young boy of 8 passing this way in 1921. As Norman and I rested on our hotel beds looking out over the harbour, we saw several British troopships sail by, their decks lined with soldiers on the way to the Far East. 'Poor buggers!' said Norman, 'I wonder how long they'll be there?' I didn't answer, not wishing to tempt fate; and look forward to being back with you within a fortnight.

This afternoon I saw a mirage, which I'm told is always an image of water, never of land or trees; certainly the mirage I saw was of water stretching all the way to the distant foothills.

Ismailia, 24 March 1945
In between courses and lectures we are continually overwhelmed

by chaps who feel they need to converse with folk from home with 'fresh minds', with people like us who have not long been out here. Lurking behind all their conversation are the questions, 'How much have I changed through being so long overseas? What will my wife or girlfriend be like now and will she still want me? Has she been faithful?' Not a word about their own behaviour! Some — those perhaps who are 'sand-happy' — are signalling, 'Tell me I'm still normal.' Our lectures on the 'release' scheme, I'm pleased to say, and especially mine on the postwar world, have been as greatly welcomed here as in Italy and our personal reception, unlike in Italy, has been both warm and friendly; so we and our mission as a whole are leaving in good heart.

One last course before we reach Cairo, where I hope to find your letters. Departure day for home and there, hopefully, some leave seems likely to come within a week. See you both soon!

❋ ❋ ❋

On returning to Northolt in London I was told, before taking some leave, to report personally to Philip Morris, the director general, at the War Office and went fully expecting to discuss the Mediterranean mission, although I had not been shown the final report, which presumably Norman Fisher had already submitted. But, after dismissing the trip in a few, congratulatory words, Morris to my surprise went straight into a discussion of the future of the army school at Cuerden Hall, where he said he had already made changes in the senior staff and decided that I was to be promoted to lieutenant colonel and would return there as commandant. Looking to an early end to the fighting in Europe, he told me that Cuerden Hall's throughput of instructors for the period of demobilization had to be greatly increased, involving an immediate crash programme in recruiting staff and erecting new buildings. Punch-drunk under these incessant changes, when I got back to Preston I found that a company of 300 'pioneers', who unfortunately came vaguely under my control, had already been located there to carry out the building work.

But on 7 May 1945 all else paled into insignificance beside the news that the Germans had capitulated, incidentally fulfilling my miserable anticipation at the start that it would take six years to bring them down. The whole camp exploded in a tumultuous, delirious day of which I can recall little except that at some stage, blind to the world, I auctioned with some panache, and evidently as to the manner born, the whole of the sergeants' mess and later, so I was told, put on an impromptu variety act which brought the house down.

During the following couple of months my time as commandant was divided between preparing for educational expansion and trying to keep the 'pioneers' steadily at work and in good disciplined order. Every evening a large number of them went on a pub crawl looking for and invariably finding a 'punch-up', with the result that, as commanding officer, I had to spend the best part of each morning dealing with offenders. Nevertheless they got on with the job of laying and installing the foundations for the huts; and I was just beginning to breath easily again when once again I was summoned to London to see Philip Morris.

There he told me that a special request for my services had been made by HM Treasury through Paul Sinker, who apparently had recently been appointed to a newly created post of director of civil service training. I recalled that just before I had left for Italy, Sinker, who was then training officer for the Admiralty, had paid a visit to Cuerden where he had spent most of his time sitting in on lectures, classes and discussions, which formed part of a general government scrutiny of training establishments. As a result he had decided to ask for my services on secondment as chief instructor of the civil service training programme which the Treasury, on the recent recommendation of the Assheton Committee of the House of Commons, was about to initiate. In addition, the move was treated as promotion and I was given a rise in salary.

Pleased to be in at the beginning of what was obviously a new, wide-reaching and important venture, I was not sorry in effect to be leaving the army and joining Sinker in Richmond Terrace in Whitehall; and I fully expected that my first task would be to produce a nucleus of training officers for the major traditional departments of state. To my surprise, it appeared that Sinker's priority was to grapple first with staff training in the departments that had grown most rapidly during the war, particularly the Ministry of Labour and those involved in communications, like the Post Office. His immediate aim for them was quickly to enlarge and strengthen the supervisory cadres and, in seeking to do this, he wanted me to look first at, and if need adapt for our own use in Britain, the 'TWI' (training within industry) and 'job instruction' intensive courses for supervisors and managers, first devised in the USA, which had largely enabled industry and government there to mobilize so massively and successfully for war.

Given a fortnight to reconnoitre these courses before transferring them to the UK and, finding them on my own criteria as a teacher to be soundly based, I spent the next few weeks modifying them for the civil service and producing a basic six-week programme for trainers, also capable of being applied later to most civil service departments. Personally I then ran the first five successive Treasury courses. One of my early visitors, Wyn Griffith, the chief training officer of the Inland Revenue, surprisingly level-headed for a Celtic bard, who had no difficulty in making eccentricity look normal, immediately involved me in his own department's plans, incidentally also introducing me to my Welsh origins. He got me to help in opening in Finchley the first training centre for income tax inspectors, an initiative my academic colleagues have always subsequently held against me. Of more widespread concern, arising from the ample evidence which was available to me in civil service files, official reports and correspondence, I was able to provide some pertinent examples of civil service gobbledegook for Sir Ernest Gowers, who, following Winston Churchill's well-known criticisms, had been commissioned to prepare for publication a practical guide for civil servants in the writing of *Plain English*; which turned out to be a minor classic, whose civilizing influence reached far beyond the service.

Meanwhile the atomic bombs fell on Japan and brought the war there to an end. At that stage we did not need the pictures of Belsen and Hiroshima to remind us that, whatever means had to be used, we were above all glad the war was over.

From the start it had been intended that once Sinker's department in the Treasury had created a general framework for civil service training and produced the first generation of training officers, it would devolve direct responsibility to the departments themselves and to a new civil service training college at Ascot, and itself would wither away. In my mind therefore there was never any question but that when the war came to an end I would leave. But Sinker, who knew that he himself would anyway soon be moving on as chief civil service commissioner, pressed me hard to stay and commit myself to a permanent career in the service. Almost at the same time, through an unexpected initiative of Bill Williams, the wartime ABCA chief and later secretary general of the Arts Council, I was invited by the large steel firm of Richard Baldwin & Company in south Wales to take on a new post as director of training, an offer particularly enticing, partly because it was already becoming clear that training within British industry was bound to play a significant role in postwar reconstruction, and partly because the salary offered was four times that which I would be receiving if and when I returned to the university. So, over a lively weekend, Dorcas and I pondered our options, she plaintively commenting that surely there was no problem, but after some soul-searching, coming to the conclusion that temperamentally we were probably best suited to, and would be happiest in, returning to the path we had chosen before the war, and that I would therefore resume my career in university research and teaching.

6

A Short Trip into Africa

In the early, so-called 'phoney' period of the war, perhaps to assuage a troubled national conscience and to replace vague, frustrated policies of the past with firmer, responsible resolve for the future, the Westminster Parliament had passed into law a Colonial Development and Welfare Act. This proposed over a ten-year period and through a programme of both public and private investment to overhaul and give shape to the British use of colonial resources in order to provide a better standard of life for the dependent peoples.

Unable until the war was over to take effective action, the Colonial Office as a first step in implementing this policy advised the four dependent East African governments of Kenya, Uganda, Tanganyika and Zanzibar of its intention to promote five-year development plans, inviting them to consider a list of topics for a first agenda, on which appeared the little known term, 'mass education', which so puzzled the four governors that they at once got together to ask Whitehall for clarification.

Evidently taken by surprise, the Colonial Office hastily did some homework, finally explaining that the term had been taken from the title of a small pamphlet, *Mass Education in African Society*, published during the war as a blueprint to initiate public discussion on postwar colonial reconstruction. Among the small group of academics and civil servants responsible for producing this were Professor Margaret Read of the London Institute of Education and Christopher Coxe, educational adviser to the colonial secretary, both passionate believers in the power of education to generate social and economic development as a means of transforming colonial societies, and in fact rather more interested in arguing theory than in offering any precise definition of 'mass education' or how it might be brought about. Whether it was sensible to try directly to change cultures that had endured in unpromising conditions for centuries did not appear greatly to concern them.

To the postwar Labour government elected in 1945 on a platform of reconstruction, both at home and abroad, and particularly to the new colonial secretary, Mr Arthur Creech Jones, formerly a leading idealistic member of the reformist Fabian Bureau, the appeal of a 'crash' programme of mass education for the largely illiterate populations of the colonies evidently proved irresistible, and he forthwith called for some exploratory action.

Although, as one of the postwar appointees to the Colonial Office's research committee on social policy, I had already got to know Christopher Coxe, it came as a surprise when, along with one of his senior civil service colleagues, Andrew Cohen, recently promoted as head of a department with responsibility for Africa, he approached me with the suggestion that, on behalf of the colonial secretary and to help the four governors, I should undertake a short reconnaissance to East Africa as a means of giving some precise definition to the idea of 'mass education' and, if feasible, to examine ways and means of promoting it.

Although my recent experiences of adult education in the army and of training in the civil service and concern about postwar reconstruction predisposed me to help, my personal knowledge of the difficulties and failures which the British had met in village reconstruction in India, especially in the work of Malcolm Darling and Francis Brayne, had made me sceptical about the validity in poor traditional societies of attempting to apply big bold policies like 'mass education'. Serious doubts too about my own personal fitness for the task deterred me, but Coxe and Cohen went on pressing, protesting that all they had in mind was a modest first reconnaissance; and to my personal disavowal argued that there were few, if any, experts in the subject. I had never visited Africa south of the Sahara and there was some possibility, I supposed, that I might bring to bear some of the British experience in India, so in the upshot, although unwilling so soon after the separations of wartime to leave my family again for any long period, we reached a compromise committing me to go in the following summer vacation for two months and to visit all four East African territories, and on my request to restrict any immediate proposals for action to Tanganyika.

Within days second thoughts took over for Coxe at once began to bombard me with books and reports, and in his excruciatingly high-pitched nasal Oxford voice plagued me with repeated, excessively drawn-out harangues on the telephone. Plainly, on the subject of educating Africans, he was a man eater who would not let go.

A confirmed and fussy bachelor with time on his hands, Coxe was at his most comfortable and best around the committee table. I never met a more quintessential committee man, a greater magician of fiddling and fidgeting, and to work alongside him was both to witness and endure an unforgettable experience.

Although a confirmed pipe smoker, he was always worrying about his health and the need to control his addiction, and, as a compromise, had carried to a fine art the whole business of preparing to smoke without ever actually lighting up. Right at the start of a committee, while the minutes of the previous meeting were being approved, he began one by one to pat the bulging pockets of his capacious Harris Tweed jacket, eventually, after several false starts, digging out a couple of pipes, a tobacco tin and pouch and a large brass lighter, all of which he placed reverently and precisely on the table before him. Somewhat anxiously he would then cast round for an ashtray and, when it was safely acquired, would at once begin another pocket search, finally, with a grunt of satisfaction, producing an ingenious metal pipe-cleaning contraption. Each pipe bowl was then subjected to a minute scrutiny, as if he had never seen it before, and to a process of scraping and tapping, invariably induced to disgorge endless bits of old ash and unburned tobacco, which he plainly regarded with intense dismay. By this time it was necessary to cast round, and get everybody else to look round, for a second ashtray.

With the tobacco well tamped into the pipe of his choice, surely the moment all present had been waiting for had at last arrived, but he would sit back and fiddle with his impedimenta, and alas, I never did see him light up and enjoy a really good puff.

* * *

As soon as the university summer term ended I therefore departed for East Africa in a two-engined Dakota plane from London, again picking up my wartime habit of sending a daily account to Dorcas.

* * *

Approaching Malta, 20 July 1947
This Dakota flies smoothly, enabling me to catch up on essential reading. To the last minute, even right into the airport lounge, Christopher Coxe has bombarded me with a stream of both relevant and irrelevant reports and letters, so pestilentially eager and helpful is he to get me properly briefed. He produced for me a copy of Richard Burton's avowedly imperialist journey in 1854, *First Footsteps in East Africa*, though in fact Burton went to Somalia and I'm going much further south, and with very different motivation; also Julian Huxley's more recent and useful *East Africa View* describing formal schooling there in 1929, which, however, does not touch the sort of questions I'm setting out to answer.

More to the point is the very recent report of A. J. Wakefield, formerly director of agriculture in Tanganyika, who recently in the space of only nine weeks produced a large report, at first sight impressive, with proposals on the practicability of a large-scale scheme by mechanization to produce groundnuts there, which apparently has already been accepted for action by the London government. I suppose he must know what he is talking about, but much of his survey was evidently done by aerial reconnaissance and I'm astonished that he does not suggest starting with a pilot experiment. He is looking for paradise now, or at latest tomorrow. I cannot understand why Cohen and Coxe did not discuss with me the relevance of Wakefield's report to what I am going out to do. By comparison, I'm still struggling with the contradiction of how *to stimulate initiative* in an African village.

Valetta, 21 July 1947
To give myself time to adjust I'm not taking the through plane, which would have delivered me straight to Nairobi, but will stop first at Cairo, then Khartoum. Here, I look out on Valetta town, which rises on a series of hills like a pile of toy bricks, its streets packed with people for it is the feast day of St Joseph. Below there are British naval warships, which give the island its *raison d'être*, sailing into harbour between the massive walls built centuries ago by the Knights Hospitallers of St John. More to the point, you will no doubt say, I've sent you food and sweets parcels to enjoy, and am thinking of you both.

Later
We're now flying over the El Alamein battlefield, a reminder of that bittersweet turning point of our war. There are no flight time-tables so I'm unsure how long I shall stay in Cairo and Khartoum. With only four fellow passengers I have space to lie down. Across the seats in front, snoring loudly, lies a white-whiskered Colonel Blimp, who has long since finished his first bottle and grows redder in the face by the hour; and behind him a shy, fair, curly-haired young English army lieutenant who palpably shrinks from the only other two passengers, both middle-aged, hard-faced, loud-voiced planters from Kenya, rather unpleasant, who between drinks proclaim to each other and all and sundry their disgust at shoddy, postwar, rationed Britain and delight at returning to the fleshpots of Africa.

22 July 1947, Khartoum
From the air the narrow, fragile green strip of the Nile looks trapped and threatened by the desert, so insubstantial, unlike the massy, man-made pyramids over which we flew into Cairo. Like Calcutta, Cairo both fascinates and dismays with its extreme contrast of luxury and grinding poverty. I had to battle my way through the crowds in the airport, a real Tower of Babel, and

again later to stroll through the shops, pestered on every side by beggars and hawkers. Prices are high, 2/– for a piece of soap, 10/– for stockings and 17/– in the hotel for three glasses of beer; but everything we can't get at home is here to be had for a price.

Near Nairobi, 23 July 1947
Travel by air is so tiring because it mostly becomes a matter of waiting. It was too stiflingly hot and humid to go out of doors at Khartoum, even to see General Gordon's statue, and just about tolerable to remain inside with a cold drink under a whirling fan.

Later I breakfasted at Malakel in the middle of the great, humid swamp of the Sudd; since when we've been flying at 10,000 feet to avoid the sandstorms and now, approaching Nairobi, look down on rolling country very like northern Westmorland, beautifully green and hilly, divided into large European farms.

Nairobi, 24 July 1947
Nairobi centre oddly enough reminds me of Buxton, much of it handsome to look at, set in soft, green upland country. This area is rich in maize and dotted with great, wide-spreading trees. Outside the centre, ramshackle African settlements, interspersed with cheap Indian, mainly shopping, enclaves, sprawl interminably. My eye was caught by the splendidly dignified, upright Kikuyu women, resplendent in animal skins, arms adorned with hundreds of bright bead bangles, and also here and there by proud, tall, muscular Masai warriors with mud-ochred hair and plaited pigtails carrying blankets and long spears.

This morning the local British director of education took me to see the secretary of the East African Governors' Conference, who is responsible for my itinerary; this of course will largely be spent in Tanganyika and is timetabled to finish about 10 September. I've also found time to visit government schools for teachers, medical orderlies and agricultural assistants; and no doubt I will be taken to see many more of these formal training centres, although they are not relevant to my purpose, about which incidentally everyone seems understandably mystified.

I've been able to arrange to have regular food parcels with nuts and raisins sent to you. I can't help comparing the luxurious lifestyle of the European women here, driving around in splendid new cars, with yours in Finchley, still queuing for rationed food. What price victory in war? What price empire? Many of the Africans, men and women, display magnificent physique and bearing, so unlike the ruling Europeans, most of whom waddle around fat and flabby with over-much rich food and drink, their women more often than not wrinkled and parched with the sun.

25 July 1947
In Kinglake's *Eothen* I have just come across a piece which you may think fairly describes my letters to you. 'Truly I may acknowledge that from all details of geographical discovery or antiquarian research, from all display of sound learning and religious knowledge, from all historical and scientific illustration, from all useful statistics, this epistle is thoroughly free.'

Last night I dined at the Nairobi Club, unavoidably comparing the cheerful servants, both African and Indian, with many of the Europeans here, the latter obsessed and bored with golf and bridge, scarcely relieved by malicious gossip. Their lush suburbia is exalted to dominion over African and Indian alike. The latter by comparison seem free from vulgarity and, although poor, are always full of spontaneous fun, which is infectious. It must be difficult to find satisfaction in working in the midst of such a gross, trivial and materialist European community.

Dar es Salaam, 26 July 1947
An early start by plane brought me here via Moshi, over wild game country but at too great a height to see much except the enormous bulk of Mount Kilimanjaro. Later on in my trip I will be visiting this area by car. We flew into Dar over the narrow, winding harbour entrance, my eye at once caught by a considerable stockpile of machinery, newly painted in red and yellow, mainly bulldozers and ploughs, which I suppose are being collected for the big groundnut scheme.

In government circles, both at Nairobi and Dar, I have to tread carefully to allay suspicion that I am here in some capacity to inspect and report on them, alarmingly reminiscent of my reception during the war at army headquarters in Italy. Dar, a town of about 20,000, enjoys a mile-wide harbour for ships of up to 12,000 tons, very crowded at present, and boasts an attractive European quarter of cream-coloured houses with red-tiled roofs over which vivid purple and yellow bougainvillaea flourish. In this, the best season for weather, it is pleasantly warmer than summer at home.

28 July 1947

Soon I leave for the reconnaissance through central Tanganyika to Lake Victoria, thence to Mount Kilimanjaro before returning here. A member of the social welfare department, Ronnie Blaxland, will act as guide. We will be travelling for two months and, so vast is this area, will see only about 1 per cent of the land and people — all so varied by region and tribe that any generalization must be perilous. I've only just discovered that the groundnut scheme falls under the Ministry of Food and not the Colonial Office and is to be managed by the United Africa Company, which has not previously operated in East Africa, hence the mysterious silence of Cohen and Coxe in London on the subject. Presumably it will be a plantation-type project and therefore reflect the interests of government from the top and not of people from the bottom.

Understandably, a general air of puzzlement surrounds my mission, for no one here has heard of 'mass education', or offers any interpretation of it except as formal adult education *à la* UK. For me, from the first overwhelming impression of the largely poor Africans living on barren, overgrazed land, suffering a normal condition of drought, no doubt perplexed by the all too evident internecine rivalries of government departments, the conviction grows that little educationally, whether formal or otherwise, can yet be attempted with any hope of success. Proposed schemes, big or small, cannot be implemented quickly, and I have no doubt that expensive, ambitious schemes ought to be avoided until pilot trials have been undertaken. One or two such ventures with the criteria for success clearly set out, small enough for local people to comprehend and ultimately manage for themselves, would soon prove what is feasible. I shall be looking for one or two tribes eager to improve themselves, like the already successful Wa Chagga coffee growers who occupy reasonably

133

fertile areas where some economic growth through irrigation or land management is feasible, into which a literacy experiment can be usefully dovetailed. A publicity campaign as an introduction to a mass literacy pilot experiment might then have some chance of making sense among village headmen and local non-officials, including the influential Christian missions. This sort of minor, controlled experiment, however, is bound to fall far short of the heady expectations of the Colonial Office and the Labour government at home, especially when compared with the groundnut project, and what I have to recommend is almost certain to come as a sobering disappointment.

The truth is that in these vast areas, as in much of India, Britain has long shouldered a responsibility far beyond its means and understanding. We have made progress in the notion of civil administration but not of development, especially in the villages. Our crime is not exploitation but neglect and, in Tanganyika for instance, no economic survey to ascertain what resources are capable of being developed has yet been carried out. Significant development will take years to organize and sustain, yet the time for Britain in its interest to depart from these and, no doubt, other colonial territories, is nigh. But I gather that the home government is actually thinking of relocating our former Middle East military headquarters down here, so seemingly means to stay for some time yet. British administration obviously forms no more than a thin crust resting on tribal enmities, which will emerge again when we go.

An American expert, by name Läubach, is to be employed to run a mass literacy scheme as part of the proposed groundnut scheme. He has in mind an 'each one, teach one' method, which is said to have succeeded somewhere in the United States. Personally, I'm sceptical of the validity of this notion and its general applicability, especially in Tanganyika where the typical village is not concentrated but loosely strung out over several miles; but it is typical of much current, airy-fairy optimism.

Mentioning Läubach reminds me of the two German Christian missionaries whom the famous explorer, Sam Baker, came across in the southern Sudan in 1861, bent on a mission to convert the Jews of Ethiopia, 'while carrying', as he said, 'a medicine chest they did not comprehend, a number of Bibles printed in the Tigre language which they did not understand, and yet, fully prepared to convert a people who could not read'.

Tomorrow I depart by train for Morogoro.

Morogoro, 1 August 1947
A cosy little railway train running along a single track brought us here overnight, shedding our coach in the station so that we washed and shaved in full view of a curious crowd of Africans. At each station one coach is dropped off, so all is well provided on starting you take care to get into the right coach!

Above us the Uruguru mountains rise sharply through thick jungle, home of tribes whose primitive farming has already eroded and ruined many of the lower slopes.

We were collected by the local, obviously much feared, Irish district commissioner, who stank of whisky but showed little sign of being drunk. Early in the evening he took us for dinner to his house, well situated high above the plain where he lives formally as a bachelor, obviously despised yet cared for by his servants. We sat there for several hours while he drank, pressing one whisky after another on us, my unsampled half-dozen glasses rapidly accumulating under my chair, and showing not the slightest inclination to order dinner. Finally, near midnight, a poorly cooked, almost cold meal was served, after which he insisted, drunk though he was, on driving us back to the hotel along a pitch-dark, narrow track overlooking a ravine. I was scared stiff.

There is only one hotel here run by a proverbial greasy Greek — short and fat, unshaven, heavy-jowled, profusely perspiring and forever rubbing his hands together. When I switched on the light in my bedroom on getting back last night, thousands of cockroaches on the walls, ceiling and in a dark-brown mass on the washbowl dashed to seek shelter in every conceivable nook and cranny. Over my bed, fortunately, there was a mosquito net, so as I undressed I put my clothes inside and, switching off the light, made a successful dive inside; then, through tiredness, I slept well and found that by morning only a couple of cockroaches had joined me!

When I mentioned mass education to our Irish host, he first

ignored the question, then began shouting, 'I build roads! That's the only worthwhile thing here! That's what I do! I build roads!' Apparently all the villagers in his district have to give so many days a year of free labour to construct his roads, which seem to wander around the district without obvious rationale, perhaps all too symbolic of what the British are doing here.

3 August 1947

I am *en route* by train to Tabora, between Dodoma and Manyoni, running along the enormous rift valley in which further south lie the great lakes, Nyasa and Tanganyika, never more than at a comfortable steady 15 miles an hour. 'Bush', about a foot high, covers the stony soil, hereabouts broken by rocky hills, no doubt home to lions, intersected, too, in every direction by dried-out river beds. This is the inhospitable territorial wilderness of the Gogo tribe, who live in shabby, flat-topped mud huts in an area into which some time ago they were pushed by their warlike enemies, the Masai.

Now and again we pass gangs of tribesmen clearing the scrub to get rid of the dreaded tsetse fly, which preys on their herds of cattle and goats. Although the land is already overgrazed, they lose no opportunity to increase their herds — their idea of riches — so the top soil is eroded and soon blown away by the wind. When rain does come it creates deep runnels and gorges, eating into the hill slopes, leaving a ghastly, devastated wasteland.

Tabora, 4 August 1947

(In pronunciation emphasis is evidently placed on the second syllable, as with most words here.)

Today, firmly brushing aside any talk of mass education, the provincial commissioner here took me fishing and shooting with his wife and two young daughters. Tell John I caught a fish which could easily have been five inches or even five feet long! And we had to take refuge in the car from a pack of wild dogs, just like wolves. Marabout and cranes were hopped round the water hole where we saw the spoor, but no other sign, of hippos and leopards.

Judging by the furnishing of his house (or should I say, natural history museum) with walls and floors covered by elephants' tusks, lion skins, giraffe shin bones, antlers of all shapes and sizes, this commissioner devotes himself single-mindedly to hunting and fishing and so has little time for road building or anything else, let alone education. Before I left he assured me with great earnestness that to achieve village uplift here all that was needed was to stock up the village shop with desirable consumer goods like radios, which would be so attractive as to persuade the locals to work hard. To my question, 'Have you tried it?' he gave no answer.

By comparison, I've been encouraged by meeting two admirably keen and devoted officials, one a young forestry officer who really grieves about soil erosion, and the other an elderly governor of a prison containing 800 convicts, whom, in the best adult education scheme I've seen so far, he teaches to read, to farm and to build houses.

Nzega, 6 August 1947

It has been a long, tiring journey along dusty tracks built of soft red soil, running for miles through bush country infested by tsetse fly. Three British families live here in an isolated pocket near a village, which actually enjoys a small village school. Their houses are built of mud, the walls whitewashed, the roofs attractively thatched, and the rooms large and airy. The husbands go on safari, hold *baraza*s to solve the problems raised by village chiefs, hunt and generally enjoy themselves. Their wives conceive, rear and nurse children (and learn to say goodbye), protect their families against scorpions, snakes, heat and boredom, and bear the brunt of what, as you know, is loosely termed *the white man's burden*!

Shinyanga, 8 August 1947

I'm sitting enjoying the morning miracle of perennial sunshine on the veranda of this quite *new* hotel, therefore mercifully free from cockroaches. As soon as we can get the jammed self-starter of the car repaired we'll set off for Mwanza on Lake Victoria.

At the tsetse research station yesterday I discussed the purpose of my mission with Mr Culwick and his wife, two scientists, by far the most intelligent, lively and well-informed couple I've met and both seething with anger and frustration at the continuing failure of their fellow government officials to cooperate, a state of affairs they claim is widespread throughout the territory. They cite forestry officers who negate the work of agricultural officers and social welfare workers at loggerheads with education officers. The difficulty, they say, starts at the top in Dar es Salaam, where each department ploughs its own furrow. They fear that the same fate will befall the groundnut scheme and have pointedly brought to my attention the importance in any proposed literacy and development scheme of ensuring that all the specialist officers in each area are brought together at the start to cooperate, preferably under the district commissioner. I had taken for granted (while noting the personal rivalries between departments) that in each district this sort of cooperation automatically happened, providing the *raison d'être* for the presence of so many specialists; but apparently I was wrong.

Oddly, most of the officials I have met make no mention of the groundnut project, which they obviously regard as having nothing to do with them. The Culwicks tell me that even soil scientists possess only a partial understanding of the processes that keep water clean and transform soil into healthy, living cover. They fear that humanity is moving into a trap created on the one side by mankind's plundering of the earth's resources and on the other by population growth, and that there is no certainty that human intelligence can ensure an escape from the sort of natural disasters which from time to time in the past have taken place. Our watchword here, they say, should be 'caution and patience', in firm awareness that we have to strive to cooperate with and not conquer nature. They have nothing good to say about the groundnut project.

In the afternoon I passed from the rational to the fantastic in coming across by chance a small gold mine started several years ago by two English families from Cornwall, the Thompsons and the Bakers. They haul gold-bearing ore up a tiny shaft in baskets, then toss it into a crusher and wash it into a solution of sand and water, which is then poured across mercury sheets. The resulting gold amalgam deposited in the form of a thin layer is then scraped off and the residual sand is treated with cyanide to leach out the remaining gold. All the machinery they construct themselves. Never did you see such a Heath Robinson contraption or such delightfully eccentric families. But they get gold; and everyone, including some very tough children, appears totally happy. Meeting them has raised my spirits, for I had been reaching the sad conclusion that the problem people out here are not the Africans or Indians but the Europeans. I have to take great care not to be too sympathetic in listening, especially to the English wives, because before I know where I am I become the recipient of every marital and personal problem. Those who are not divorced seem to be estranged or coupled up with someone else; and all seize on me as a suitable confidant. Why are these rootless, unhappy Europeans apparently so eager radically to change the Africans, most of whom appear to be placidly content?

Mwanza, 9 August 1947
Downhill, down ever greener valleys, to this densely settled, busy, formerly German government centre. Its streets are lined with big cassia trees, surrounding attractive European houses set amid palms and perched on small rocky hilltops. Nearly all the provincial and district officers continue to treat me with the deepest suspicion. Since 'mass education' makes no sense to them they conclude it must be a cover for some kind of covert inspection on behalf of headquarters or the Colonial Office. To disarm them occupies a day and a lot of forced smiling, which makes my cheek muscles ache.

Out here, where climatic changes can be extreme and prolonged, man is obviously the intrusive element, taking short-term views and capable unknowingly of upsetting the natural long-term equilibrium. For instance, where the herds of cattle overgraze the land desert-like conditions soon begin to emerge, though remarkably, not far away, left to itself, nature preserves a green and flourishing habitat. Large development schemes, however well intentioned, are therefore bound to be unforeseeable in their effects; and plans to change people and their environment ought initially to be small-scale and experimental, in scope no more than the people can comprehend: for example, building quite small tanks to collect water, if and when it rains, and providing a deep, piped well for each village would serve to catch the people's imagination and support, and might well prepare the way later for bigger changes. As an example of poor, unimaginative development policy, I have visited a government demonstration farm here; it produces splendid crops and marvellous quantities of manure using some complicated ideal formula, all actually produced by the labour of local Africans who are employed there, but the same people do not apply any of these methods on their own small farms nearby. Presumably what happens on the government farm is beyond their personal means and comprehension.

12 August 1947
Aboard a wildly rocking train as we approach Tabora, I am completing the first half of my Tanganyika trip and now beginning to envisage the shape and direction of proposals which I hope to agree with government here before I leave.

I've had no news from you or from outside for a week and eagerly look forward to getting your letters; and also finding out how that great experiment, the handover of power in India, is proceeding. It will be the first and biggest of a long succession of British colonial departures in the years ahead.

14 August 1947
We've reached Arusha (the halfway point between Cairo and the Cape, 2450 miles each way), an attractive holiday hill town, with not one but *two* hotels, standing high on Meru mountain and therefore often in cloud. At present, apart from the occasional European farmer, the town, as they used to say of London in August, is empty. However, we are in fact in the midst of the Masai, the most exotic, haughty Africans I've ever seen. Both men and women carry much of their worldly wealth on them in the form of a myriad of bright beads — red, brown, purple and yellow — and bangles of copper round their wrists, necks and ankles; and most wondrous of all, some wear large, cupped bangles hanging in grossly distended ear lobes. I saw one man carrying a scroll of paper in one lobe, no doubt some government report which is already earmarked and pigeonholed!

The Masai tribesmen, largely pastoral, are grouped by age, the pre-warrior set easily distinguishable because they dress and mould their hair in red clay; the warrior set, all very tall, wearing long pigtails and each carrying a large brown blanket on one shoulder. I could mistake them for Hollywood's version of the noble Red Indians.

On the way by car from Dodoma we intended to stay the night at Kondoa, but found that the district commissioner had unexpectedly gone off to Dar to get married, so decided to press on, only to be further delayed by a puncture. We are crossing mountainous country, with deeply eroded valleys and widespread dust-bowl conditions, all the lower slopes lacking contoured irrigation channels and overgrazed by large herds of cattle. Rain, if ever they get any, must run off this land like water off a duck's back.

Soft soil roads, furrowed and corrugated by motor traffic, created a rough, noisy ride, so we made slow progress. Near midnight we saw ahead, stretching right across our path, a forest fire which seemed to extend the length of the horizon, turning the sky into a vast blazing canyon. Animals streamed across the road, caught momentarily in the headlights, and I was able to spot wild cats, bush buck, rabbits galore, giraffes, jackals and several snakes. Although frightened that the fire might catch us or cut us off, we just got through safely, the bush hereabouts having fortunately been well cut back on each side of the road, but the smoke, brown and acrid, coated us in grime, not the usual ruddy-brown dust. Despite the sudden appearance of so many animals, this is an empty, godforsaken area.

Arusha, 15 August 1947
The large local population of Indians, Hindu and Muslim, many of whose forbears first came to work on the railways, some also as soldiers, have been celebrating India's and Pakistan's independence. Much disliked by Europeans and Africans alike, the Indians, who perform essential work as shopkeepers, railway workers and technicians, themselves reproduce the Hindu–Muslim rivalries of their original homeland, so each held its own separate party and invited me. I enjoyed one Hindu's peroration, no doubt aimed at unfriendly Africans, 'I was born on this mountain, I live and work on this mountain and I will die on this mountain.' I

have no doubt that when independence comes to British East Africa the inevitable pluralist struggle for power will lead to political trouble between Africans and Indians; and unfortunately the limited nature of British political experience, which rarely extends beyond the much vaunted, often irrelevant Westminster model, offers only a superficial and not a lasting solution.

With their customary good eye for a site, the Germans founded Moshi, a delightfully elevated, cool, green heaven, its snow-capped mountain suspended above the clouds. Chagga women, carrying enormous bundles of grass, toil slowly uphill to feed their cattle, which are kept in huts high on the mountain — a practice which evidently started as a defensive measure against the raids of their neighbours, the Masai. In a neat rotational system, manure from the cattle is later shovelled from the huts downhill to fertilize the fields below.

With my own mission here much in mind I'm now trying to pinpoint one or two circumscribed and not too heavily populated areas in which to try pilot experiments. Any widespread attempt to achieve mass literacy would prove impossibly expensive and be short-lived, even if anyone here (or elsewhere) possessed the know-how, and without some associated economic development the people want for themselves, would lead nowhere.

Korogwe, 18 August 1947
In the light of what I said in my last letter I've been excited today to find an area inhabited by the Wa Pare tribe — some 10,000 or more strong — which may well form an encouraging context for an experimental development scheme incorporating a literacy pro-gramme.

We climbed by car to a plateau some 500 feet up on the north Pare mountains, using a zigzag track more like a loose scree on Wastwater than a road, and with one or two breath-catching slips and skids got safely up and later down again.

On top, in a fertile, extensive, level, well-watered and populated area, we met several headmen of the Wa Pare tribe, who seemed intelligent and go-ahead, eager to compete with the success of the Wa Chagga tribe across the valley, who have made good in growing coffee on the slopes there.

Most of my conditions for a successful literacy experiment can be applied here — a healthy farming economy and a go-ahead, ambitious tribe living in an area sufficiently set apart so that a measurable programme can be satisfactorily mounted, monitored and assessed. Moreover, the local district officer seems enthusiastic and the Europeans we met, including local mission folk, showed interest.

One European planter expressed the doubt that 'It will take months to organize', to which I was pleased to respond, 'All the more reason for making an early start.' I feel greatly cheered by today's discovery, which marks a turning point in my mission.

Tanga, 20 August 1947
I've reached the coast and am delighted to see and plunge into the ocean again after covering nearly 2000 miles overland by train and car. Do you recall marching down to Tanga in Brett Young's story about the expulsion of the Germans from Tanganyika during the First World War? My room overlooks the harbour, which is lively with yachts and a populous bathing beach, and, picturesquely in the middle distance, stands a wooded island crowned with a dazzling white lighthouse. Originally the town was founded by Arabs and, although cosmopolitan, bears their dominant trading and religious stamp.

This evening I make the half-hour hop by plane to the small island of Zanzibar, returning tomorrow to Dar es Salaam, where I look forward at headquarters to discussing my findings, and, if possible, agreeing on practical proposals for one or two experiments which will include literacy campaigns in Tanganyika, before departing for Uganda, Kenya and home.

Dar es Salaam, 24 August 1947
In meetings with senior members of the secretariat today I've agreed to propose a couple of experiments, one affecting up to 100,000 Africans, the other about 20,000, both to my mind rather on the large side. I insisted on criteria I consider to be of fundamental and general importance, discounting any idea of mounting mass literacy schemes in isolation, divorced from a contextual plan for feasible, local economic and social development. I there-

fore urged that the term 'mass education' be dropped altogether and replaced by the more intelligible, wider concept of 'social or community development', which I also hope to get accepted by the colonial secretary in London. I have stressed, too, the high importance of the specialist officials involved in any such scheme working as a team, under a single leader, normally the district commissioner, and the desirability of prefacing any proposed experiment with a publicity or public relations campaign to inform and gain the understanding and support of village headmen and prominent non-officials in the area, including, for example, taking them by bus to let them see for themselves what is being proposed. It may then become their own scheme, the precondition of success.

Of the two schemes recommended, the first forms part of a long-term programme to move a large number of Africans from their mountain terrain, which their herds of cattle have already over-grazed, down to the plain and then to 'rehabilitate' the vacated area before returning them. Although a literacy programme will be included, I fear that movement on such a scale and the ensuing confusion may well undermine it.

But in the second experiment to be centred on the go-ahead Wa Pare people on their high plateau, I am much more hopeful of achieving measurable, lasting progress in literacy as part of a land management programme.

Incidentally, during our discussions I learnt that the heads of the specialist departments here in Dar, namely education, social welfare, agriculture, forestry, medicine and veterinary science, have never yet held a joint meeting, which goes some way to explain why the cooperation of specialists in the districts is so defective. And no one even mentioned the big groundnut scheme!

In one sphere at least I have found myself on secure ground, quite at home, for in my travels I have discovered that each district headquarters, of which there are over 50 in Tanganyika, has for many years past had to maintain a history of the African tribes in its area. Most contain unique material contributed over the years by a succession of often dedicated officers. If we wish at the school in London to help create and teach a history of Africans (as distinct from Europeans in Africa), these materials would prove a revealing counterpart to whatever may in due course be discovered through the recording and elucidation of the oral history — poems, narrations and songs — of the tribes. I have therefore arranged through the chief secretary to have these historical sections from all the districts typed and copied to our library in London.

Entebbe, Uganda, 29 August 1947
My flight here in a small, two-engined De Havilland 'Rapide' from Moshi was memorable. We left very early, before 6.00 a.m., and on starting I happened to mention to the pilot, a young South African, that so far I'd hardly seen any big game. After Moshi, since I was the only passenger, the pilot said he would remedy that; so flying at about 300 feet instead of the customary 7000 to 8000 feet, skirting the hills as if they were small pimples, he took me over vast herds of zebra and buck, at one time chasing a large, galumphing, dark-brown rhino, lots of giraffe, which sometimes stood, heads erect, disdainfully resenting our intrusion, and athletic ostriches, which raced us for miles, but, alas, no elephants.

I started without breakfast and had nothing to eat or drink on the flight and, with the heat of the plane and the excitement, got dehydrated. I was programmed to lunch with Sir John Hall, the governor, at 1.00 p.m. at Government House, Entebbe, but, because of our flight detour, landed late, so had to be rushed directly by car to the lunch.

There I was met on the steps by a young enthusiastic ADC waiting to hustle me in to lunch, who, learning how parched I was, promptly produced a large glass of what I took to be water but which too late, for by then I had downed it, I found consisted largely of gin. In no time everything and everyone at that large lunch party became rather dim, floating away, so my memories of Governor Hall and his guests are vague in the extreme. I remember telling myself, 'Don't talk! Don't talk!' and somehow got through without disgracing myself. Back in my hotel room I fell on the bed as if poleaxed!

Winston Churchill in his *African Journey* described Entebbe as 'a death trap from disease', but everyone here — African, Indian and European — looks healthy enough, and the setting too is handsome, with smooth lawns sloping down to the lakeside forming a rich green backcloth to the white egrets daintily picking their way through the trees.

Over the next week here and in Nairobi, along with the respective secretariats, I hope to run through the findings and conclusions I have reached in Tanganyika with the government there before making for home.

Nairobi, 4 September 1947

As a child in India I experienced the unpleasant underside of empire and here in East Africa, in meeting 'the British imperial top brass', political, administrative and military, I've seen the flip side; and on the whole I am dismayed at their poverty of vision and lack of vigour against a background of an excessive, indulgent and easy-going life. The stuff of empire is gone! What will these long-serving ruling families turn to when the empire is wound up? Moneymaking?

Whenever meeting colonial service officers in the districts here I try to find out how much they know about relevant, earlier British experience in the empire generally, especially India, such as the experiments in village uplift described in F. L. Brayne's small book *Socrates in an Indian Village* or Malcolm Darling's more recent efforts in the Punjab, in which he wisely attempted not so much to reconstruct as to recondition the village, but no one here seems even to have heard of them. It is as if the raj had never existed. So much for empire! Officials and scholars in West Africa have, for example, long pontificated about the brilliant originality of the idea of indirect rule, seemingly unaware that two-thirds of India always remained under indirect princely rule. Before leaving London I took the trouble to spend an afternoon in the British Museum library hoping to find what I expected to be a rich literature comparing British administration in India and Africa, and could find only one short article by Lord Hailey, and that on the subject of comparative legal jurisdictions. I suppose the deep gulf which always existed between the India Office and the Colonial Office in London in part accounts for this. But what a misnomer to talk about a 'British empire', which anyway was cobbled together while the British public was looking the other way; and it is unlikely to linger long in British memory. In an empire on which 'the sun never set', how lamentable not to have created a permanent training centre in Britain where 'best practice' in government and development from all the poor, colonial areas can be explained and analysed to the new, eager officials.

I am not sorry to be leaving for home tomorrow!

※ ※ ※

No sooner had I got back to London than Christopher Coxe, an eager beaver if ever there was one, caught me by phone, pressing for a report, which he said was immediately needed as part of the colonial secretary's proposed new five-year development package for Tanganyika. As I had already agreed on proposals with senior officials before leaving Dar es Salaam and also wanted to clear my own desk before the start of the university session in October, I was able, within a week, to let him have a brief summary of findings, which he later welcomed as 'crisp, cogent and convincing', though I suspect he would have been happier with a much more detailed account. Almost by return Cohen called me in to discuss it, an experience so unexpectedly bizarre as to be unforgettable.

In physique over six feet tall, bulky and awkward, with powerful shoulders and ruddy face always thrust forward as if in argument, he looked a tough customer. Apart from work, his abiding passion was cricket and the comment once applied to Warwick Armstrong could equally have referred to him, 'No ball that he drove and no deck chair that he sat on was ever the same again.'

Making no effort to set me at ease, he plunged straight into my report, meanwhile disconcertingly prowling round his office, abstractedly picking up one object after another and scrutinizing each one minutely, as if it formed the vital evidence of some crime, before precisely replacing it. On his desk lay a plate of sandwiches, which as he spoke he broke up and gobbled untidily, at each huge bite scattering a shower of crumbs and meat on the carpet. When taken by a particular question he gnawed savagely at his fingernails as if biting his way to an answer. Seemingly unaware that his mannerisms were distracting, that he seemed remote, he yet ap-

147

peared master of the subject and by the time I left, although I had got in only a few words edgeways, I felt satisfied he fully understood my report. But there was not a hint of any action to follow.

A couple of weeks later, however, I was invited to meet Mr Creech Jones, the colonial secretary, who praised my report because it offered a completely different approach from that of the groundnut project, which, he hastened to explain, was being run not by the Colonial Office but by the Overseas Food Corporation. He agreed that the vague, misleading term of 'mass education' should be dropped in favour of 'community development' and that the two proposed experiments in Tanganyika should proceed. Before we parted he said, too, that on the basis of my report he was minded to prepare a dispatch to urge this policy generally in the other British colonial dependencies.

He was as good as his word and within six months the dispatch went out, quoting extensively from my report. In it, using my words, he advised 'all governments to address themselves energetically to the practical problems of community development', which was defined as

> a policy to promote better living for the whole community, with the active participation, and, if possible, on the initiative of, the community; but if this initiative is not forthcoming spontaneously, by the use of techniques for arousing and stimulating it in order to secure its active and enthusiastic response to the movement. It includes the whole range of development activities in the districts, whether these are undertaken by government or unofficial bodies ... in the field of education by spreading literacy and adult education.

As an unexpected bonus, shortly afterwards the United Nations adopted the policy of community development as one of the main strands of policy to uplift the Third World. But one or two swallows never make a summer, and some practical follow-up was obviously needed if good intentions were to be given any chance of being turned into effective policy.

The first signs were promising, for by the following summer

Mother and Father, 1920

He loved his engine

ABOVE. At the Lucknow Residency with the flag never lowered, barely discernible, 1924
BELOW. Rock Ferry High School prize-giving, 1930, with the Headmaster (left) and Alec Ramsay in the background

Staff and students of the School of Oriental Studies, the greatest bunch of eccentrics, 1938

Dorcas and Lance–Corporal Philips, 1941

ABOVE. The Front-line University wrecked by German shell-fire, 1944
BELOW. The teaching staff at the Army School of Education,
Cuerden Hall, 1944

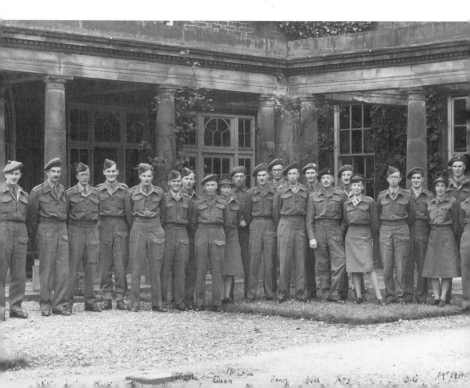

With a family to face the postwar world, 1946

John ready for school, 1956

The Chancellor opening the library of the School of Oriental and African Studies, 1976, attended by the Chairman and the Director

With the Chancellor, HRH the Queen Mother,
at the students' union, 1976

"Better do it my way, squire, before my mate comes back!"

Print No. 2/300   John R. Edwards Jedd

R.C.C.P. 1978-80.

Safeguards for the suspect. Courtesy of. "Police Review", 1979

ABOVE. Visiting the Chief Constable of Sussex, Sir George Terry,
and his colleagues, 1980
BELOW. The Royal Commission in retreat, 1980

February 5, 1982, 30p

POLICE REVIEW

Sir Cyril Philips

Society's punch bag: an interview with the Chairman of the Police Complaints Board

Chairman of the Police Complaints Board, 1982.
Courtesy "Police Review".

Cohen had initiated a series of Colonial Office annual conferences on current topics of significance, which usually met at Cambridge, aimed at bringing together colonial service officers on leave, along with specialists both from the service and outside whose expertise was relevant. For the first gathering, which consisted of a couple of hundred participants, 'The encouragement of initiative in African society' was the chosen theme, with an invitation to me to give the opening keynote address.

My message was deliberately couched in blunt terms. External resources were never likely to become or be made available on a scale significantly to raise the standards of all the poor peoples and countries of the undeveloped world. Colonial populations existed for whom little could ever be done and, if India's experience was anything to judge by, mass famine would from time to time still occur. Big schemes like the groundnut project in Tanganyika, the primary purpose of which anyway was not the uplift of Africans but the production of fats for Europe, related to Western ambitions and modern technology rather than to the peasantry's needs and values, and proposals, as in Burma for instance, to build a massive dam drowning a river valley would devastate the village economy.

More modest efforts devised for the village level, incorporated if possible into a general policy of community development capable of being understood by the villagers — involving, for example, small river dams, tube wells and pumps for irrigation; cooperative banking for credit and seed purchase; and small literacy projects directly related to these efforts — offered lasting promise because their motivation would be cooperation with and not the conquest of people and nature. In short, I urged, small is sensible.

My audience sat silent, as if stunned, and there was little discussion. Afterwards Margery Perham, celebrated for her writings on West Africa, told me that my message and steely objectivity alarmed her, which I thought probably reflected the audience's general reaction.

Twenty-five years later, the economist E. F. Schumacher, in a widely read much-discussed book, *Small is Beautiful*, picked up this thesis of the likely destructive effect of large Western-style projects on poor societies in Latin America, Africa and Asia, urging instead that emphasis be placed on development policies and technologies appropriate to the understanding and needs of the people. 'People', he said, 'matter more than politics and economics, more than markets and profits, and the forces of trust and comradeship are as important as competition.'

But still another score of years was to elapse before the prime movers — the World Bank, the United Nations and the American Bureau of Reclamation — began to admit that their large dam-building policies, for instance, could no longer count on political or public support and would be modified accordingly.

Capitalizing on my lecture, Christopher Coxe asked me to run a summer seminar lasting six weeks on the same subject for a small group of senior colonial officers especially brought to London from British East and West Africa, which at some personal sacrifice I repeated in the two following summer vacations.

Although in no doubt about the strategic role such study groups could play, it was impossible for me to go on repeating them, so, in searching for an alternative, I approached Cohen through Coxe to suggest that the obvious desideratum was a permanent centre for the study and practice of development in British colonies and other countries of the Third World.

Although this idea had obvious attractions, Cohen, despite my plea that he was really only touching the surface of problems, remained convinced that the annual conferences were offering a more direct, flexible and wide-reaching influence on the British colonial service. I therefore brought my own series of seminars to an end.

Ten years later, by which time Mrs Barbara Castle had become minister for overseas development, he returned to the idea of creating a permanent centre, which was finally set up at Sussex University, inviting me to serve as deputy chairman, which I did for the following 14 years. That their partnership should have become known as 'The Elephant and Castle' was both apposite and amusing, but from my personal experience of elephants, at least in India and Ceylon, I had no doubt that they felt their way and trod far more delicately than Andrew Cohen.

But the most heart-warming postscript to my East African mission was added long after Tanganyika, in its new form of Tanzania, had achieved independence. Asked to take the chair at a lecture to be given by a distinguished Tanzanian, I discovered in subsequent conversation that he had first learnt to read and write in the mass literacy scheme I had initiated there.

7

In Search of Asian History

As the war came to a close and already living in lodgings in central London, I had no difficulty in quickly picking up relationships with colleagues at the School of Oriental and African Studies,* whom I found to be cock-a-hoop in just having regained from the wartime Ministry of Information the complete use of the school's new buildings on the university's Bloomsbury campus. To discuss the future I sought out my old chief, Professor Dodwell, still head of the small History Department, discovering within the first few minutes' conversation that he would shortly be retiring. To my question of whether in the light of my long absence from the department he thought I had any chance of succeeding him, he shook his head discouragingly, 'It won't be the same job,' he added, 'because the field of study and description are about to be changed from the British in India to the more general subject of Oriental history.' This was an unexpected, unwelcome setback, for my own special interest and prewar studies lay in the former, not the latter, and I had no pretensions to becoming in the true sense an 'Orientalist', requiring a command of one or more classical Indian languages. As if that was not discouragement enough, he quickly went on, 'Of course you have to face the fact that the administrative headship of the department will go with the title,' adding, with a hesitant, questioning look, 'You might I

---

* The School of Oriental Studies had in 1938 become the School of Oriental and African Studies.

suppose manage the academic side, but I'm not sure about the administration.' At that lordly judgement I really had to smile, for the department under him consisted of no more than one part-time and two other lecturers, including myself, both of us still on war service, an administrative responsibility which I must confess did not seem all that daunting or beyond my capacity.

Concluding from these Janus-style utterances that I had nothing to lose, I put in for the professorship and was successful, even though I nearly blew the final interview through not at once realizing that one of the senior members round the table, Dr Harold Claughton, then principal of the university, had spent his early career in India and was the same Claughton who had edited a calendar of Persian correspondence. However, I was able to rush home to Dorcas and, wild with delight, share 'the good news of a dream come true; for the future in the distance, and the good that we could do'.

Now assured of an academic career, I spent the summer evenings in a highly competitive hunt for a house in the London suburbs, hastily snapping one up in Eastcote, only in the following very severe winter to find the suburban trains so frequently disrupted that it became necessary to go through the dismal process all over again, this time finally getting the family settled in East Finchley near to central London, where we happily stayed for the following decade.

The bustle of the postwar period soon overtook us. Pleasingly, I received an approach from Sir Reginald Coupland, famous as the government's constitutional guru on imperial policy, asking whether I would write a short history of modern India for inclusion in a new series he was editing. There could have been no better stimulus to make up the lost years and, although rusty, I set to work, burning the midnight oil. All went well until I reached the closing phases of the British-Indian story, for at the time it was still far from clear whether and when the British government would make up its mind to quit India and, in the process, perhaps divide the country.

Long convinced that in its own interest Britain could not hold on after the war and that its policy could not reconcile the Hindus and Muslims, I was in no doubt by the time Mountbatten went to

Delhi as viceroy in March 1947 that partition in some form, probably into two successor states, was certain, and committed my history to that view before those events actually took place.

My little book therefore was ready for publication soon after the Act of Indian Independence and, given the untoward circumstances, proved right in its conclusions, and timely and adequate for its purpose, finding a ready market and being translated into a number of European and Asian languages. With this behind me, I felt ready to relaunch myself into university teaching.

In the aftermath of war, poignantly aware of friends and families who had been killed or injured while we had survived more or less intact, Dorcas and I, like many of our generation, vowed to do our best to keep faith and to deserve our good fortune. It was a simple joy still to be in the land of the living, to have the opportunity to make something good out of the gift of life, to help to make a better world. Already blessed, moreover, with a young son, John, and shortly, too, a baby daughter, Meg, with and for whom to face the future in a new Britain and Europe, we found delight in being together again and at last taking charge of our own destinies.

It soon became obvious that the quick succession of two devastating world conflicts, precipitating Britain's economic decline, had gone far to crack the mould of British power and empire, and that the *pax Britannica* had already given way to a new world order. Far from the popular view that Britain had won the war, it had in fact just about managed not to lose it, and in straitened circumstances had to face a postwar challenge to fashion a new, much-reduced base of national power and influence. It was a time for fresh thinking, hard work, experiment and adventure, and in our own sphere we relished the prospect.

Because of the massive changes in Asia and Africa brought about by the war, nowhere in our universities was there a greater opportunity for fresh thinking than in the range of studies covering those peoples. This posed a particular challenge to the school, which had emerged from the conflict as little more than a glorified training school for the armed services, and raised the fundamental question of whether the objective and serious study of Asia and Africa, large parts of which still remained under

154

British imperial rule, could be implanted into British higher education.

One of the disasters of war that had most shaken Britain was the military collapse in 1942 in Malaya, Singapore and the Far East; and in the inevitable ensuing *post mortem* more than one influential finger had been pointed at the earlier, prewar failure of British political and intelligence services accurately to assess Japanese strength and intentions. It was claimed, moreover, that precisely the same British failings were still to be seen in our policy and practice in the Middle East and Africa. In part response, towards the close of the war the foreign secretary, Anthony Eden, who himself enjoyed the unusual distinction of having taken a degree in Persian studies, set up a departmental committee with Lord Scarbrough, a former governor of Bombay, as chairman, along with a large heterogeneous group of specialists, some on Asia and some on education, including my friend and wartime boss, Philip Morris, recently appointed vice chancellor of the University of Bristol. Their task was to advise what contribution the universities could make in helping British government and business avoid the errors of the past and prepare the way for creative change in British attitudes and policies towards the emerging nations of the Third World.

In an ambitious, yet in some ways incoherent and unconvincing report published in 1946, seemingly cobbled together to reflect diverse interests, some primarily concerned with Britain's future role in international partnership, some with the need to use academic scholarship as the foundation for wider changes in British national attitudes and expertise, a massive increase in the state funding of Asian and African studies, and also in the Slavonic and east European fields, was recommended. No convincing explanation, however, was offered to show how academic development would or could lead to the committee's objectives. Nevertheless, the new Labour government, alight with zeal for every kind of postwar reconstruction, accepted the report lock, stock and barrel, promptly allocating lavish, earmarked funds for the purpose to be expended through the national University Grants Committee.

For the London School of Oriental and African Studies, which at least already enjoyed the advantage provided by an established administrative framework and a cadre of some 30 or so members of the academic staff, this generous policy offered a wonderful opportunity for rapid expansion. Earlier, on putting its own proposals for the future to the committee, the school had been told to go away and double them, at the same time being advised that if any major field within its Asian and African purview was not covered elsewhere in Britain as, for example, the little known, minor and as yet unwritten languages of Africa and Southeast Asia, it should assume responsibility. In this lordly style, with expansion as the watchword, and virtually treating education as an automatic panacea to bring about desirable economic and social change, the door was thrown wide open.

From its first modest beginnings in 1917 during the First World War the school's base had rested in philology and the study of the classical Oriental languages; later some general linguistic and phonetic studies had been superimposed, and, specifically to meet the needs of probationers in training for the Indian civil service, there was a modest addition of several modern Indian languages and a spot of history and law. During the war this side of its work languished, but as the fighting spread in the Far East intensive training courses for several thousand translators and interpreters in Chinese and Japanese had been introduced, no doubt immediately valuable for the war effort, but in the school itself producing an academic hotchpotch, in no way offering an appropriate postwar university base on which to build for the future.

Nevertheless, as the newly appointed head of a very small history department of three, already purporting to provide for the history of Asia as a whole, this invitation to go for expansion could scarcely be resisted, even though it distracted me from the quiet period of readjustment which, as a scholar, I badly needed. Moreover, the framework of departments and the organization of policy at the school left the existing director along with his eight heads of department, including myself, as the arbiters of policy as a whole; so willy-nilly from the start I was drawn into time-consuming responsibilities far beyond the range of history, including a frantic routine of interviewing prospective staff and students in all studies.

But the school was facing the opportunity of a lifetime at a
period when Britain at home had to reconstruct its domestic policies, including the character and scope of higher education, and
was looking abroad to set in train the process of shedding what
had now become the incubus of a restive, largely Asian and
African, empire. In this context it was desirable for universities,
especially the school, not only to extend the conventional frontiers
of British studies but also, at the same time, to seek the means of
playing a part in changing traditional British governmental and
social attitudes towards the former colonial peoples and their
cultures, consistent with the process of decolonization which obviously lay ahead.

Already administering a system of quinquennial awards for universities, the University Grants Committee, along with the federal
University of London, of which the school was a constituent college, were able and ready to provide the recurrent funds the school
had asked for to meet the proposals put forward for expansion
separately by each department. Unhappily, the aggregate in no
way represented a considered strategy and, indeed, the director,
Professor Ralph Turner, himself a Sanskritist and dedicated lexicographer who might and ought to have provided this, showed
little interest in fields of study outside his own, with the result that
each department, including my own, was allowed to go its way
without much regard being paid to the creation of coherent
patterns of studies calculated to attract British students.

Unlike most of the subjects taught by the school, the subject of
history of course enjoyed the national status and advantage of
being already widely established in British universities, so there
existed a pool of able candidates, many with recent and relevant
war service overseas, from which to recruit into our Asian and
African fields.

In the first round to provide for Indian history, for example, we
found no difficulty in harvesting a rich crop of young scholars
with first-class degrees and wartime personal experience of India,
including notably Kenneth Ballhatchet, John Harrison and Peter
Hardy, all happy to grow to maturity and high reputation there.
They were soon also to be joined by Lyn Basham, somewhat
older, who had spent the war in the London fire service, whom I

persuaded to use his great gifts and exchange his early ambitions as a novelist to resume his prewar study of Sanskrit and early India. We soon shook down into a team which became widely known and respected internationally. Likewise, in the Near and Middle Eastern historical fields a quick start was made, but candidates for the Far East were slow to come forward. There were no plans for African history and no mention had been made of it in the Scarbrough Report. In the light of what I had learnt from my two timely visits to North and East Africa in 1945 and 1947, there was no question but that in due course we would have to make good this omission.

At the start, the department effectively consisted only of myself and Dr Bernard Lewis, slightly younger, who, although still away on war service, had in fact been my chief rival for the professorship. He might well have resented my preferment, yet there was not the slightest animus and we quickly became and have remained lifelong friends. Bernard was one of the very few British students who had graduated before the war at the school. Capitalizing on the initial advantage of a Jewish background and knowledge of Hebrew, he had gone on to achieve a first-class and higher degree in the history of the Near East and also an enviable command of Arabic and Turkish; and his abilities and qualifications were so obviously outstanding that I sought the earliest opportunity to get him established beside me with the rank of professor. It was an undoubted advantage, too, that the centre of his interest should lie in the Near and Middle East, complementing my own primary concern in India and the Commonwealth. Between us, in the decade that followed we succeeded in building a large department, which soon began to attract staff and students worldwide.

Since our aim was to cover the history of the peoples and dominant cultures of Asia (and later Africa) extending from early times to the present day, including therefore the civilizations of China, Japan, Southeast Asia, India and the Near and Middle East, we had to recruit and train for each of these areas at least five specialist teachers. Once achieved, we would be able within the existing framework of the University of London's degree system to offer an undergraduate degree course combining the study of any one of these areas along with that of British and European history, which was already available at other colleges in London. In so doing, and for the first time in Britain's universities, an intellectually stimulating and liberal study of the history of traditional Asian cultures would be dovetailed with that of the dominant, modern material culture of Europe.

Before the war, students, mostly mature in age, working in the department had come primarily from India, some also, though relatively few in number, from the Near East, their purpose usually being to acquire postgraduate training in research as a means to achieving senior status on their return home. Assuming that in the immediate postwar period this pattern would soon re-establish itself, we had to find senior established scholars not only capable of guiding these students but also of supervising the early careers of the young British recruits to the staff who would later bear the brunt of the teaching. But established scholars were few and far between and difficult to attract.

By a stoke of good fortune Dr D. G. E. Hall, already well known for his pioneering research into Burmese history, had recently returned to Britain and was willing to join us; and we were also able to negotiate the temporary transfer from King's College of Professor C. R. Boxer who, after an early military career, had specialized in the history of the early European companies in the Far East. Otherwise there were no short cuts and no alternative but to recruit and train new young recruits virtually from scratch, a process which would obviously have to continue for at least a decade.

As anticipated, within the first three years the intake of students for research degrees resumed its prewar pattern, yet on a much larger scale (quickly exceeding 60 in number), drawn mainly from India, with a welcome fresh sprinkling of Americans, Canadians and Australians, but not a single British student, forming a total commitment, however, which made great demands on Lewis and myself. Unlike the United States, graduate studies in Britain had not advanced sufficiently, especially in the absence of any provision of taught courses for Masters' degrees, to enable us to form an American-style graduate school combining a base of taught courses with individual research supervision. But, with this in mind as a long-term objective, I was able to bring to bear my own experience in the army and civil service in introducing a seminar system for all our research students, providing group discussion to reinforce the prevailing traditional method in British universities of individual research supervision. For each of our five major civilizations of Asia this required a separate seminar devoted to the subject matter of that region's history and, to provide both a general context and focus over so wide a field, I introduced a central seminar chaired by myself and attended by all our younger colleagues, which specialized in historical method. Out of this seedbed the department grew to maturity.

It was an advantage that as a constituent part of the federal University of London, which in its other multi-faculty colleges already included eight departments of history, we were able to reinforce and diversify our own programmes by inviting scholars of world renown from these established fields of study. In our second session, for example, we learnt much from Professor Hale Bellot's analysis of new historical methods in American history and had the benefit of Professors Vincent Harlow, Gerald Graham and Sir Charles Webster's expertise in the fields of British imperial and diplomatic history. Through these comparative reconnaissances it emerged clearly that in a world that is largely multicultural, the interpretation of human history cannot be either a linear or a single projection, but must be textural in nature; shot silk not yarn, the colour, the interpretation, changing with the point of view.

Through our discussions we also came to understand that the story of history was never likely, as Ranke and his followers in the nineteenth century had assumed, 'to be able to show how things really were'. Historical accounts tend more often than not to be about the preoccupations of historians rather than any simple search for objective truth. New Western models, for example, were already jostling for dominance — Marxism and the class struggle, as well as Braudel and his school, which played down the traditional treatment of men and events as 'surface disturbances, crests of foam that the tides of history carry' and stressed instead the significant influence of the world's broad climatic and demographic changes. But the message above all, which emerged loud and clear from our discussions, was that the prime role of the historian is to try to explain the past, what people thought, felt and did, not to exercise moral judgement but to understand it better.

Because each generation establishes its own viewpoint, complete objectivity remains in a liberal society no more than an inspiration, an ideal to be sought. Most influential on our methodology were the ideas of Karl Popper, then a colleague at the London School of Economics, who argued that historical accounts or statements really constituted imaginative conjectures or hypotheses that had still to be tested by finding and bringing together facts, both old and new. We may launch our experimental toy boat and if it leaks can try to repair or replace it. The simplicity of this analysis of the process of conceiving and writing history cohered closely with my own everyday experience, and it was around it that I built my own course on historical method.

In teaching adults, both in the army and civil service, I had long since realized that one casual assumption about its nature, seemingly shared by many of my colleagues and by most of those who had previously taught me, was false, namely that what a lecturer or writer sought to convey could be and was usually absorbed *en bloc* by his audience. In looking for more accurate explanations, I came across Angus Sinclair's short lucid book *Introduction to Philosophy* describing the way in which he believed we actually learnt things, which corresponded much more closely with my own understanding. In any serious enquiry, he said, learning takes place through a process of selecting and grouping ideas and facts, largely in terms of our existing knowledge and experience, and in such a way as can also be assimilated into and is comfortably acceptable to our emotional makeup and motivation. This struck the right note and provided the context for my own teaching, which of course had to take account of the experience of students brought up in the previously dependent countries of Asia and Africa, who usually arrived holding strong feelings of resentment at the patronizing attitudes of many traditional Western writers on the Orient with whose works they were familiar. Their minds were further conditioned by nationalist fervour and an inclination to embellish and romanticize their own national past. Not to take

161

into account these differences in their approach and perception would have spelt certain failure, as would have been the traditional university reliance on lectures. These latter we moderated by making extensive use of question-and-answer techniques and guided discussion to bring to bear the students' own experience, and by placing our main emphasis on learning rather than teaching.

As only one of the nine departments of history comprising the London History School, it was also rightly incumbent upon us to obtain prior approval from the widely representative University History Board for our senior appointments and also for the curricula of our courses for undergraduates, so at the start it was a severe disadvantage that only Professor Lewis and myself were in place on the board to promote the still relatively unfamiliar fields of Asian and African history. When one of the board's senior members, Professor Lillian Penson, then head of the History Department at Bedford College, with whom as an examiner I had become friendly before the war, suggested I should take on the onerous secretaryship of the board, I therefore jumped at this opportunity to put our own studies into the centre of university affairs, even though for the next three years it meant setting aside every other weekend to grapple with the administrative details of the board's considerable weight of business. Nevertheless, it took me in due course to the chairmanship of the board and went some way to confirm the department's status in the eyes of the other history departments and of the higher committees in the university.

In the years immediately following the war the monthly meetings of the University History Board were graced and enlivened by scholars of brilliance and high public repute who created a splendid forum of debate and drama, exciting as much for the quality of argument as for the clash of personalities.

Dominant by force of character and presence was the youngest, Professor Lillian Penson, then in her forties, whose breadth of vision, command of facts and cogency usually carried the board. She kept her feet, too, firmly on the ground and one of her practical asides stuck in my memory. 'Remember,' she said, 'Whatever the merits of your argument, most people in the last resort usually vote according to whether they like you or not!' Always at each other's throats, two colleagues from University College, Professor John Neale, famous for his Elizabethan studies, whose beaming cherubic face was belied by his hard pebbled eyes which never smiled, and Professor Hale Bellot, who disdainfully treated every move and every word of Neale's with suspicion, seemed to gain pleasure in differing about everything. Aloof from the fray, tolerant and watchful, Sir Charles Webster, an experienced diplomat and scholar in that field of study, seemed never at a loss in producing a formula to break any and every stalemate.

It came as some surprise to me, however, to realize that these leading historians of the day, who by profession were dedicated to the pursuit of truth and understanding, did not thereby appear to be better people or more sensible in their personal relationships than other ordinary folk.

While winning the favour of the London History School, my department suffered a particularly savage and damaging rebuff at the hands of Professor Galbraith, director of the London Institute of Historical Research, one of its most influential figures. Within the walls of that famous institute it had long been customary for most of the senior history research seminars from the colleges to gather. Although warned that he was 'tough, smart and abrasive', I had sought him out to put what I thought was the quite reasonable request that my own department's main seminars on Asian and African history should join the others, mainly in Western history, in the institute. 'How many students would you be bringing?' he asked. 'About 60,' I replied. 'Where from?' 'Mainly Asia and Africa,' I said, upon which, with his face flaring red, he jumped to his feet shouting, 'You would drown us, and anyway I don't want any bloody niggers here!' Without another word I left, accepting regretfully that, unlike every other major field of history in London, seminars on Asia and Africa for the time being at any rate would have to remain within the confines of my own college.

Another attempt in the same period to place Asian history firmly within the traditional British framework of historical study also came to nothing. Taking advantage of a move by the prestigious and influential Royal Historical Society, whose council I had recently joined, to launch a series of handbooks for distribution to

its large membership, most of whom were of course primarily concerned with Western history, I got my young colleagues at the
school to join me in preparing a *Companion to Oriental History*
to add to the series, but although this was accepted by the
society's council and widely circulated, the influence I had hoped
to bring to bear in taking the subjects of Asia and Africa into the
heart of the society's lecture and publications programme proved
minimal and failed to take hold.

Since neither the Scarbrough Committee nor the school had
made provision for the study of African history, it was not long
before I personally made the move to fill the gap. In the existing
favourable financial climate funds for the purpose were easy to
come by, but it was essential first to get the approval of the
university's Board of Studies in History and, in the process, to
explain that the study of African history, as distinct from the
traditional study of European influence in Africa, would involve
an enquiry into and reconstruction where possible of African
tribal histories. This, I argued, would form a valid field of history,
at least suitable for study by graduate students. Materials in
European languages, Arabic and some African languages such as
Hausa and Swahili abounded, but many of the lesser African tribal
languages still remained unwritten, although often the tribes
themselves had long maintained and still preserved oral traditions
in the form of epic poems, songs and stories. Establishing and
interpreting this record had proved a slow and difficult process,
but scholars in France and South Africa, and also work in the
United States on the Red Indians, had led the way in interpreting
tribal oral traditions and had already demonstrated the feasibility
of making use of these kinds of materials, and there seemed no
good reason why the British should not follow suit.

Such strong doubts were at once raised in the history board by
colleagues in the English and European fields about the suitability
and feasibility of the subject that it began to look as though the
matter would be deferred indefinitely; but, as can sometimes
happen, a chance incident, in this instance the quotation of an apt
illustration I had come across in the essays of Thomas Carlyle,
magically turned the tide of opinion. 'Some nations', he had written, 'have prophecy, some have not; but of all mankind, there is

164

no tribe so rude that it has not attempted History, though several have not arithmetic enough to count Five. History has been written with quipo-threads, with feather pictures, with wampum belts; still oftener with earth-mounds and monumental stone heaps whether as pyramid or caiver.' Amused and apparently impressed by Carlyle's benediction, doubts seemed suddenly to fade and the board, while still scarcely enthusiastic, offered no further obstacle.

In the first trawl to find researchers and teachers in this field, we at once struck lucky in recruiting two young energetic scholars of ability, Dr Roland Oliver and Dr John Fage, both of whom went on to earn international reputations in laying firm foundations in Britain for the study of the history of Africans, the former later holding the first chair of African history in Britain, and the latter becoming the head of a new influential Centre for West African Studies in Birmingham.

In the postwar era, as the direct Western political domination of Asian and African peoples was drawing to its close, historians worldwide were naturally prompted to ask what effect this great change was likely to have on the presentation and teaching of history generally. At the school the question assumed immediate practical importance for me when Cambridge University Press invited me to bring up to date its standard six-volume history of India, the modern part of which, as a corporate enterprise, had been produced and edited between the two world wars by my predecessor, Professor Henry Dodwell.

From a first cursory examination it was evident that so great had been the shake-up in national attitudes (especially brought about by two world wars) that no process of touching-up could render the volumes acceptable to postwar Britain, or for that matter to any other Western country, still less to Indians or Pakistanis. Largely written by Westerners in the heyday of Euro-pean dominance over Asia and profoundly Euro-centred, in outlook it bore the stamp of British imperial attitudes and that overweening sense of Western cultural superiority which had grown in the nineteenth century. Nothing short of a completely new account reflecting the significance of the indigenous cultures and the rise and achievements of Indian and Pakistani nationalism would serve and, as I had to advise Cambridge University Press,

British scholars were too few on the ground and anyway not yet fully equipped to do this.

As a preliminary to putting forward an alternative, up-to-date and acceptable historical framework, I cast round to assess what contribution Indian and Pakistani scholars and writers, past and present, had already made and were now making, and the extent to which, over the centuries, historical standpoints, both in India and outside, had changed. To my surprise I discovered that there was a remarkable dearth of such work and that most writers in these fields, including those in the West, had shown little awareness of changes in the past in the nature of their historical heritage. Each succeeding generation appeared to produce its own story and interpretation in disregard of its predecessors.

It was abundantly clear therefore that some survey of the nature of past historical writing was an essential prerequisite to any new attempt to write a major, new history of India. Moreover, in discussion with those of my close colleagues whose concern was primarily with the peoples and cultures of the Near and Far East, it soon emerged that my findings, which related to Indian history, could also fairly be applied to modern Western writing on the peoples of Asia more generally, and that because of the many close cultural links between the dominant civilizations and peoples in Asia, especially through the wide spread of Buddhism, Islam and Christianity, and the similarity of their experiences under Western dominance, it would be both feasible and fruitful to project any such investigation of historical writing not only into India, but also into the Islamic world, China and Japan.

But any enterprise on this scale that would have to call on the services of scholars worldwide, in due course bringing them together in London, was bound to be very expensive. Failing to get a response from British foundations, I turned to the Rockefeller Foundation in New York, having recently become acquainted with two of its senior officers, John Marshall and Chad Gilpatric, whom I had met when they were touring Europe on the look out for projects to encourage Asian students and scholars. In Gilpatric, who was young, idealistic and vigorous, I found a responsive spirit and, through his advocacy, gained the funds to launch our venture over a three-year period, culminating in the summer of 1956 in a conference attended by over 100 scholars, both Asian and Western, including many of the world's leading authorities. In outcome, through the Oxford University Press we produced four large volumes on the nature of historical writing on the peoples of Asia, analysing how it had changed through the ages, which formed a landmark in the subject. Besides creating a new plateau of learning and understanding about our heritage as historians, for the decades ahead it acted as a springboard for younger scholars everywhere.

Appealing to a wider public, reaching beyond the normal reach of academe, the timeliness and imaginative force of this concept and the extent to which it had quickly encouraged scholars from Asia to start rewriting their own history, precipitated a flow of articles and programmes in British newspapers and on radio. One detailed and perceptive analysis of its general significance in particular, written by Dwight Macdonald, well known as a brilliant journalist and the editor of the New York magazine, *Politics*, caught the attention of politicians and public both in London and New York. Attributing the undoubted success of the conference to my method of preparation, especially the extent to which it had been guided into processing the bulk of its work before it actually met, Macdonald drew attention to its timeliness not only in countering Eurocentrism but also in correcting a tendency on the part of the rising generation of Asian historians to romanticize their own past. These contributions, he said, were outstanding, offering lessons not only to scholars but to political leaders as well.

While the conference was still sitting, presumably arising from the favourable publicity it received, I was summoned to lunch with Her Majesty the Queen, who was entertaining a party of Arab ministers at Buckingham Palace. The large party sat down at an open square of tables, but because my seat with an Arab both to right and left happened to be on the side facing the queen, we were served last. The service was slow and the main course had only just reached us when, apparently having finished her own meal, the queen rose, no doubt to go to some other official appointment; as we abruptly got up the Duke of Edinburgh, who had spotted what had happened, cheerily called across, 'Did you get enough to eat?' Unable on the spur of the moment to summon a suitable reply, I looked to my neighbour who, muttering under his breath, was giving vent to short explosive barks which sounded suspiciously like oaths, but as they were in some Arab dialect the duke I suppose was no wiser than I. No doubt deeming discretion the better part of valour, the duke did not wait for a reply.

My colleagues and I found quite as much enjoyment and value in planning and developing these ventures in cooperative research as in the scholarship itself, so these golden years shine bright with joint achievement in which the difference between teacher and taught virtually disappeared. Staff and research students at every level of achievement came together, not in a relationship of knowledge, on the one hand, to ignorance, on the other, but as a joint enquiry into largely unsolved problems. We thus realized that the essence of the department lay not in its range of subject, quality of mind or completeness of knowledge, but in its corporateness.

Our graduate students went home carrying aloft the banner of devoted scholarship and teaching, some in time to become professors and vice chancellors, others to rise high in the world of politics or as civil service heads, others to become tycoons in the world of business and in the press, or as radio and television stars. But most vivid in memory for me are Bankey Misra, who first came at the age of 40 and went on into his nineties still exploring the dynamics of Indian administration, Sri Ram Mehrotra, who risked blindness in his determination to complete a monumental history of the Indian National Congress, Damodar and Devahuti Singhal, who arrived as budding politicians and departed as scholars, and so remained until their premature deaths, and brightest and best, Eric Stokes, whose career I had helped to nurture in Singapore, Salisbury, Bristol and finally Cambridge, who wrote with brilliant originality before dying of cancer at the early age of 50.

Immersed as I was in corporate research and teaching, my own personal research had to take second place, but to keep abreast of scholarly and political developments in India, Pakistan, Ceylon, Singapore, Malaya and Hong Kong I began the practice of paying regular short visits, which often led to further new joint historical enterprises, more often than not supported by funds from the Rockefeller Foundation. One of the most useful programmes allowed me to pick out for support and advanced training some 30 of the most promising young historians in south and east Asia to come to my department in London. Some years later it was satisfying to find that at one period every single member of the history departments in the universities of Hong Kong, Colombo and Singapore and many in the Indian and Pakistani universities had benefited from that experience.

Personally most enjoyable were the safaris I took part in with Ceylonese and south Indian district officers touring the hill villages around Nuwara Aliyah in Ceylon and the country around Madras. On these I started lifelong friendships with Rajendra, a Tamil who later went on to take charge of the Ceylon Treasury, and G. C. Mendis, a former student who back home had earned the title of 'the father of Ceylon history'. Together we explored Anuradhapura and Polonnarua, the long-lost Buddhist cities in the jungle. It was on these journeys through the countryside that I first began to appreciate how relatively superficial British rule and law had been in their effect on the lives of most Indians. From Delhi, the capital, and from the British archives the British rulers looked impressively powerful — their influence bound to be deep-seated and lasting — but seen from the villages they seemed little more than interesting passers-by whose memory would soon fade.

At the northern extremity of the subcontinent I took my family by car across the arid plains of Pakistan to Peshawar, dust-covered and golden in the evening sun, where we stayed in the former colonial Dean's Hotel, caught in a time warp, still with three ancient, tottery, grey-haired British musicians performing 'Tea for two and two for tea'. At first light on the following morning, with a district officer and armed guard we mounted the Khyber Pass, passing through the tribal territory of the Pathans and the gun-making town of Landi Kotal where every man carried a rifle and bandoleer. From the top of the pass, which formed the mountain frontier, we could just discern in the early morning light the shining minarets of a mosque on the road to Kabul, vividly recalling my boyhood wonder at the futility of the long-forgotten 'Great Game'.

On our return to Lahore to catch the plane to Karachi, we were waiting on the airport's runway when a large black limousine, pennant flying, drew up, disgorging the vice chancellor of the local university resplendent in his bright-green robes of office. With a flowery speech he then presented me with a sizeable oblong package. Within was a silver miniature replica of the enormous cannon, popularly called Zam-Zam, which for centuries has been kept in the city centre as a symbol of Sikh power. Aboard the aircraft, finding the gun awkward to bestow, I pushed it under the seat. At Karachi, amid the usual scramble to disembark, my wife made her way to the doorway, beside which two large armed guards had taken station, presumably there because of the recent spate of hijackings, when, with an afterthought, she turned and called to me, 'Don't forget your gun!' Everyone froze, on which without ceremony the guards promptly seized both of us and hustled us off to be interrogated. Needless to say, no one there had ever heard of Zam-Zam. By way of explanation I would dearly have loved, but lacked the courage, to quote to them the splendid opening of Rudyard Kipling's famous novel, *Kim*, in which his young hero is first introduced perched on Zam-Zam's barrel outside the Lahore Museum.

> He sat, in defiance of municipal orders, astride the gun Zam-Zammah on her brick platform opposite the old Ajaib-Gher — the Wonder House as the natives call the Lahore Museum. Who hold Zam-Zammah, that 'fire-breathing dragon', hold the Punjab; for the great green-bronze piece is always first of the conqueror's loot.

Privileged in receiving a personal invitation from Jawaharlal Nehru, the Indian prime minister, I attended the great annual gathering of the ruling Indian National Congress at Bombay, joining the members of the working committee in cabinet, where they bickered and quarrelled like schoolboys until the headmaster, Nehru, spoke. Immediately afterwards, in the first of many visits, I met the Indian president, Dr Radhakrisnan, the notable philosopher whose son had been a student under me, and then completed the double by going straight to an interview with General Ayub Khan, the president of Pakistan, refreshed not so much by their easy accessibility as by their helpful attitude towards scholarship and scholars and an undoubted interest in our work, so different from my dispiriting experience with leading politicians in London.

Vivid is my memory as a guest of Sarojini Naidu, the celebrated Indian poetess and nationalist politician, then governor of the state of Uttar Pradesh and chancellor of its university. At a unique and moving ceremony she conferred degrees on all 15 members of the Congress Working Committee, including Nehru, who had negotiated Indian independence, watching with tears in my eyes as each one in turn reverently knelt before her to receive a last blessing, for I knew that she was dying of cancer.

While the enmity between India and Pakistan kept erupting into war and dominating the news headlines, my department was frequently approached by the BBC networks to give talks and join in broadcast discussions; I often found myself paired with Malcolm Muggeridge, which was rather like riding pillion on a motorbike on a skid pan. Under one producer, Jean Rowntree, a weekly evening series I gave on the Home Service on the policies and performance of Asian leaders proved extremely popular, landing me with a fan mail. It was not difficult to fit this radio work into my daily routine, but a brief excursion into the world of television offered much greater difficulty.

Invited by the producers of Panorama to join James Mossman in vetting some 16 hours of film recently brought back from India and China by a German news team, we prepared in detail two programmes. At this period the presenter was Richard Dimbleby, then at the peak of his reputation, whose habit it was to turn up to rehearse his role about an hour before the live presentation, and for his introduction on India we had arranged a floor setting displaying a large ground map of that country on to which under an overhead camera Dimbleby was to walk. But at this he recoiled, 'I won't do that,' he said, 'I'm going bald on top!' Such interest as I started with was further quenched by the need to spend such a disproportionately large number of hours on what after all were ephemera; and any illusion of popular appreciation was completely extinguished by a friend who, when asked what he thought of the programmes, replied, 'Very interesting, and my wife liked your tie!'

At a meeting in Delhi in 1963, Jawaharlal Nehru mentioned

casually in conversation that he had not long to live, but felt satisfied to have bequeathed a worthy personal literary record of his life; he then sharply demanded to know why we professional historians had not made greater efforts to make sure that those who had played a prominent part in the fashioning of Indian and Pakistani independence and the handover of British power would leave some personal account of their roles. This struck a welcome chord, for I had already been turning over the idea of creating a small unit to tape-record historical memoirs of the chief players in those events. Once again I turned to the foundations for funds, Rockefeller and Leverhulme joining in providing support over a period of five years for me to gather a small team of international specialists to meet regularly in London to study the partition of India of 1947.

In the literature so far published on this subject, attention had focused on the central role of the British and the Indian National Congress, especially the parts played by British leaders and by Gandhi and Nehru, but by comparison our early recordings and researches brought out the obstinate and decisive role played by Muhammad Ali Jinnah, the founder of Pakistan, in his last few years dramatically transmuting from constitutionalist into revolutionary, mobilizing Muslim nationalism to fight for Pakistan and delivering the terrible challenge, 'If not a divided then a destroyed India', which neither the British nor Congress dared answer. We struck lucky too in coming across a pile of gunny sacks in a rat-infested cellar in India containing the somewhat tattered papers and correspondence of the All-India Muslim League and in arranging to have them secretly moved across the border to the University of Karachi in Pakistan, and to train the staff, again with funds from the munificent Rockefeller Foundation, to get them safely housed and preserved.

It was from the personal interviews I was able to organize with prominent British, Indian and Pakistani politicians of the partition episode that our most original discoveries came.

One of the big puzzles of the immediate prewar years was why the Government of India Act of 1935, designed as the grand climacteric of British policy in providing for a federation of India to hold together the British provinces with the Indian princely states, was never fully carried into effect. Initially much of the blame had been laid at the door of the viceroy, Lord Linlithgow. But, discovering in our enquiries that the arrangements Parliament had proposed to bring the Indian princely states into a federation were in fact too complicated to work, we challenged Rab Butler, who, as the minister chiefly responsible, had joined us. In response he claimed that it was the responsibility of his London officials who 'were out of touch and at fault', but one of them, Algernon Rumbold, who also was present, at once demonstrated in detail and much to Butler's discomfiture that, on the contrary, it was the London politicians not the officials who miscalculated. But in any event, with that failure the chance, never strong, of a purely British solution to India's political future had finally gone.

The underlying message that emerged was that the adversarial and two-party concept had so deeply infused both the politics and legal system of the British that they seemed quite unable to grasp the need for (and merits in multi-ethnic societies of) pluralistic systems, so in defence of empire they too readily resorted to the tactic of divide and rule; thus in Ireland, Palestine, Cyprus and India, each attempt to hand over power ended in partition.

Most provocative, yet instructive, were the sessions we were able to arrange with Lord Mountbatten, whom as a young boy I had first seen with the Prince of Wales on a destroyer sailing down the Ganges and who, as viceroy, had presided over and played so large a part in negotiating the partition. Puzzled in our first meeting by the large number of discrepancies between his account and what my own group had already established, I persuaded him to bring together the small personal staff of advisers he had taken with him to India, including Sir Ronald Brockman, his aide-de-camp, General Erskine Crum, his military adviser, and Alan Campbell Johnson, his press officer. Step by step with the aid of a chronological analysis especially prepared by Erskine Crum, we established that the face-saving idea providing for both partition and independence for India and Pakistan within the Commonwealth, which all parties in India and in London, including the hitherto obdurate Winston Churchill, were willing to accept, had originated with an official, V. P. Menon, and not with Mountbatten himself, as he had originally implied.

When pressed about allegations that, contrary to the initial promise all parties (including Mountbatten himself) had made not to seek to alter Lord Radcliffe's award on the proposed new frontiers, he had intervened at the last minute to modify in India's favour the proposed line in the Gurdaspur area of the northwest, Mountbatten indignantly denied the charges. When later we put the question to Lord Radcliffe, who had personally drawn the frontier lines, and in particular when Sir Olaf Caroe, a devoted supporter of Pakistan and former governor of the North West Province, angrily repeated the charge, it emerged in Radcliffe's evasive and unusually rattled response that just such an intervention had indeed occurred; as was confirmed 30 years later when the documents became public.

This alteration in the award proved later to be decisively advantageous to India in the war with Pakistan in leaving a vital, strategic road in her possession.

Outside, the seminar stimulated a great output of new work on the partition. The British government, through the good offices of a personal friend, Sir George Tomlinson, a senior official of the Commonwealth Relations Office, began publishing official papers, producing 15 volumes of British documents on the episode; and a new generation of British, Indian and Pakistani historians published studies of the last three viceroys — Linlithgow, Wavell and Mountbatten — and fresh, detailed accounts of the role of the Indian National Congress, the All-India Muslim League and the British government.

In these research enterprises I had deliberately given primacy to the training of my younger colleagues and, with it, to the creation of a team spirit in forming a reputable school of Asian history in London. My own personal research necessarily took second place. But it was essential in giving leadership not only to convey a sense of mission but also to demonstrate my own continuing commitment to research, so in the time I could spare I made every effort, fragmented though my working days had become, to continue with research and writing, particularly concentrating on the publication of original materials to create a published documentary base for students. As part of this I edited and published in two large volumes the correspondence of Lord William Bentinck, the governor general of India between 1828 and 1835, under whose rule the British first seriously tried to come to grips with the question of whether and how far they should venture by deliberate policy to try to change traditional India.* In his poor strategic sense and lack of practical grasp Bentinck was a failure, but for his moral courage in facing the questions raised in a clash of cultures he emerged as the man who in his day did the greatest honour to Europe in Asia.

But my most considerable achievement as a new partner in a historical profession in Britain, which still in general confines its attention to a remarkable degree to the history of Britain and Europe, was to have given the lead in making the search for and coverage of the history of Asian peoples a notable part of recent historiography as a whole. Moreover, this was done in the light of what was happening worldwide, when the time was ripe to replace the Eurocentric outlook of the past generation and, for example, to range far beyond the bounds of the British Indian raj into the history of Indians proper. Pleasingly, this side of my life was rounded off when the Asiatic Society of Bengal, first founded in 1783 and therefore one of the oldest learned societies, elected me an honorary fellow for 'outstanding contributions to Indian history and historians'.

After a decade of corporate activity I was just beginning fully to commit myself to my own personal research when I reluctantly had to switch the focus of attention to my own general future, for Sir Ralph Turner, who had been director of the school since 1937, announced that through ill health he was thinking of retiring and, as one of the younger members of staff already occupying a senior influential position, I knew that if I threw my hat into the ring my chances of succeeding him were good. Even so, I was taken by surprise when one morning, following a committee meeting, the chairman of governors, Lord Scarbrough, took me on one side and

---

* The documentary base for students also included *Fort William–India House Correspondence 1782–86* (Indian National Archives, 1963); *The Evolution of India and Pakistan 1858–1947* (Oxford University Press, 1962); *The Partition of India, 1947* (Allen & Unwin, 1970); and *Indian Society and the Beginnings of Modernisation, 1830–50* (SOAS, 1976).

asked whether I was interested in succeeding Turner and, several months later, after a brief interview, offered me the post.

In the event, to get committed in this way was not as straightforward as I had anticipated, because in the interval the electors to the newly created Smuts Professorship in History at Cambridge made me an attractive offer, and in the same week I received an exploratory letter from Professor John Fairbank, the doyen of Asian studies at Harvard University in the United States, enquiring whether I would be interested in going there.

To commit myself to the school implied acceptance of a largely administrative rather than scholarly role, devoting myself in future primarily to institution and programme building, allowing little time for personal scholarship, whereas either of the other posts would have demanded and facilitated full-time historical study. But by this stage the searching challenge of raising the school and its studies into a secure position in British higher education and firmly establishing the serious study of Asian and African peoples within the British school and university system had begun to dominate my thoughts.

By this time too I was beginning to sense that I felt most fully extended in trying to bring together and inspire others in a common vision, and in mobilizing and combining the necessary supporting resources in money, materials and buildings to enable them to reach their full potential as scholars and teachers.

Moreover, my family was enjoying life in Mill Hill in north London and our two children, John and Meg, were just settling happily into new schools; so with Dorcas's warm support, I took the decision to commit myself to the school. But just when our hopes for the future were riding high, the scourge of malevolent fate suddenly struck, sweeping aside these dreams forever, savagely turning our euphoria into despair.

On a cold, foggy afternoon in mid-November 1956, I was urgently summoned from a meeting in the university to John's school in Mill Hill, where apparently he had suffered a serious accident. Met by an agitated, grey-faced headmaster, I was rushed to John's bedside, where he lay, still and pale, though quietly smiling. Apparently he had been playing football when one of the players had casually lashed out at the ball, which struck John a heavy blow on the chest, knocking him to the ground, where for some minutes he lay immobile before it was realized that he was seriously hurt. In fact he had suffered a heart attack and, although appearing to make a quick recovery, some months later in the school's swimming pool again fell down unconscious. Soon afterwards, early one Sunday evening at home, he collapsed again and, several minutes later, gasping for breath while Dorcas was still frantically trying to summon a doctor, died in my arms. He was 11 years old.

On getting back home after the service of cremation, we were met on the doorstep by Richard Robbins, John's art master, who held out an armful of what turned out to be watercolour paintings. 'I thought you would like to have these,' he said, 'all done by John in the last few months and so good that I've been hanging them around the school.' From his irrepressible habit of drawing lovely illustrations in anything he happened to be reading and on the walls of his bedroom, we knew that John had distinctive, promising gifts as an artist but had not realized that towards the end his talents were flowering so richly. On the contrary, from a school report we were beginning to fear that his powers of concentration were failing. In it Richard Robbins had offered the exasperated remark, 'He has succeeded in occupying the whole term in setting up his tapestry loom,' and the headmaster capped a long list of 'Could do better' with, 'But he still eats a good school dinner!'

On a dark, bitterly cold January morning, the frozen ground white with hoar frost, we scattered John's ashes along the banks of the River Cam at Milton where in the side streams we had spent so many happy hours fishing for stickleback and watching the crested newts and the wondrous water spiders rising and falling in their diving bells.

John's sudden death devastated the family, precipitating throughout the next few years a tale of family woe. Dorcas's mother, Emily, who had nursed him in wartime through his early difficult premature months, thereafter enjoying an especially close, almost conspiratorial relationship with him in weekly letters and secret plans for birthdays and holidays, suddenly seemed to lose interest in life and died of an internal haemorrhage. Fits of vertigo afflicted me, especially at night and on first rising and whenever I sat down, turning my numerous committee meetings into one long ordeal. Then Dorcas, who always felt guilty about having delivered John prematurely as a baby, was stricken with what turned out to be a disabling attack of rheumatoid arthritis, suffering grotesquely swollen hands, one finger or another subject to continual, agonizing dislocation, and worst of all, distortion to her knees and ankles so that she was at times only able to shuffle about backwards. When the doctors said that little more could be done to help her, I put together a large metal container in which to heat wax which, when coated on her limbs and insulated by wadding, soothed her pain, and bit by bit, with the aid of regular doses of aspirin, the swellings went down so that, although still halt and lame, she managed by strength of will once again to get about.

With the approach of spring and hope rising eternal, I recalled from wartime service in Italy the restorative charms of the Amalfi coast south of Naples, caressed by the warm sun and azure sea, bright with orange and lemon groves, blue wisteria and flowering red hibiscus. Able once again to travel, we took a short, healing spell there, soon discovering a welcoming hotel for future holidays on the beach at the then little-known village of Positano. Slowly, through the next couple of years she turned the corner to health, so that with a determined effort we were again even able to walk and enjoy the high ridges of the Lake District. But, to control the continuing pain, she had to persist with a daily, large dose of aspirin and it was only much later we realized that there was a terrible price to pay.

8

To be a Founding Father

To be appointed director-elect of the school as it turned out some 18 months before Sir Ralph Turner finally made up his mind to retire, although pleasing to my ego, was not all that good an idea, for it meant that in daily sessions with him I spent a lot of time just sitting and kicking my heels.

By nature taciturn, even shy, a member of some fundamentalist sect with a sombre view of life, he had an unlimited capacity for sitting silent, alternately stroking his beard and drawing on his pipe. Needing a lot of time to come to the point, like King Philip of Spain whom in appearance he closely resembled, even to the Vandyke beard, he was always wrestling with his conscience. Somewhere deep down in him there seemed to be a kindly person struggling to get out, but although over the previous ten years I had frequently lunched with him, never once had he enquired about my family or given any hint that he knew I had one.

During the war Ralph Turner had performed a signal service for British Oriental studies in persistently pressing government for support and then in opening the doors to many young scholars, but, lacking strategic grasp and the will to be decisive, he had failed to take good advantage of postwar opportunities for development.

Convinced though he appeared to be that the school was in good shape, it was clear to me that in passively presiding over uncontrolled growth he had got the school stranded in a blind alley. Whatever, as director, I might have in mind, the truth was that the school was already locked into a traditional, heavily linguistic mould, and although it could fairly be described as the foremost place probably in the world for the study of Asian and African languages, it had also become, through the lack of students, financially unsustainable. Many languages had been introduced, which like Cambodian, Burmese, Tibetan and Yoruba for instance, could not be expected to provide the basis for Western students of a liberal education. Moreover, as someone bitingly remarked, the school was little more than a departmental expression, only held together by the heating system.

One of the root causes of this imbalance of studies (which had occurred too in several other universities including Oxford, Cambridge and Durham) was the Scarbrough Committee's original declaration in 1946, made no doubt with the most generous intention, that Asian and African studies in British universities should be fostered 'if necessary independent of student demand'. Without elucidation, the committee apparently proceeded on the assumption that supply in the course of time would create demand, but there was still no sign of this and in fact student numbers were actually falling; when I took over there were in total no more than 22 undergraduates, although something like 1000 were needed to give a respectable ratio to the number of staff. Accordingly, the cost per student place had become astronomically high, by a considerable margin in the arts the most expensive in the country. Moreover, there had been no open debate among the largely young staff about the general implications of this trend. On asking Turner personally what purpose and function in his view the school should primarily serve, I got the reply, 'To be a repository of Oriental learning.' As an indefatigable lexicographer, I think, along with many of his linguistic colleagues he must have regarded the school as a kind of massive dictionary or encyclopaedia, always there and useful to be consulted if required. But to me it resembled rather a large raft with no rudder, slowly drifting in the prevailing currents without direction or anchor, lucky in that so far the elements had been friendly.* How could this academic

---

* A detailed account of the school between 1917 and 1967 is to be found in my *The School of Oriental and African Studies*, University of London, 1967.

hotchpotch be transformed into a coherent institution to attract students to the serious study of the peoples of Asia and Africa?

In British society, moreover, which in the winding down of empire was undergoing the painful process of becoming for the first time markedly multi-ethnic and multicultural, a unique opportunity had arisen to study and explore the interplay, past and present, between Western European culture and the older Asian civilizations. If well taught, those graduating in these studies from the school need be no less intellectually equipped than students in other fields and would stand in no different case in their need for subsequent professional training before finding their future walks of life. In short, although its studies were bound to be regarded by the public as unusual and specialized, they need not be regarded as unduly exotic or esoteric, and the school ought not and need not be conceived as a repository for pure specialists.

There was one further essential component. As director-elect waiting in the wings it became crystal clear to me that we could never take serious study and teaching to the highest level in the existing run-down and inadequate buildings, which even lacked, for example, language laboratories and a library building worthy of the large and valuable collection of books and materials that ought to form the dynamo for good scholarship. Given a new setting, we could hope to develop a curriculum of studies capable of attracting a substantial body of students to enjoy some familiarity, some vision of greatness, with the best in human achievement and character.

However, possessing no capital funds to purchase sites in central London or erect new buildings, the school had already got scattered in penny packets throughout Bloomsbury, with its original modest central building still in the fragmented run-down state in which it had been left by the Ministry of Information at the end of the war. It was little consolation that the chairman of the University Grants Committee, in explaining why he was unable to give the school any money for renovation or new building, reassured my governors that 'Your new director has a genius for improvization.' Evidently, salvation would have to come through self-help, and if we had relied on British sources alone, the school, like the empire, would simply have withered away.

181

As an early signal of intent I did manage from our own meagre resources to scrape together the paltry sum of £13,000 to put an extra floor on the original building and to refurbish the corner site in the adjacent Gordon Square where we had undertaken to display a recent, priceless gift of Chinese ceramics. But a simultaneous approach to the principal of the university, Sir Douglas (Jock) Logan, for help in reserving for the school the vacant adjacent site in Woburn Square met with a typically ebullient, discouraging response that if we could quickly raise our own funds for building then some priority might come our way, but otherwise, with comparatively few students, we must remain low on the university's lengthy priority list.

Although at first sight not unlike the fictional Billy Bunter of Greystoke's — short, rotund, peering owlishly through thick spectacles, yet with immense ability and energy — Jock Logan was a truly formidable character, acknowledged to be the arbiter of university policy. It was my misfortune as honorary senior treasurer of the London University Union to have crossed him about his lax attitude to grossly extravagant student union bonanzas and personal participation in their unsavoury parties, and his absurdly ambitious ideas of exalting student sporting fixtures between London and Paris into some kind of Oxbridge competition. I had also joined with Colonel Manning, the union chairman, in telling Logan that some of his officers had their fingers in the union till, which he believed impossible. Logan did not lightly forgive or forget, and it was my fear that the school would be made to suffer.

Accepting that the university's door was temporarily closed, I took the dilemma to my own governors, telling them that we needed to raise more than a million, delighted in response to find that the deputy chairman, Sir Percival Griffiths, and the treasurer, Sir Fred Pedlar, both with business and City interests, were willing to make the effort and were at once successful in enlisting the leadership of the widely popular Sir Neville Gass, then chairman of British Petroleum.

Private fund-raising by British universities was still in its infancy, but from a recent visit to the United States I knew that if we hoped to mount a successful appeal it was essential first to obtain a really big opening gift that could be used as an inducement and marker in whipping up support. Disappointingly but perhaps predictably, because we had a daunting case to argue, the committee's efforts in the City of London failed to mature, and in some disquiet and without high expectation I turned to the Rockefeller Foundation, which over the years had given such generous backing to our studies. Knowing, however, that the foundation's trustees maintained a rigorous long-standing policy not to provide money in Europe for 'bricks and mortar', I sought out Chad Gilpatric, one of the senior Rockefeller officers and a personal friend, to help in mulling over the problem; together we came up with the idea of pitching the appeal on the school's needs not so much for a general-purpose building as for a new library to house the school's superb collections. In turn this idea apparently caught the imagination of the president, Dean Rusk, who persuaded his trustees to make an exception by offering a large pump-priming gift, which over the following couple of years enabled the school from other donors to put together a building fund of well over £3 million, large enough in fact to induce the somewhat surprised principal, Logan, to arrange for the allocation of the Woburn Square site to the school.

Coincidentally and quite fortuitously, stung by recurrent and increasing criticism in the press of the University of London's slow progress in developing its Bloomsbury campus, especially in completing its Senate House complex, the university had just commissioned a new notional plan for future building on the campus, in which, if any departure was to be sought from the much-criticized original Holden design, attention was directed to the school's Woburn Square site as offering the architectural point of transition. Seizing on this as an unexpected and golden opportunity to jettison already completed design plans for the school's new building, which had slavishly copied the Senate House model with gloomy interior wells and overlarge, wasteful corridors, I got the governors to commission Denys Lasdun, well known for his skill in working in a transitional architectural context, to produce a completely new scheme. Charging him to treat our library as the heart of the new building and to anticipate the changing needs of a college whose teaching needs were growing rapidly by rendering the interior structure as flexible as possible, Lasdun responded by designing a pleasingly internal and external, cellular structure making extensive and ingenious use of concrete, his favourite and relatively inexpensive medium.

But if the school's extension was in any real sense to create a desirable and 'studious grove of academe', it was essential first to restrict or preferably exclude altogether the growing stream of traffic, which in ever-increasing numbers was pouring northwards past the school from Russell Square through Woburn Square. But neither the Ministry of Transport nor the Camden Council regarded such a change with favour, requiring a traffic survey extending over several years to assess the effects, which imposed on the university a large charge to produce some compensatory widening of Bedford Way, which Camden required as a condition of its approval.

Stimulated by the university's well-publicized proposals and just as the school was ready to start building, articles began to appear in the press attacking the scheme as a whole, soon joined by academic voices, especially among our neighbours, University and Bedford Colleges. Sharpest of the critics was the Georgian Society led by its president, Sir George Summerson, making the accusation that the traditional and much-admired Georgian squares of Bloomsbury were being destroyed piecemeal by the university.

In some disquiet, fearing that the school would never get its new building unless convincing and public explanations were quickly given, I invited the protesters within and outside the university to meet Lasdun, who for his part was eager to answer his critics; between us we demonstrated that the original Woburn Square of the early nineteenth century, which the opponents of the scheme, especially the Georgian Society, seemingly wished to preserve, no longer existed, having been destroyed by wartime bombing, the decay of most of the original houses through age and damp, and the subsequent erection of the Courtauld and Warburg Institutes. I was able to show, too, that an exercise especially conducted by Lasdun at my request on the feasibility of preserving the admired Georgian façades had revealed that this would not only radically reduce the available building space but unacceptably treble the cost.

Despite this last-minute effort some 30 members of the two

colleges who enjoyed membership of the university's Convocation, representing the very large, influential association of former graduates, exercised their right to call an extraordinary general meeting of that body with the purpose of bringing the university's building plans in Bloomsbury to a complete standstill while a fresh review was undertaken.

Although Convocation did not in fact possess the power to define or reverse university policy, with members well placed in the two power centres of the University Court and the Senate, it was obviously well poised both to agitate public opinion and to embarrass the university, which would not have been able to ignore an adverse vote; and if this were to happen, the cost to the school, which had already committed large sums to site clearance and foundations, would undoubtedly be calamitous.

Convocation's meeting, which took place in the following week, attracted a crowd of about 1000, mostly members, but also including groups of students out for some fun, completely packing the main hall and overflowing into adjoining areas. No preparation that I was aware of had been made by Jock Logan to co-ordinate the university's responses, so I went to the meeting uncertain what would happen and what part, if any, I ought to play.

From the start the gathering crackled and fizzed, the students foot-stamping and endlessly chanting 'Up Woburn Square', 'University out', and for the opening half-hour, despite calls for calm by the chairman, Sir Charles Harris, seemed likely to get completely out of hand.

First to speak were Jock Logan and Lionel Elvin, director of the Institute of Education, whose proposed new building on the east side of the square was also placed in jeopardy, but over the growing hubbub neither could be heard, and both made the mistake of trying to shout down the hecklers, which served only to provoke a majority of the audience to join in the row. Speaker after speaker followed, some, like George Summerson, being listened to in comparative quiet, but most not, so that the meeting seemed inexorably to be going the way of the protesters.

Quite uncertain what I would do or say if given the opportunity, I kept signalling to the chairman, but not until well after nine o'clock, by which time the audience was beginning to sound and look exhausted, did I get my chance.

Amid catcalls as I walked to the platform, it suddenly came back to me that in the previous month at Convocation's request I had addressed their quarterly meeting with a set-piece account of the school's special role in the British educational system, putting it into the context of the university's own long and unique record in initiating higher education in the Third World. This had proved so much to their liking that at the close they had given me a standing ovation; so on the spur of the moment, as I mounted the platform, dropping any idea of trying to put a rational case, I decided simply to hark back to that occasion, calling on them in terms owing more to my Celtic than academic background to keep tryst with me and the school. As I spoke, complete silence fell for the first time and, after a minute or two, bursts of applause began to break out, and as I returned to my seat a thunder of stamping accompanied every step. The chairman seized the moment to close the debate and take the vote, which upheld the university's position by a majority of no more than 11.

On the following morning the meeting was reported in a news article on the front page of *The Times*, citing my emotional appeal as the decisive factor in rescuing the university. However, later that day, along with the chairman of the Court, Sir David Hughes Parry, and Jock Logan and Lionel Elvin, I was urgently summoned to the presence in Whitehall of Mr Robinson, the newly appointed minister of planning in the Labour government.

Flanked by his officials and advisers, no doubt for effect, he at once demanded 'What does the university propose to do now?' Our spokesman, Hughes Parry, wise in the ways of Whitehall and too hardened a campaigner to be flustered, allowed a seemly interval before smiling sweetly in reply, 'Nothing different,' and with another telling pause, 'After all, we won.' As if looking for support the minister turned to his group frowning and shuffling his papers, then finally relaxing, 'I agree,' he said, 'a majority however small, even one, is decisive.' But on arriving back at the university there was a note from him to say that while the government proposed to take no action on developments in Woburn Square, it had placed schedules on the adjoining Gordon

Square imposing restraints on the university's proposals in that area. But I could rest content knowing that the school's new library building, which also provided for our own expanding needs, had been saved, albeit by the narrowest of margins; I have often reflected since that my intervention at that meeting may well have formed the most practical, single contribution I ever made to my college.

Although the struggle for sites and buildings had proved more exacting and time-taking even than I had at first anticipated, I was soon to discover that opening up new fields of study capable of attracting substantial numbers, especially of new British students, was a no less intractable problem.

To bring down the existing student unit cost of the college to a level acceptable to the University Grants Committee, an undergraduate body of about 1000 was needed along with a new range of subjects in the modern field, including the social sciences, to attract them. But since neither the uncommitted financial resources nor the teachers of the required disciplines of study and with the necessary linguistic knowledge and skills were available, the only alternative was to seek private funding as a means to introduce fresh areas of development. This course was dictated, too, because I had to work with an awkward bunch of heads of department, including several formidable characters who, under Turner, had got used to getting their own way and had gained a stranglehold on policy. The most senior and most cussed was John Firth, something of a loose cannon, who had openly scorned and flouted Turner. But I had a soft spot for him because he was willing to be friendly and every day as head of linguistics insisted on explaining to me interesting new theories on that subject, which, as Dr Jowett once said of Gladstone's views on Homer, 'were impossible singly and mutually destructive of each other, but he still persists in holding them all'. But it was the two professorial prima donnas, John Brough and Malcolm Guthrie, the former opinionated in the overriding value of intellect, the latter a former missionary in West Africa convinced that God was always on his side, who posed a serious threat. They were determined to go on enlarging their already overgrown language departments, thus pre-empting all hope from school funds of diversifying our studies.

Fortunately, before becoming director I had already been able to forge relationships with senior officers in both the Rockefeller and Ford Foundations in New York, especially John Marshall, Chad Gilpatric and John Everton. I was lucky too in my timing, for my first tentative feeler happened to coincide with a move by a small group in Harvard University, led by the sinologists Professors John Fairbank and John Lindbeck, to set up in Hong Kong a documentary centre on China. Knowing that I was already a governor of the new Chinese University there, they came to me for advice and help and, on a quid pro quo basis, we found little difficulty in concocting a reciprocal Anglo-American scheme, not only to achieve what they had in mind but also to link it with my own programme to enhance British studies of the modern Far East.

Gaining the support of Fairbank proved a coup of importance reaching far beyond the immediate objective, for throughout the United States his standing and academic leadership were highly regarded, readily commanding the financial backing of the large American foundations, including Ford. A small Anglo-American steering committee, jointly chaired by Lindbeck and myself, was soon set up to meet every six months, alternately in London and New York, the virtual impossibility at the start of finding suitably equipped British members being made good by the willingness of other senior American scholars and administrators to join in; consequently, the Hong Kong information and training centre quickly opened and plans were prepared to start new Far Eastern programmes, not only in the school but at several other British university centres.

One afternoon during a joint committee meeting in New York, I paid a customary briefing visit to see Jim Slater, who in a refreshingly bluff, generous manner was administering this programme at the Ford Foundation headquarters. Previously, in early morning meetings over breakfast at Brown's Hotel in London, I had got to know him but had not realized how pleased he was with the progress of the Anglo-American programme until in greeting he startled me by saying, 'My trustees meet in ten days' time still with well over half a million dollars uncommitted in the Far Eastern allocation. If within the next half-hour you can set down your own plans for the further development of British studies on the

Far East, we'll see what we can do.' There and then, with his secretary as typist, I drafted my submission, with only a slight hitch when in signalling the end of the first sentence I said 'Stop!', on which she gently murmured, 'You mean, point!' Three weeks later the foundation gave the school getting on for a million dollars to put the programme into effect.

With these funds we took the essential preliminary step to open the way to an undergraduate programme by instituting a cadre of training lectureships, handsomely endowed, to attract first-class candidates already established in their Western-based disciplines of economics, politics, social studies and geography, and willing to undertake the additional hard labour of learning Chinese or Japanese from scratch, a preparation which might well extend over three or four years. At the same time we stocked the library with reference and contemporary materials in Chinese and Japanese previously unavailable in Britain, which helped to provide a distinctive linguistic backing for the school's work in the social sciences.

In the first trawl for candidates we attracted Ken Walker, who had previously been studying the economics of afforestation in Britain and who in going on to study and publish on the economy of China later progressed to a professorship and the headship of the department, and Chris Howe, who followed in his footsteps and helped to lay wider foundations.

When these and other recruits returned from their first phase of training in Hong Kong and Harvard, momentum was maintained in London by bringing in Professor G. C. Allen of University College, who specialized in the economy of Japan, and Richard Harris, leader writer on the Far East for *The Times*, to run a seminar programme. In this way, piece by piece the jigsaw was put together.

Always nagging at the back of my mind was the worry that it would fall to me within the next few years somehow to find from the school's own over-committed funds the resources to absorb these recruits into permanent posts and also to search for a senior economist or political scientist with the international standing to lead the group and gain the confidence of the university's social science faculty as a whole. For advice I turned to an old friend,

Lord Robbins, the doyen of economic studies at the LSE with whom I had earlier worked at Chatham House, who had the bright idea of negotiating the appointment jointly at our two colleges of Dr Edith Penrose, an American then engaged in research into Middle Eastern oil economics at Johns Hopkins University in the United States, and who it appeared was about to join the LSE. Once in post, as we had foreseen, she was able to devote her considerable energy full-time to the school, and took charge of the department, which rapidly grew in size and reputation.

Within the school this line of policy was never going to enjoy an easy ride, for suspicion and opposition towards the scholarly status and educational role of the social sciences lingered in the strongly entrenched language departments and, unhappily, personal dislikes soon got mixed with academic quarrels. Nevertheless, through her appointment we were able to unlock university doors in the social sciences, especially in introducing quite new subjects and courses that I had feared would long remain closed to us. With this minor triumph I felt like the orchestral conductor, Sir Thomas Beecham, who, after a discordant start to a concert, was able to assure his first violinist, 'Don't look round, I think they are following us now.'

Among the first of the staff recruits to this programme and initially by far the most promising, Malcolm Caldwell scarcely fulfilled our intentions, for in making use of the springboard we provided he not only contrived to attract a great deal of unwelcome public notoriety in Britain but himself met a tragic fate in Cambodia, which created much international speculation. In him Mr Hyde truly and unhappily turned into Dr Jekyll. At his first interview his performance was the best I had ever encountered. Tall, clean-shaven, with bright, intelligent, brown eyes and a neat head of close-cropped, dark-crinkly hair, dressed in a black morning jacket with striped grey trousers, carrying a rolled umbrella and bowler hat, he at once impressed by his knowledge and sense of *gravitas*. Already established as a principal civil servant in the Scottish House and Health Department, the argument he put to change careers and fit himself to study the peoples of Southeast Asia was persuasive, and well confirmed by his progress during the following couple of years. He then went on to work in the field and to Harvard for further study under Professor John Fairbank.

At the start of the following session, on entering the senior common room I saw a tall slim figure, casually dressed in United States Air Force knee-length boots and a leather jacket over the collar of which curled a mass of long hair, whom I did not recognize but who seemed vaguely familiar, and several minutes passed before I realized with a shock that it was Caldwell. I soon learnt that he was an avowed communist, already playing an active role behind the scenes among the growing body of student militants at the school and in organizing a so-called Communist University in a house in the neighbouring Gower Street.

Some months later as I was changing planes at Bangkok airport we met quite by chance on the tarmac, his destination apparently being Cambodia. Later I read in the press that, confident of his friendship with the communist leader, Pol Pot, he had gone there to arrange the release of several imprisoned Europeans, but in the process, in somewhat mysterious circumstances, was shot dead.

In trying to comprehend the complete transformation of so promising a scholar I wondered whether his commitment to communism had taken place in Edinburgh in the civil service before he joined the school, or whether it occurred during his course of training at the school and in the United States. If the former, he had given not the slightest indication at that first interview and, if the latter, there was not the slightest outward sign of what was happening to 'the man within'.

Although the school had succeeded in achieving a remarkable breakthrough into the social sciences, it was only too evident that British universities generally were still lagging far behind the Americans in the study of contemporary Asia, especially the Far East, where Japan's remarkable recovery and the communist revolution in China demanded study. Britain's universities had failed to exploit its earlier role in those countries, even though a rich accumulation of relevant materials for study had come into existence in Hong Kong. In an Anglo-American meeting in New York I happened to learn by chance that the Ford Foundation was eager to divest itself of direct responsibility for the management and publication of the *China Quarterly*, perhaps the best-known journal on modern China, which for some years past they had been supporting, and, realizing how greatly its acquisition would raise the school's reputation, I managed to persuade the foundation to accept a mutually advantageous package in which the school took over the *China Quarterly* and the foundation offered to fund a programme in Britain for the study of contemporary China, probably to be incorporated in a new institute to be set up at a selected British university.

An associated approach I had made to the British Foreign Office to engage its interest produced a committee, including a former diplomat, Sir Roger Stevens, who had become vice chancellor of Leeds University, which, while supporting the package, showed marked reluctance to associate the venture with the school on the grounds that it was too traditional and over-committed to linguistic studies. When it became clear that no money from British sources or through the Foreign Office would be forthcoming, I made up my mind to go directly to Jim Slater at Ford with the suggestion that the school was capable of carrying the whole programme, an offer which, to my delight, he accepted without hesitation; he then persuaded his trustees to make a first grant of $350,000 for the purpose.

Finding a director for the proposed institute and a new editor for the *China Quarterly* proved extremely difficult, but we had a lucky break when Dr Stuart Schram, an American working in California and widely respected for his work on modern China and in particular on the career of Mao Tse-tung, offered his services as director, a boost which enabled us to entice David Wilson (later the governor of Hong Kong) to transfer from the Foreign Office as editor. Under them the *China Quarterly* took on a new lease of life. The establishment of the institute was warmly welcomed too, not only in the United States but also, to our surprise, by the communist government of China. Fortified also by funds for training fellowships from the Volkswagen Foundation in Germany, its work soon began to expand; but, disappointingly, a simultaneous attempt I made to lay the foundations for a similar effort in the Japanese field failed, not for lack of funds but for want of suitable British candidates to man the programme.

By this time the school's growing reputation and its well-developed facilities for research were beginning to attract established scholars of the highest repute from other British universities, including for instance the Near Eastern specialists Professors Charles Beckingham, Edward Ullendorff and Donald Wiseman, and also from the United States, Professors Stuart Schram and Vatikiotis, both political scientists. Moreover, several of our most promising younger scholars, although receiving invitations to join Oxford, Cambridge or Harvard, which at one time they would have accepted with alacrity, chose instead to stay at the school.

The original eight departments had increased to eighteen, now including geography, social studies, politics and economics, art and archaeology, ethno-musicology and the study of religions, all together attracting student numbers approaching 1000. The school's library had also achieved a range and importance sufficient to earn recognition as part of the British National Library. To outward view therefore the school appeared to be well on the way to becoming one of the leading centres of the highest competence, if not yet excellence, which the Robbins Report had said Britain should create and support. It was my encompassing aim to achieve that!

Within the school itself, however, the challenges created by the rapidly growing number of British undergraduates had exposed widespread weaknesses in teaching. It was hardly to be expected that members of staff recruited initially for their research potential, single-mindedly seeking to be scholars, would automatically or quickly establish themselves also as good teachers, so I brought to bear my own wide experience of training adults in methods of instruction by introducing an annual, short course, incorporating also the opportunity to record and study personal performance on video, taking it for granted that the departmental heads would encourage their new members of staff to join in. But the response was disappointingly slow and patchy, some of the heads apparently assuming that by some magical touch their own new recruits were instantly transformed into competent teachers, others asserting that experience alone would do the trick and one airily inviting me not to despair because 'even a healthy forest needs areas of deadwood!'

In pursuit of true excellence all through we were evidently

committed to a long haul, so despite the obvious unease of most of the heads I started the practice of formally visiting each department every second year to discuss academic problems in general and to keep up pressure for improved performance. But the high degree of self-satisfaction, even at times complacency, especially evident among the younger members newly joining the staff made me aware that the policy of setting out to provide the best possible conditions for work and offering the most generous resources for research with, for instance, fully-paid overseas research leave every three years carried no guarantee of success and might even prove counter-productive, undermining initiative and fostering 'the comforts of unreason'. Time alone would tell. Certainly there would be little point in maintaining a highly specialized college like the school unless it achieved the highest standards.

With many of my generation I had reluctantly accepted that the best hope of achieving a peaceful future for the Western world rested largely in a policy of nuclear deterrence and a persistence in the 'cold war'; it was therefore with a mixture of surprise and pleasure that I received a cordial, official message from Professor Gafurov, my opposite number in Moscow, saying that his government would support an annual exchange of staff between their Academy of Sciences and the school. This duly came into being and, with an occasional hiccup, continued while I remained director. But while attending a meeting of the Congress of Orientalists in Moscow, which happened to take place just after the Russians had shot down the notorious American U2 spy plane, I found the greatest difficulty in getting an appointment with him, even though previously he had agreed that I should make a presentation to the academy of a complete set of the school's publications. Meanwhile, from the moment of my arrival I was being pestered by the close attentions of a Russian dressed in the proverbial dark raincoat and trilby hat, claiming to be a guide, who first thing every morning was waiting for me in the hotel foyer and, despite my protestations, stayed with me throughout each day. On the last morning of the conference it occurred to me to ask this individual whether he could arrange for me to see Gafurov and, within an hour, a large black limousine with darkened windows arrived and proceeded to take me at high speed across Moscow. Just as I was getting alarmed, wondering where I might end up, we stopped at a tall, yellow-bricked building — shades of Lubyanka — where I was instantly rushed in to the presence of Gafurov, who sat waiting with a languid interpreter and a steaming samovar from which he elegantly served tea in tall glasses set in silver filigree holders. But my journey was fruitless for, despite every effort, Gafurov never allowed the conversation to go beyond pleasantries. Months later the gift of books was duly noted but never formally acknowledged.

Soon after my return to London an emissary from Gafurov paid me a visit to say that Moscow University wished to confer an honorary degree on me on condition that in return Gafurov would receive a London degree. When I explained that the London system could not be made to work in that way, he promptly raised the odds by adding that the offer would also provide for the publication and sale in large numbers in Russia of all my books.

Coincidentally, I got involved in academic combat with Sir Anthony Blunt, director of the London Courtauld Institute (not yet publicly exposed as a spy for the USSR), who was arrogantly using that institute's majority on the university's Board of Studies in the History of Art to create a monopoly in that field of study, even claiming the right to take complete control of courses and admissions in the Oriental and African fields in which in fact they enjoyed little competence. Later, as vice chancellor, when accompanying the chancellor, the Queen Mother, on a routine visit to the Portman Square headquarters of that institute, I had occasion to warn him that the lease of their highly expensive building would soon expire and could no longer be borne by the university, so it was imperative for the institute to move to its new purpose-built quarters already provided by the university on the Bloomsbury campus. 'Over my dead body,' he angrily retorted. I would have taken a stronger line still if at the time I had been aware that he had also installed himself, presumably at the university's expense, in a comfortable, male *ménage à deux* on the upper floor in Portman Square. Soon afterwards, after he had been publicly exposed as a spy, the removal of his professorial title by the university constituted no more than the rough justice he deserved.

The school's increasing involvement in modern and contemporary studies happened to attract the attention of Senator Jackson of Washington, USA, who was visiting Britain on a campaign to improve the effectiveness of NATO. Offering a ready supply of funds, he challenged me and my colleagues to produce some practical guidance for that body's armed forces in making effective use of Asian and African languages, to which I responded by mounting a conference of experts from all 17 NATO countries which, after much wrangling, especially with the French, produced a report setting out a programme of language studies in key areas for NATO, indicating where grammars, dictionaries and reading primers were still lacking. Lord Eccles, then British minister of education, possibly prompted by a laudatory article on our work in that week's *The Economist*, without warning descended on me to find out what it was all about, but on hearing the subject matter plainly thought it unimportant and something of a bore, and departed as hurriedly as he had arrived.

In my capacity as director it often fell to me to meet government ministers, much the most enjoyable of these occasions being termly lunches, which I was able to arrange with the frequent succession of secretaries of state for education, each of whom on taking office became the school's official visitor. One such Labour ministerial incumbent, Edward Short, who in early life had been a primary school headmaster, took it upon himself to berate us soundly for enjoying expensive language laboratories while there were still 'so many primary schools without lavatories', while his successor in the same government, Shirley Williams, hastened to reassure us that we 'were worth every penny'. The most perceptive of these visitors was Mrs Thatcher, who did the school a favour by urging me to build up a collection of Oriental and African paintings, and which now form such a strikingly attractive feature of the school's décor; in response we introduced her to the world of Chinese ceramics. Greatly taken when she first came by her intelligent questions and willingness to listen, we were later dismayed at the change the exercise of power had wrought, transforming her into a convinced prima donna of politics, no longer asking questions but delivering assertions as if laid up in heaven. Every schoolboy knows that power corrupts, but for her it had confined as well.

Success in attracting to the new Master's degree in area studies sizeable numbers of mature students, especially North Americans, to join several hundred British undergraduates straight from school resulted in an uneasy, unstable mix. Some of the incoming graduates turned out to be Vietnam draft dodgers and militants from Europe, which in the climate of revolt then rapidly spreading through universities in the West landed the school in deep and surprisingly stubborn trouble.

At the start of the 1968/9 session, following long-established practice I invited the officers of the students' union to join me over morning coffee in order to agree on a timetable and agenda for our customary regular monthly meetings. Normally this student group consisted of no more than five or six but on this occasion my secretary, Nora Shane, came in to warn me that about 15 had gathered outside. While she was speaking a motley crew, mostly men, led by a burly, frizzy fair-haired and bespectacled individual whom I had never seen before, roughly pushed past her, promptly with his colleagues sitting down on the floor. Dressed in a dirty, khaki army greatcoat which reached nearly to his feet, contemptuously brushing aside my attempted greeting, he announced in a rasping American voice, 'I'm Gillespie, president of the union. We've come to tell you that the director has too much power around this place and we mean to change things.' Abruptly, without another word, all then filed out.

To my surprise, within a week, this group had somehow or other persuaded the union to vote to close down the students' coffee shop and bar and to picket the refectories, all of which were alleged to be charging excessive prices. From then onwards through many weary months, on one spurious pretext or another, they and their small clique of disciples kept the school in a state of uproar, which the majority of staff and students seemed to regard as unimportant, carrying on as though nothing untoward was happening, and although discussing the disruption doing nothing whatsoever to counter it.

Along with a handful of senior colleagues I spent many hours, informally and in committee, mostly on quite insignificant minor matters such as the fair price for a cup of tea, trying to discover what they were really protesting so violently about, hoping to achieve some meeting of minds. With our exceptionally high ratio of staff to students, about one to five, it seemed unlikely, as in the University of California, that our emphasis on research in particular could have roused the agitation, and they never complained about it, so ultimately and reluctantly I concluded that they hated what we stood for. A few seemed set on destroying the college, many more were simply enjoying an 'ego trip', while the majority were willing now and again to join what they obviously thought was a great lark. If this lot were at all representative of the generation that had grown up since the war, I feared for the future of my country.

Session by session for several years one militant group after another, never more than a tiny minority variously claiming to be Maoists, Stalinists, Trotskyites, Anarchists or Nihilists, each apparently freely able to tap and on occasion even steal funds from the students' union, which by law were paid by British local authorities directly to that body and which amounted to some £30,000 annually, exploited every opportunity for disruption. They produced political news sheets, posters and magazines of every description, mostly trivial and always obscene, and even went so far as to organize weekend training courses on methods of agitation and disruption. They supported a Communist University in an occupied house in nearby Gower Street and several times, no doubt for light relief, threatened my wife by telephone. They also contrived, invariably on specious grounds, several destructive occupations of the school's premises. On the occasion of the Vietnam march through central London, for example, the students' union, anticipating a bloody battle with the police, offered the marchers the general use of the school's library accommodation as a temporary hospital, and among other ploys took advantage of a 'demo' about Makerere College in Uganda to besiege the neighbouring Senate House building, in the process battering down doors and manhandling and injuring the attendants. Several of the worst offenders from the school were later tried and imprisoned, and some were deported.

In the early stages of the student militant movement a group of students, including some from my own college, on some vague pretext occupied the new university students' union headquarters building in Bloomsbury and, as the union's senior treasurer naturally concerned about the security of the building, I went there early on the second evening. It was cold and foggy, inducing a motley crowd of London's dropouts to congregate there sitting huddled on the steps, others sprawling fast asleep in the entrance. Along the corridors, stinking with the stale smell of tobacco, 'pot' and body sweat, several groups of students had bedded down, many still absorbed in petting and some in coupling. In the main hall beyond, where a radio was blaring out a *paso doble*, dancing figures could dimly be seen through the thick atmosphere, their faces shining with perspiration, the harsh lighting giving them an abandoned, sheep-like look. On the platform, each with his own separate microphone, three speakers, frantically competing for attention, cavorted and raved.

Several days later, when all had departed or been evicted, it fell to me, as treasurer of the union, to assess and pay for the damage done — it amounted to over £15,000.

It passed my understanding that such privileged and presumably intelligent persons could go on behaving in so barbarous, petty, yet destructive a manner and that in the face of this the majority of students and members of staff could so casually, often even apathetically, carry on turning a blind eye. They were all thieves of time. I was taken aback to discover that in admitting new students several of the school's academic departments were ignoring adverse reports on their previous behaviour at school and in other universities, even though some had been thrown out, and that when I tried to persuade the Academic Board to give a ruling that the whole person including character and behaviour, not simply his or her academic performance, should form the appropriate criterion for admission, I was voted down. This I considered to be the ultimate *trahison des clercs*.

However, in thwarting one occupation after another I got some small consolation in that I perfected my skills at speedily obtaining court writs, on one occasion within a record 24 hours, which *in extremis* gave me the right to call for police assistance otherwise not available on the campus; two incidents provided some wry amusement — at that time in short supply. On the occasion of the quinquennial visit to the school of the University Grants Committee, at which it was important to make a good impression to ensure a high level of future funding for the school, I learnt that our militant students were planning some disruption. Beforehand I therefore approached the UGC chairman, Sir Kenneth Berrill, to find out whether he regarded the occasion as primarily his or my responsibility and was relieved to hear that it would be his meeting and that come what may he was determined to see it through. However, knowing how unbridled the militants' behaviour could be and without telling anyone, I took steps to have a convoy of taxis waiting in readiness out of sight. When the great day arrived a full turnout of 15 UGC members was surrounded as it entered the conference room by a jostling crowd which shouted down Ken Berrill's repeated attempts to open a dialogue. When I managed to reach him, telling him that in anticipation of this contretemps I had made arrangements to switch the whole programme to the headquarters of the UGC itself, he and his colleagues gladly accepted the offer, after which the day went according to plan.

On another occasion one of the more tiresome of the succession of militant union presidents announced that he proposed to give a practical demonstration to all new students of how to take over empty accommodation in Bloomsbury as 'squats' and, with a large expectant crowd following him, duly made his way to a nearby, newly completed and as yet unoccupied block of flats, where he proceeded to break down one of the doors. But within minutes, to his bewilderment, several vans full of police drove up and unceremoniously ejected everyone, the president having unwittingly chosen for his demonstration a building designated to accommodate police cadets. Having frequently tried in vain over many months to get the Home Office and the police to respond to my own appeals for help, I could not but savour the speed and marvel at the unceremonious vigour of the police's reaction.

As an ultimately decisive factor in this long-running, often absurd struggle, but always costly both in money and time, the balance of advantage lay on the side of the administration not the militant students; and when the gamut of disruption had been run, when every tune and note had been played, incidentally producing a lot of fun as well as damage, the agitation slowly faded like a nightmare at the opening of day. Sadly, the freedom to do what they liked and the encouragement to express themselves had not been balanced by any sense of moral discipline and, however well-intentioned, however lofty the declared aims, the movement, especially among American students, was motivated for much of the time by hate.

* * *

In June 1961, out of the blue I had been rung up by Sir Keith Murray, widely known and respected as an energetic, liberal, forward-looking chairman of the prestigious UGC and, much to my surprise, asked whether I would be interested in serving a term of five years on that body. Assured that he wanted me not in reference to Asia or Africa but for general academic reasons, I accepted without hesitation because to a specialist like myself not only was the role certain to prove challenging and generally instructive, but my presence was bound to draw the attention of a wide, influential circle to the rising significance in British education of the need for the serious study of those great areas and peoples in the world outside Europe and North America. In the event I went on to serve for the unusually long term of ten years in what proved to be the most expansive decade in British higher education since the war.

On the committee I found myself in the company of members already committed to an ambitious programme of creating entirely new universities from scratch and, having myself been so completely immersed in the Asian and African fields, at first found it difficult to adjust my horizon. At that time in its varied experience and abilities the committee was strong, with Eric Ashby, Willis Jackson, Bob Hunter, Arthur Vick and Asa Briggs on the academic side, reinforced by leaders in public affairs of the calibre of Geoffrey Heyworth, then chairman of Unilever, Lady Albemarle and Ronnie Edwards, soon to become chairman of the Electricity Council. It was a joy to work under Keith Murray, who treated everyone on equal terms, and we soon became good friends.

Outstanding by virtue of his moral courage, he was the embodiment of Chaucer's 'parfit gentle knight loving chivalrye, trouthe and honour, freedom and curtoisye'. He had been in post since

1953 and had become a committed expansionist well before I joined, seeking considerable growth in the number of university places, convinced too that many fields of study in existing universities, especially in the form of the dominant single-subject honours degrees, constituted an outdated, restrictive mould which needed to be broken. This, he and most of his committee had concluded, could best be done, perhaps could only be done, by creating entirely new institutions providing new types of undergraduate courses and, in so doing, in Asa Briggs's words, expanding 'the frontiers of knowledge' and 'redrawing the map of learning'.

From the vantage point of the school, where our study of Asia and Africa had long been pushing across existing frontiers of knowledge and opening fresh fields by combining subjects in new ways within the flexible degree framework of the University of London, I felt bemused by the single-minded and rather exaggerated claims implicit in the committee's approach and, as a graduate of the civic University of Liverpool, could not but wonder why a much bigger role in any expansion was not being given to all the flourishing civic universities. But I was too much of a new boy, too much of a specialist, lacking sufficient breadth of academic experience to challenge what had become conventional wisdom though, in the light of my personal experience of the high cost of initiating quite new studies, I made no secret of my reservations about the practicability in so short a period of trying to create and maintain at a high level so many new costly institutions.

Nor did I find reassurance in some of the heady expectations then being publicly voiced — the new vice chancellor of Essex announcing that he was looking forward to British universities of 20,000 students in size, comparable with the large American state universities, and the recently appointed vice chancellor of Warwick seeking the UGC's financial support to install basic services on his new site, ultimately to support a student community on at least that scale.

Sir John Fulton, the bubbling, always enthusiastic vice chancellor of the recently created University of Sussex, excited by his first visit to Hong Kong, called one day to tell me that he was at once proposing to introduce a programme at Sussex for the study of

To be a Founding Father

Far Eastern art and archaeology, only to drop the idea like a hot potato when I explained some of the difficulties, especially in the Chinese and Japanese fields, in finding trained staff and the high cost of acquiring a teaching collection of *objets d'art* and building up a specialist library.

In the work of the UGC I was able to offer from personal experience advice on the short- and long-term problems to be met in creating university studies from scratch, and was greatly concerned therefore to learn that the proposed original capital sum to be allocated to buy books for the central library in each new university and presumably intended to cover the whole field of human knowledge amounted to a miserly £250,000, the more so because I knew that my own college library on Asia and Africa alone was already spending annually that amount on current acquisitions. Although this capital allocation was subsequently increased, it was still inadequate in the arts and social sciences to maintain research at an international level. Moreover, to protect the best of existing British departments in universities like, for instance, Imperial College, the LSE and some specialist institutions, it seemed to me that an enhanced general level of funding and fees was required, perhaps allowing the rest to find their own level in the way the liberal arts colleges in the United States had done. But so far as I can recall, these alternatives were never fully set out, studied or radically analysed in full committee.

In any event, the acceptance by government of the proposals of the Robbins Committee on Higher Education, which added to the existing seven new universities, and the decision of the Labour government to create in addition the Open University, further compounded the national financial problem. In the back of my mind lurked the very real fear that in this ever-expanding system there would be no place for expensive specialist institutions like my own school.

With heavy commitments in time and energy within the University of London's federal system, I was hard put to meet the demand the UGC made on its members. My diary for this period records an average commitment of some 40 days in the year. Apart from the monthly day-long meetings of the main committee with agendas to be predigested and then cleared, and several additional subcommittees, there were visits to be undertaken to the 80 or so grant-receiving institutions. However, this was a small sacrifice to be set against the opportunity of moving from a wholly specialized routine into the consideration of much wider educational questions in the company of so able, lively and congenial a group. Looking back, one can see that it was a golden era in higher education for, given a large degree of discretion by the Treasury in administering a quinquennial grant period for recurrent expenditure and a triennial grant for forward 'building starts', both the UGC and the universities were able in partnership to plan and look well ahead with confidence, which enabled them to keep their programmes for growth in steady movement and reasonably good balance.

But as the national economy began to slow down, this admirable five-year forward-planning system slowly became a hostage to fortune and when, following the Robbins Report, the UGC was made part of the Ministry of Education's responsibility rather than that of the Treasury, it was only a matter of time before a more restrictive, shorter, even yearly grant system on a par with the rest of the state education system was introduced.

Moreover, the quintessential UGC doctrine that its role was simply to act as a buffer between the government and the universities, in the process preserving 'academic freedom', although not difficult to justify in times of plenty, was bound to be challenged in any national squeeze. In upholding this policy, moreover, the UGC usually shrank from any public admission of *dirigisme*, so that when forced to make hard choices, for example which of the various expensive schools of agriculture or veterinary science to favour or abandon, it squirmed and agonized for years. Another clear weakness was that in stressing the value of quinquennial visitations in assisting each university to clarify and justify its policy, it simultaneously shunned all appearance of adopting an inspectorial role so that in practice we as members could never be certain that policies projected and agreed with a given institution at the start of the quinquennium had in practice been persisted with or successfully achieved by the close.

In an unusual primary role, which by good fortune happened to come my way while on the committee, I became the exception

proving the rule for, in relation to my own extra-European concerns, I was given the opportunity to promote national policies,
which in fact were both *dirigiste* and inspectorial; and to do this
with the tacit approval of Sir Keith Murray and his successor Sir
John Wolfenden.

Matters relating to Asian and African studies rarely if ever found
a place on the main UGC agendas and in joining the committee I
had taken this for granted. But it so happened that, in refreshing
myself on the details of the formative report of the Scarbrough
Committee of 1946 on these studies, I noticed that a review of
progress after ten years was provided for. That period had already
elapsed without appropriate action, so I reminded Keith Murray
and, though taken aback, he raised the question with government.
In response the UGC was empowered to conduct the prescribed
review, which in further discussion with him enabled me to get the
terms of reference extended to cover not only a review of the
previous decade or so but also consideration of desirable future
developments. In agreeing to this generous extension Murray
bluntly warned that 'no vested interests' would be given a place on
the Review Committee, adding, 'and that includes you!'

In the event, although with evident difficulty, a small committee
was put together consisting of Sir William Hayter (formerly
ambassador in Moscow and recently appointed warden of New
College, Oxford) as chairman and four members, none of whom
had any first-hand teaching experience in these specialized fields.
Fortunately, and what later turned out to be of critical importance, Mrs Elizabeth Layton, an economist who had previously
done some work for the UGC, was recruited as secretary.

Thinking to get them off to a good start I invited William
Hayter and his colleagues to a meeting at the school, finding to my
dismay and embarrassment that they had never previously met,
but before the meeting closed I made a point of arranging for
Elizabeth Layton to pay another, early visit at which I was able to
explain in detail how expansion under the Scarbrough proposals
had become seriously unbalanced not only at the school in
London, but also at Oxford, Cambridge and Durham.

For some months I heard nothing further until a somewhat
worried Elizabeth Layton phoned to say that she was concerned at

the committee's slow progress and that, despite or even because of its short visit to the United States, she feared that no discernible clear strategy for the future of Asian and African studies in British universities seemed to be emerging; and she asked for an early personal meeting. This gave me a chance to illustrate in detail the three salient weaknesses in the postwar growth of Asian and African studies in Britain: first, the failure to attract students, which was threatening long-term growth; second, the reluctance of already established centres, including my own, to introduce modern and especially social science studies capable of providing a suitably broad educational base to attract students; and third, the decision under Scarbrough to concentrate on specialist institutions in London, Oxford and Cambridge without extending these studies into the big undergraduate departments in the civic universities, which had in effect created a gulf students were finding difficult to cross. For good measure and to redress a serious omission in the Scarbrough Report I got the school's librarian, Jim Pearson, to prepare a paper on associated library needs, which with little change was later included in the published report.

There could be no doubt that the report of the Hayter Committee, finally appearing in 1961, owed much to Mrs Layton's drive and perceptive grasp of what was needed. Within the Asian, African and Slavonic fields an expansion of modern studies with emphasis on the social sciences was recommended, not only in existing centres, especially the school, but also in new centres to be created in some of the large civic universities. The government's quick response through the UGC was to provide generous funding for these purposes, on which Keith Murray asked me to chair a small subcommittee (drawn from a group of suitably experienced academic members outside the UGC) to put flesh on the report's bones and, over the following five years, to administer the national programme.

Universities were asked to put in bids to set up teaching and study centres for one or other of the main regions of Asia, Africa and the Slavonic world, with a guarantee of support to strengthen library holdings and to provide travel funds for research in the field. In this approach the newly established universities were not included because they were free to deploy their own funds as they chose, and Sussex, for example, in setting up a School of Asian and African Studies, had already taken such action.

From the numerous bids Leeds was selected for work on China, Sheffield on Japan, Hull on Southeast Asia and Oxford and Durham on the Near and Middle East. Oddly enough, in the light of Britain's imperial tradition, especially embodied in the British raj, the 'jewel in the crown', no proposal for that region came forward; and indeed at that time Oxford was actually engaged in abolishing its longstanding Indian Institute. It seemed to me quite indefensible in the light of Britain's imperial history not to include a new university centre for this region of south Asia so I cast round and through two friends at Cambridge, Nicholas Mansergh, professor of Commonwealth studies, and Dr Eric Stokes, a former student of mine, exerted pressure there to elicit a belated proposal, which my committee accepted. Later this centre turned out to be one of the great successes of the whole venture.

Similar support was given in African fields of study to Birmingham and Edinburgh and, in the Russian and Slavonic fields, to Birmingham, Swansea and London; on a comparable scale, funds for new staff appointments, research travel and library materials were also provided for my own London School of Oriental and African Studies. Through the following five years my committee regularly visited all these centres, helping to recruit senior staff, watching progress and, on several occasions when performance fell below promise, doing the unexpected in cutting grants.

Arriving just at this juncture, these fresh, earmarked funds at the school proved a godsend. They enabled many of the scholars and teachers whom several years previously I had recruited for training on temporary contracts using Ford Foundation moneys to be given an assured future; and allowed us to introduce a range of courses on modern Asia and Africa in the social sciences, especially for undergraduates, and to develop a Masters' degree programme to enable graduates to transfer from more conventional Western fields of study. Piece by piece the component parts were being put in place to form a graduate school on the lines of the best American university practice.

Within the University of London, in particular, parallel developments in the Russian and Latin American fields of study opened even wider horizons, encouraging Dr George Bolsover, 'Honest George', and Professor Robin Humphreys, the 'Father of Latin American Studies in Britain', respectively directors of those area institutes in London, and myself to work together so closely and effectively that in some quarters we became known as the 'Three Musketeers'. We succeeded in projecting throughout the federal university a Master's programme in area studies, covering all the major regions and civilizations of the world, including North America and Scandinavia, in which teachers of seven of the other London colleges at once agreed to take part. But at the LSE, where several departments sought to develop an exclusively collegiate curriculum, we met hostility and not even the deliberate invitation to Professor Leonard Schapiro of that school to chair the committee supervising the federal programme as a whole brought about a change of attitude.

Despite this setback, the exceptionally rapid growth in the numbers of students attracted to these area programmes gave rise to discussion of the feasibility of creating a new London School of International Studies on the model of the successful institution in Columbia University, New York. But to this senior members at the LSE were totally opposed, as became evident when I visited that college to suggest that there was no reason why such a federal programme should not be centred at LSE itself. However, the financial storm clouds forming on the university horizon and our awareness that the schools and institutes that would be involved were already highly expensive places persuaded us reluctantly to drop the whole idea.

Aware that the era of university expansion was drawing to a close and with only four more years of my directorship to run, I decided that it was high time to make sure of consolidating the many central developments introduced by me into the school in the previous busy decade. But events did not quite turn out that way.

For reasons that will be explained in the following chapter, I had become vice chancellor of the university in September 1971 and, for the next five years, had grappled with the complexities arising from the reform of the university's federal constitution. Although the vice chancellorship was supposedly part-time, it had gradually occupied me fully, so it was with difficulty that I managed to go on chairing the school's committees and generally keep an eye on developments there, and, looking ahead, the best I could hope for was to be able quickly to pick up the reins again when my duty as vice chancellor was over.

Unfortunately, shortly after my return, the school and I myself personally suffered an unexpected blow through the sudden retirement because of ill health of Lord Radcliffe, the chairman of governors, who had originally accepted that appointment on my direct appeal and had been foremost in urging me to take on the vice chancellorship.

Short and sturdy in physique with a kindly square face and grey eyes that glinted with hidden strength, he at once conveyed an immensely impressive sense of *gravitas*. Frequently used by government as a constitutional adviser, he had performed an exceptional service in the partitioning of India in 1947 when, at the height of the summer in Delhi, he had shut himself away to work alone and in the short space of six weeks drew the lines of division which today, despite two subsequent wars, still form the frontiers of India and Pakistan.

He was one of the most delightful persons it had ever been my good fortune to work with and had become a close and dear friend, and in particular as a former deputy chairman of the University Court had always encouraged me to continue in my role as vice chancellor.

He was succeeded by Lord Gore Booth, who had distinguished himself as head of the diplomatic service. It was an appointment which roused mixed feelings in me. Over a period of 30 years we had often met and I had greatly admired both him and his wife Pat, especially their bearing on great state occasions when together, a tall, slim, elegant pair, resplendent in their glittering decorations and bold blue ribands, they recalled the great, fast-fading glories of the imperial raj. But between his cavalier regality and my humdrum republicanism there existed a gulf we never succeeded in bridging. We first fell out over my condemnation of the confused British role in negotiating the partition of India, and again later when I criticized the Commonwealth Relations Office for failing to take steps to provide a permanent and suitable home

for the India Office library and records in London, not least for
ignoring the offer I had succeeded in negotiating with the
University Court of a free site on the Bloomsbury campus. Instead,
to consign those massively rich and wonderful collections of
Britain's imperial story and experience in Asia to a rented section
of a box-like office block in Blackheath Road, remote from the
centre, constituted to my mind not only an inappropriate setting
but an inglorious postscript to the demise of the raj. When Gore
Booth became head of the diplomatic service my attempt to
persuade him to make use from time to time of members of the
school's academic staff as temporary cultural attachés in some of
Britain's embassies in Third World countries, following the
successful practice introduced by the Americans and Australians,
was dismissed with a contemptuous, 'Don't you know we are a
professional service?'

So far as I was concerned these differences, however, were 'old,
unhappy far-off things, and battles long ago', things of the past,
best forgotten, but I quite failed to perceive the depth of his
resentment.

Immediately following his induction as chairman, he told me
that, unlike his predecessor, he proposed to take an active part in
the day-to-day running of the school, brushing aside my plea that
such a course was bound to cause confusion; before long he began
to pay unannounced visits to my office and, perhaps prompted by
senior colleagues irritated by my prolonged absences, gave the
impression that he was determined to put and keep an ex-vice
chancellor in his place. Only later did I discover that his eyesight
was fast failing and that he already knew he was going blind and
therefore may well have been hoping to find in the role of
chairman one activity he could sustain.

An untimely incident at the start of his chairmanship compounded this unhappy relationship. Following my return as
director, I had arranged for the long-postponed opening of the
school's new library to take place with the university's chancellor,
Her Royal Highness the Queen Mother, performing the ceremony.
On hearing about this, a small group of about 20 students seized
the opportunity to occupy and barricade the senior common room
and adjoining administrative offices, including my own room —

incidentally disrupting the arrangements for the final degree examinations — and justifying their action as part of some national protest about an alleged inadequacy in the number of teacher training places in the United Kingdom, a matter which had little to do with the school. Unfortunately, Gore Booth happened to be with me when this occurred and, obviously upset, suggested we forthwith postpone the Queen Mother's visit. Confident from past experience that the occupation could swiftly be brought to an end, I refused, then at once began to set in train the well-established routine of obtaining a court writ which, if the need arose, would enable me to call on the services of the police. Plainly aghast at this and my rejection of a similar plea from the vice chancellor, Gore Booth walked out with the warning, 'It's your head not mine!'

In the event, several hours before the Queen Mother's arrival the court bailiff served the writ and the students sheepishly filed out, only to take up position in the entrance hall routinely chanting the usual 'No victimization'. But they were at once completely disarmed by the Queen Mother's customary charming smile and her beeline to shake their hands. After that the visit went off smoothly according to plan. As she was leaving, the chancellor turned to Lord Gore Booth with the comment, 'Well, you dealt with the students!' and, seeing him hesitate, I intervened, 'Yes, Ma'am, it was game, set and match!'

But after this episode I noticed that an ultra-cautious, even cantankerous spirit had crept into the school's governance, quite alien to the expansive, visionary spirit which had animated the previous 20 years. A generous offer of three-quarters of a million pounds for the erection of a badly needed hall of residence for students, which I had been able to negotiate with Lord Murray, who was acting for the university's anonymous donor, and a proposed gift of some thousands of pounds to be used to help students in need, and also options which I had acquired for a site for the hall, along with an adjacent plot for a future training centre for business courses and adult education, were all one by one and in quick succession and much to my chagrin rejected out of hand by the governors, suddenly growing hesitant about future commitments. Beginning to feel like 'a dreamer of dreams, born out of due time', and unwilling tamely to acquiesce in so radical and premature a shift of direction, also belatedly beginning to realize that, after five bruising and frustrating years as vice chancellor, I was in need of change and rest, I came quickly to the conclusion that it would be right to give way to younger leadership, perhaps better attuned to the approaching national economic and financial downturn.

Although uneasy about rumours that government was considering a policy of early retirement for senior professors, which at a stroke could well wipe out the best part of a generation of scholars at the school, which it had taken 20 years to bring together, I was content to go, satisfied that I had done my best; delighted, too, to be able to hand on to my successor a parting gift from the Rockefeller Foundation of £100,000 for research and development. But Gore Booth insisted on having the last word, casually in a personal aside remarking, 'Of course we'll be giving you a farewell present', adding, as I turned to go and as if I were some untrustworthy spendthrift, 'But, mark you, not more than £100!' So, as never in my wildest dreams I could have imagined, weary in spirit and sick at heart, I bowed out.

9

Into a Federal Maze

The five years I served as vice chancellor of the University of London could hardly not be momentous for it was a time of acute crisis for this federal university. Not having sought or experienced a managerial role of this magnitude, from the start I felt doubtful about coping with what was surely the most onerous post of its kind in Britain, for within the British system of higher education the University of London was unique in forming what in the United States would have been called a multiversity; and with some 35,000 internal and about the same number of external students, it was the only one in Britain comparable in variety and size with the large state universities there.

The part I was called on to take cannot readily be understood without giving first a brief description of the university, even though for so large and complex an organization and subject one runs the risk of having to give overmuch detail.

Although having worked ever since 1935 within the federation, I differed little from most of my academic colleagues in the constituent colleges in remaining extremely vague about its extraordinary variety and how precisely it functioned. It had long been a standing joke among us that only the widely known principal of the university, Sir Douglas ('Jock') Logan, who had been in the post since the end of the war, knew about these perplexing matters, which anyway were best left to him. Yet personally I could claim less excuse than most, for I had been privileged to see the university at work from both academic and administrative standpoints, having long served with the other heads of schools on the Collegiate Council and also with my professorial peers on the Academic Council, whose primary and important function was to ensure the maintenance of the standards of the university's courses, degrees and academic staff. This latter council also had to face the almost impossible task of trying to give some coherence to the policies and activities of the 66 large and busy subject boards of studies, each of which, as in my own field of history for instance, brought together teachers in the colleges or schools, as many were described, from the same respective subject departments throughout the university.

Decisions and proposals from these two senior councils, along with those from a myriad of other boards and committees, found a meandering course on to the agenda of the Senate, declared by statute to be the supreme university authority, but whose monthly meetings, undisturbed by debate, simply acted as a forum of record and rarely lasted more than 15 minutes; and with a bit of luck could be dispatched in 10.

But not until first becoming a member of the relatively small University Court in the late 1960s did I realize that it was this body, composed partly of lay, partly of academic members, that formed the real power house of the university, controlling its finances and, through a confidential process, usually, but not always after hearing the Senate's views, allocating funds among the constituent schools and programmes. To outside view the system could not but appear something of a mystery.

Of the thousands of internal teachers, however, few acquired personal experience of the Court, leaving the great majority puzzled by the process through which, shrouded as it was by a network of senior committees and councils, the Court actually made its financial awards, and thus for most the federal system remained a vague notion rather than a reality.

The general public, too, could be forgiven for assuming that the massy, square-towered Senate House in Bloomsbury was what essentially composed the university, although in fact nearly all the teaching and research were conducted in the 34 schools and colleges and the other 40 or so constituent institutions and programmes scattered in and around Greater London.

In one very important sense it was true that the Senate House did represent the university in that it embodied the concept of the highly reputable, coveted University of London degree, internal and external, and also of course accommodated the senior councils and the offices of the vice chancellor, principal and supporting central administrative departments.

Within the central London area, two large multi-faculty colleges, University and King's, stood as the twin pillars around which the federal university had first grown; also prominent within London were the large, more specialized Imperial College of Science and Technology and the London School of Economics; and also to the east in Mile End Road, the rapidly expanding multi-faculty Queen Mary College. Reflecting their size and importance, the heads of these five colleges enjoyed membership, along with the university's vice chancellor and principal, of Britain's national Committee for Vice Chancellors.

In central London itself, a number of smaller, multi-faculty colleges had found a place within the federation, including Birkbeck, Bedford, Westfield and Queen Elizabeth Colleges; and also several highly specialized centres of teaching and research including, for example, the Courtauld and Warburg Institutes, the School of Oriental and African Studies, the Institute of Education, and a variety of postgraduate institutes, many world famous, like the Institute of Historical Research.

Situated well outside London were the Agricultural College at Wye in Kent, the field station of the Royal Veterinary College at Potter's Bar, the Marine Biological Station on the River Clyde in Scotland and, perhaps most unusual of all, the British Institute in Paris.

Long regarded as the university's 'jewel in the crown' was the very large medical faculty based on 12 notable undergraduate medical schools which were closely linked with prestigious teaching hospitals, including the famous Bart's, Guy's, St Thomas's and the Middlesex. Grouped, too, with these were several dental schools and a variety of postgraduate medical schools, one of which, the British Postgraduate Medical Federation, acted as an umbrella for a number of specialized, research institutes. Also closely associated with this faculty as a whole were the School of

Pharmacy and the Royal Veterinary College, and the pre-clinical medical teaching provided by several of the large multi-faculty colleges.

* * *

Like their teachers, the great majority of the 35,000 or so of London's full-time internal students pursued the bulk of their studies within the walls of their own respective colleges, having little contact with or awareness of the federal organization.

In the decade following the government's acceptance in 1963 of the far-reaching expansionist proposals of the Robbins Committee on Higher Education, the colleges and institutes, including the medical schools, which were already training about one-third of the country's doctors, took full advantage of the supportive flow of government funds and, with little central university direction or control over the emergence of new subjects and departments, it was inevitable that in the major fields of study much duplication within the London schools should occur, producing, for example, nine separate large departments in history, and similar proliferation in medicine and most other subjects.

In the 1960s so extensive generally was the spread of teaching and research within each of the respective colleges that inter-collegiate teaching proper had gradually shrunk to a comparatively small part of the university's total operation, involving the college teacher on average in 1970–1, for example, in no more than one hour a year and the student on average in only three to four hours annually, reflecting that in the sphere of teaching the organization was already becoming loosely confederal in nature.

In the national system of university education London therefore loomed large, absorbing by the early 1970s rather more than 20 per cent of all recurrent government grants administered through the University Grants Committee. Although exercising under the UGC a quinquennial system of funding, which within the prevailing philosophy of academic freedom encouraged a high degree of local initiative, the London federal centre did not attempt any strict discipline of academic planning and, from as early as 1969, began to accept the targets set by the UGC for all proposed future

216

growth in the number and mixture by subject of student places in London, and from the way things were going, in particular the acceptance of an arrangement for a distinctive separate allocation to Imperial College, it seemed only a matter of time before the UGC would begin to take responsibility for making its quinquennial allocation, not simply to the federal centre in the Senate House, but directly to each of the schools, or at least to the five largest. Clearly, if this were to take place, the role of the federal centre and the nature of the federation itself would have to change radically.

It came as no surprise therefore when in 1962 the report of the Robbins Committee publicly called on London to take an early fresh look at itself with a view to changing its constitution and the nature of its administration or face an independent external enquiry. The university's response, jointly made with the UGC, was to invite Lord Murray, who had recently retired after ten years' outstanding service as chairman of that body, to conduct an enquiry into the future governance of the university; and with members to assist him of the calibre and experience of Professor Sir William Mansfield Cooper, Sir Frederick Dainton, both former vice chancellors, and Lord Cole, a leading industrialist, high public expectations were naturally raised of an early redefinition and perhaps new lease of life for a reformed federation.

In this context, somewhat to my surprise, I was approached in the summer of 1971 by the retiring vice chancellor, Sir Bryan Windeyer, in the company of Sir Charles Harris, a former vice chancellor and still serving as chairman of Convocation, the university's influential association of graduates, with the suggestion that I should agree to let my name go forward as the next vice chancellor in order primarily, as they put it, to supervise the introduction of the anticipated major proposals for reform and reorganization of the federation that would shortly emerge from the Murray Committee.

Not envisaging myself in such a role in London and indeed in recent years having already turned down several similar offers from outside, including one from my own Alma Mater, Liverpool University, I threw cold water on the idea, countering that the task could only be handled with success by someone, unlike myself, who enjoyed the vantage ground of one of the larger multi-faculty colleges. But, declining to be put off, they claimed that my long experience of both senior councils was an inestimable advantage, the more important because the long-serving principal, Jock Logan, would shortly be retiring. For me this was far from providing an inducement for, although greatly respecting Jock Logan's remarkable abilities, in my years as director I had never found his aggressive, often abrasive style to my taste and doubted whether for his part he would like working cheek by jowl with me. But they had done their homework, promptly producing a note and a phone call from him saying how much he hoped I would serve. I was left to weigh my duty.

Ever since becoming an assistant lecturer in 1936 I had prized my association with this famous university. Within its scope there was room for the widest diversity and highest specialization of studies, talents and ambitions, encouraging cross-fertilization to produce teaching and research of the highest quality. What it missed in cohesion as a university it gained in the creative mixture and tension engendered by many remarkable diverse intellectual interests and scholars of great distinction. Although conscious that I knew little or nothing of several of its important faculties, in particular medicine and the natural sciences, I valued their international reputation and wished to ensure their future prospects. The university's record too as a pioneer in extending higher education worldwide, acting as midwife in the birth of many universities, both in Britain and in the Commonwealth, its innovations in distance learning, notably through the external degree system, and its early liberality in opening wide its windows and doors to women and to all religions and races, was outstanding. Moreover, it had created a generous and liberal setting in which highly specialized schools like my own and the numerous medical research centres could find the sort of springboard without which they might well have faltered.

So generally impressive was its record that an effort to preserve the federation made good sense, but in my view only if the great majority of schools were agreed on this and meanwhile accepted the need to strengthen the centre to control proliferation and further unbalanced expansion. From my experience on the UGC I had little doubt that the large and accelerating expansion of recent years, coinciding with the devolution of responsibility for teaching and research to the colleges, was imposing too great a strain on the centre's ability to maintain any effective financial control and was threatening the federal university's future viability.

As a member of the national UGC, while also serving as chairman of the university's Collegiate Council, I enjoyed an unrivalled opportunity to look at the problem from both ends and became seized of the urgency of the financial threat to the federal university. Therefore, in 1968, I attempted to bring the question before the heads of schools by introducing a paper sounding the alarm and calling for a more manageable arrangement, for example by dividing the federation into five or six groups of roughly comparable size. This could be done either on the basis of integration or of an association between schools for collective planning, which would make it much easier to plan and control development.

But my initiative was ill-timed and too hastily mounted. The schools were too preoccupied with the drive for the devolution from the centre of responsibility for teaching and research and the council gave my proposal only superficial attention. With hindsight I believe the university then lost the best and most timely opportunity of radically rethinking and reaching agreement on the character, scope and reorganization of the federation, and might have been well placed to put a generally agreed proposal to the Murray Committee, which was shortly afterwards set up to consider the university's future governance.

All that, however, was water long since under the bridge. The Murray Committee no doubt would offer a solution and therefore, although stoically and with some reluctance, I allowed my name to go forward. I was duly elected as vice chancellor to take office in the following September, 1971, by which time everyone confidently expected that the Murray Committee's proposals would have been delivered.

However, being realistic, it would have been naïve of me to assume that, in so large and complex a federation, any role that I personally could play would prove dominant or decisive. The appointment as vice chancellor, as laid down by statute under the terms of the Hilton Young Report of 1926, was unpaid and part-time and lasted for a period of only two years, subject also to annual election. Anyway, in practice the office had long been generally regarded as predominantly ceremonial, useful of course in that it involved the chairing of many senior committees but otherwise mostly calling for the skills of a congenial host. In the somewhat dismissive view of Lord Annan, provost of University College, the job essentially was 'to act as the university's stomach', by implication leaving the direction of affairs at the federal centre to the principal, though for my taste I preferred Anthony Trollope's more indulgent job description of 'a good digestion, genial manners and above all a thick skin'.

By the time I took office we were still awaiting the Murray Report, so for some months I was able to confirm and enjoy the customary quiet, undemanding nature of the job.

A good part of my first autumn term was spent in visiting the administrative and service departments of the Senate House, which included anything up to 600 or 700 members — the first time evidently many of them had seen a vice chancellor, let alone shaken him by the hand.

An early taste of the role was also provided by Jules Thorn, founder of the Thorn electrical empire, who approached me directly, hinting that he might make a large benefaction to one of the medical schools. He invited himself to lunch in the Senate House, only to become indignant when accidentally jostled by a crowd of students. 'If you want to know how to behave,' he shouted after them, 'come and see my work people.' Taking his word I went to his TV factory at Linfield, where with great pride he showed me the original, small, carefully preserved wooden hut in which, as a Jewish refugee from the Nazis, with only a boy to help him, he had started to manufacture the ceramic components of electric light bulbs, the start of his fortune and industrial empire. 'It's just as it was,' he remarked, 'though somebody now dusts around and cleans the floor.' In return I invited him to see the university's priceless collection of Chinese ceramics, amid which, while pausing in turn to admire each of the beautifully shaped and glazed bowls and vases, he invariably asked before moving on, 'How much?' Later he took me to his penthouse office in St Martin's Lane and, after much beating about the bush, asked whether I could arrange a personal meeting with the chancellor, Her Royal Highness the Queen Mother. Jokingly I told him, 'If you really want to get to know her, why not buy a couple of racehorses and join her at the races?', advice he later apparently took. Hungry for public honours, he did succeed in landing a knighthood, though not the barony on which he had really set his mind; and on our side the medical school duly got its benefaction!

By tradition, each November, brightly relieving the dreary proceedings of Senate councils and committees, the honorary degree ceremony was held in the Senate House presided over by the chancellor, Her Royal Highness the Queen Mother. Her presence and, during my time as vice chancellor, an outstanding succession of public orators, Joel Hurstfield, the Tudor historian, Sydney Evans, the theologian, and 'Tats' Tattersall, the administrator, combined to make these corporate gatherings the brilliant, high point of the university year.

On these occasions, as the several gaudily gowned processions of faculties and councils made their way towards the assembly hall in the Senate House, it fell to me and the chancellor to bring up the rear, our own cue to start moving always being the opening strains of Elgar's *Pomp and Circumstance*. It was then her invariable practice with her fan to tap me on the shoulder, whispering 'Under starter's orders', on which we fell into line with the graduands who were to be honoured. On one such occasion, the poet W. H. Auden, only too obviously drunk from having partaken over-freely at dinner and trailing far behind his group, was tottering towards us along the corridor. Reaching us and facing the dauntingly wide staircase down which his part of the procession had already proceeded, his nerve suddenly failed and, falling on his knees, he made a terrified grab for the handrail, desperately refusing to move. By the time I got to him and persuaded him to let go, his part of the procession had long since disappeared into the assembly hall, so with my arm around him we staggered drunkenly down the stairs where, offering a prayer, I pushed him into the central aisle up which, with many a helping hand, he staggered before being unceremoniously hauled on to the platform, where he promptly went to sleep. For the second time that evening the Queen Mother tapped my shoulder. 'Who is that odious little man?' she asked. 'One of your new honorary graduands, Ma'am,' I replied.

✳ ✳ ✳

When I got down to work an unwelcome surprise awaited me, for I found that Jock Logan, the principal, was a very sick man. Punctilious in his morning visits to brief me, I could not but become alarmed when in the course of discussion he frequently fell asleep, sometimes in mid-sentence, dropping off as though poleaxed. Bemused and perplexed, I used to let him have his doze, relieved that after about ten minutes or so he would blink, yawn prodigiously and then carry on as though nothing untoward had happened. Later I was told that he was probably suffering from an incurable disease, perhaps narcolepsy. It soon also became clear, however, that he was by no means abreast of current university, particularly financial, business and when asked for up-to-date résumés of one or other subject of concern, there invariably ensued a long delay before it was forthcoming, and, for example, on the very important question of how much the medical faculty was then costing and likely to cost in the next couple of years, it took three months to get a considered response from him.

From recent experience of Court meetings, this confirmed what I had already begun to suspect, that the command of the financial affairs of the university was slipping from Jock's grasp, leaving Hamish Stewart, the clerk of the Court and in effect Logan's deputy, with the unenviable task of trying to pick up the reins, a process which few outside the University Court could have realized was taking place.

Not that this caused me personally any intrinsic difficulty, for Hamish and I, with wartime experience in the army in common, not to mention the relative merits of Crystal Palace and Tottenham Hotspur football teams to argue about, along with a readiness to laugh at ourselves, had always got along well, but it did go far to explain the recent lack of any obvious central and firm control over university policy in general, particularly the total failure while resettling priorities to bring university policies and costs together at an early stage, a function which normally lay in the hands of the principal. Although Hamish found himself at a disadvantage in not commanding the authority of the principal in being able as a member of all Senate committees to take formal initiatives on academic policy, he did successfully maintain a detailed financial record and programme, largely modelled on that of the UGC and, in the absence of any long-term strategy to govern priorities, devised a method of simply aggregating pro-posals, whether emerging from the UGC, the Senate House or the colleges, leaving decisions on priorities to be taken somehow or other, at the last possible stage, usually in a hurry, by the University Court. Since the Court's business was always regarded as confidential, no one outside, and especially the heads of schools, were given much chance of understanding how these particular priorities had been reached.

Within a federal system, which for success, especially in the allo-cation of funds, must rely on fairness, openness and accountability at the centre, such a clumsy, closed process was bound to create suspicion and discord, which kept coming to the surface in caustic debate in the meetings of the heads of schools and sooner or later was bound to lead to a crisis of confidence. The LSE in particular, notably while Sir Sydney Caine was director, persistently criticized the balance of the detailed allocations without ever being able to bring about radical change in the system.

Had the Court itself in its own procedure been working effec-tively, some of these defects might have been ameliorated. In principle, the idea of rendering the university through the member-ship of the Court responsive and accountable to public opinion was obviously sensible and right, but the practice fell far short of what was needed. To outsiders the Court looked reassuringly impressive, with a majority of illustrious lay members, including in my time as vice chancellor, for example, Lord Scarman as chair-man and the Lords Plummer, Rippon and Shawcross, Sir Reg Goodwin and Sir Peter Parker among its members. But lacking an established system of forward planning, with no firm strategy on priorities and facing an increasingly sophisticated system, they often found themselves lost in a fog of uncertainty, having to leave important decisions to be settled by the minority of academic members, who usually constituted the very groups that had initiated the proposals.

On the academic side in the Court we were no doubt remiss in not fully exploiting the expertise the lay members could give, as became plain when in a crisis we did in fact get round to asking the deputy chairman, Sir Peter Parker, to relieve the university of a financial incubus by selling off two loss-making companies, Dillons' Book Shop and the Atlas Computing Company, which had earlier been incautiously established, yet predictably had failed to run profitably. But this was exceptional.

Because so large a proportion of its budget was absorbed by London, the UGC, in preparing proposals for the 1972–7 quinquennium — and no doubt alerted by experience gained by the chairman, Sir Fred Dainton, as a member of the Murray Committee of the weaknesses in London's system of planning and control — took the initiative in suggesting a financial limit of 5 per cent on future growth. Such a rough-and-ready criterion, although constituting some improvement on the wasteful free-for-all of previous quinquennia, at once provoked the medical schools into protesting that it was impossible to manage within this quantum, so, though obviously doubtful about the wisdom of the proposal, the UGC agreed to allow the university to put forward a quite separate submission for medical education.

But in response, when the UGC's allocations were finally revealed to the university, the proposed increase for the medical side proved to be so large in proportion to that for the 'non-medical' side — 19 as compared to 9 per cent — as to create, especially within the large multi-faculty colleges, instant alarm and uproar, which could only be contained by forming an emergency *ad hoc* committee, which I had to chair, to rework the two allocations into an acceptable general package. So considerable in fact were the variations we then had to devise that Sir Fred Dainton protested, summoning me to explain and justify our decision, and, though finally accepting that within the UGC's own doctrine of academic freedom the university could assert the ultimate right to manage its own affairs, made it abundantly clear that while he remained chairman there would be no repetition.

Personally I believed that, through the devolutionary policy originating in the 1960s, an acceptable balance between the powers appropriate to the federal centre and to the colleges was in the process of being struck, although still missing were a generally agreed strategy and adequate central control to keep the development of the faculties and studies in fair proportion and to prevent undue duplication and proliferation. But economies achievable through major restructuring in and between colleges, which in time would no doubt be needed, would have to await the outcome of the Murray enquiry.

In this conviction I felt encouraged by the coincidental and helpful change being brought about in the composition of the Collegiate Council through the arrival of a quite new generation of college heads (much more managerially sophisticated than their predecessors), including the Lords Annan and Flowers, Sir Harry Melville and Dr Ron Tress, who soon indicated that they were not prepared to put up with continued delay or muddle in the central allocation of university resources. They had no hesitation, for example, in welcoming my proposal of a very simple device to introduce forthwith an advisory committee jointly to represent and report back both to the Court and Senate, which would not only bring academic and financial policy together, but also, unlike virtually every other change of importance, did not require a change of statute. But no sooner had I signalled my intention than a somewhat agitated Lord Murray sought me out in my office, begging me not to act because it would pre-empt one of his committee's most important forthcoming proposals. Reluctantly holding back, I felt bound nevertheless to get the Senate House and its administrative staff ready for this obvious and necessary change.

But, to my surprise, on calling together the senior officers — Jock Logan, the principal, along with the clerks of the Senate and Court, Leigh Pownall and Hamish Stewart respectively — I found them decidedly reluctant even to meet. When at long last we got together round the table, the meeting proved disastrous. To the principal's opening demand that in serving the proposed new committee he must have a new planning unit under his personal control, completely separate from the Court Department, Stewart quite reasonably responded that his department already possessed the required information and experience and that such duplication

225

was unnecessary and undesirable. Pownall said not a word. At this point, emitting a series of enormous yawns, Logan abruptly fell asleep and, with both Stewart and Pownall obviously unwilling to proceed, I saw no alternative but to abandon the meeting; in fact I never saw any point in calling that triumvirate of officers together again.

Jock Logan's proposal would no doubt have had the unacceptable effect of creating two rival empires, yet the suggested alternative of putting the advisory process wholly into the hands of the Court Department would simply have extended its powers, further undermining the Senate's statutory role in academic policy. In any event Logan's illness really ruled him out as arbiter, so, although with little conviction, I cobbled together an arrangement appointing the two clerks as joint secretaries of the new advisory committee, thus in principle protecting the formal position of the Senate, though fully aware that on most matters the initiative and effective authority would rest in practice in Stewart's hands. With this decision Logan finally moved to the sidelines, where he occupied himself in writing a memoir.

While still awaiting the Murray proposals, my discussions with Stewart gradually revealed that the university was rapidly falling into even deeper financial difficulty than I had first realized, largely through the escalating and to some extent uncontrollable recurrent and capital costs arising on the one hand from the medical schools and on the other from four recently created computer programming centres.

Of the latter, three had been set up in the colleges, the fourth at the centre, this one incidentally also servicing other universities in the south. Managed by a powerful committee representing competing users it had been pushing demand ever higher, and because for some reason the annual estimates were still based on the initial scale of capital investment, amounting to about £12 million, little attention was given to the future recurrent implications of growth. Since for most academic users the sky appeared to be the limit and the user committee prevaricated about devising any acceptable method of controlling expensive computing time, the university was landed with a heavy and seemingly limitless financial commitment. My enquiries also revealed that even those three schools that had established their own computing centres were vague about the resulting future financial commitments.

Nor were the heads of those multi-faculty schools which were closely linked with the medical schools in providing pre-clinical medical education, conversant with the general developmental costs currently being put forward by the medical schools themselves. Moreover, since no ceiling had been placed by the University Court on the scale of future development of the medical schools, the Court Department had adopted the practice of simply accepting and carrying forward all new proposals for buildings, so on my estimation the sum for the medical side already amounted to about £40 million, which would have pre-empted the whole of the university's total allocation from the UGC for all building purposes whatsoever for a decade ahead. In short, within the existing system, we were accelerating towards financial breakdown.

Rumour of my concern must somehow have reached the new minister of health, Dr David Owen, because he urgently called me to a meeting to discuss the question, at which, after first bitterly complaining about the disproportionately high costs of London's hospitals, he floated the idea that the university should consider transferring two of its medical schools to other universities, one to go north and the other to the southeast. With so much already on my plate, and indisposed to get into argument, I simply indicated interest in any proposals he might put forward and, as I expected, heard no more from him.

Fortunately, on the university's existing large commitments to the arts and sciences we avoided similar difficulties because, in planning ahead for the division of student numbers for the 1972–7 quinquennium, I had been able in good time to put in place an advisory committee to reconcile the bids of the 11 multi-faculty schools. With this modest operation in mind, while still awaiting the report from the Murray Committee, I was able to sketch the sort of planning structure that would be needed at the federal centre to produce a more sensible, coherent and general system of financial control for the university as a whole, which would have to take something like the following cumbrous shape, indicating just how complex and probably unmanageable the federation had become.

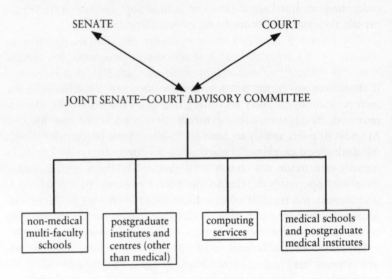

In parallel with the need to control computing costs it would also be necessary to start rationalizing the university's 66 libraries, which included, besides the large central collections in the Senate House, several of established international standing, like those of the LSE and of the School of Oriental and African studies, both of which were highly expensive.

My chief concern, however, was how to present and negotiate this formidable proposal with the heads of schools, who were only just beginning to appreciate the seriousness of the financial position, and still more to explain and justify it to their administrative and academic colleagues, who were completely in the dark, despite the monthly bulletin I introduced to keep all university members briefed on the current position.

Moreover, they all shared a vested interest in wishing to carry still further the devolution of responsibility for teaching and research from the federal centre, which had been the mark of the last decade, so any suggestion of introducing a firmer central system of financial control ran the risk of being seen by them as a threat to that policy. Nothing could have been further from my own purpose, but I quite failed to realize how far and how easily my motives and proposals might be misinterpreted.

* * *

If there was any uncertainty about the views of the generality of members about the way forward for the federal university, it was removed by their instant, virtually unanimous reaction to the Murray Report, which in December 1972 had finally landed on my desk. A quick glance through its 300 pages and its 200 recommendations made my heart sink, for it heralded nothing but trouble. Apparently dazzled by the potential in so large and varied a university for the role of central planning, not only in achieving economies of scale but also in charting future development, the report proposed for these purposes a substantial strengthening and enlargement of the federal centre as the chief means of bringing about some measure of rationalization and economy. Many of its proposals for restructuring and perhaps amalgamating colleges would in any event have been thrown up in the course of time, but the total objective was put so crudely by the Murray Report, with so much stress being laid on their priority to expand and strengthen the federal centre, that it gave an overwhelming appearance of wishing to reverse the devolutionary process of the past decade. Incidentally, to my disappointment, the proposal to divide the university into five or six groups was summarily dismissed.

To my mind the Murray Committee's notion of the federal university was invalid, seeming to envisage some sort of ship of state, well capable with a captain of authority on the bridge of finding a direct route to defined goals. I thought they would have been nearer the mark if they had seen as a model the *Kon-Tiki*, Thor Heyerdahl's raft, a large, unwieldy structure made up of a mixture of large and small logs, loosely roped together, moving hither and thither with the currents and only occasionally capable of taking an agreed direction.

It was incomprehensible to me that a committee under Lord Murray, which included such able and experienced members as Sir William Mansfield Cooper and Sir Fred Dainton, both of whom had already seen service as vice chancellors, and Lord Cole, who was a highly successful industrialist, should have so misread the situation. Perhaps Lord Murray's recent successful term at the head of an exceptionally proactive national UGC directing university expansion throughout the United Kingdom had encouraged him in an exaggerated notion of what could be achieved through a strong lead from the centre, and both he and subsequently Fred Dainton could be forgiven for long since having lost patience with the confusion and failure of the ineffective London Senate House machine. Whatever the explanation, the plain fact was that the committee had confused the federal system with the role of the federal centre, failing to distinguish clearly between them and therefore completely underrating the extent to which many of the functions of the Senate House had already been devolved to schools, and equally important how far such a process could usefully be taken in future.

In a forthright condemnation of the report, Lord Annan declared 'This puts the clock right back,' a view which over the next few months, in more measured terms, was formally repeated by the governing bodies and academic boards of the 34 federal institutions and also by the 100 or so university committees to which the report had been sent.

No doubt gratified by the committee's confidence in the future role of the Senate House, Jock Logan still thought something could be saved from the report, but I thought it was more likely to provide the last straw for the federation, and quoted to him:

> A twister of twist once twisted a twist,
> And the twist that he twisted was a three-twisted twist,
> But in twisting the twist one twist came untwisted,
> And the twist that untwisted untwisted the twist.

Although there was no doubt about the initial hostile reaction of the members of the university, six months were to elapse before the formal responses from the constituent institutions reached the Senate House, leaving me in a dilemma, for my commitment in taking on the vice chancellorship had in effect been within my two-year term to make a start in giving effect to the Murray

proposals. Now the critical question to be faced was whether anything worthwhile could be rescued from the débâcle.

As a part-time, unpaid vice chancellor, dependent on the support
and goodwill of my own college, appointed for no more than one
year at a time, with the chief executive, Jock Logan, far from well,
I simply did not command the authority, means or time to embark
on the necessary process of restructuring or regrouping the colleges, especially the expensive medical schools, and of tackling the
even more urgent matter of the university's spiralling costs, both
capital and recurrent.

In any event there was no obvious, quick way forward because
the heads of schools and the senior university councils were only
just beginning to grasp the severity of the university's financial
crisis and, to make matters worse, had already got caught up in a
lively debate among their academic colleagues, who plainly
relished the subject, about the purely constitutional implications of
the Murray proposals for the future of the federation.

In the first responses to the Murray Report the only thing in
common was the unanimous wish of the schools to retain the
federation, in particular to maintain the standard of and their
commitment to the prestigious London degree, so I was driven to
the conclusion that my most useful and perhaps only contribution
in the remainder of my short term as vice chancellor would be to
concentrate on producing a revised federal constitution as an
alternative to Murray, which no doubt would require a new act of
Parliament to be made effective. Simply to throw in my hand at
that juncture was out of the question and I sought comfort in
reflecting that I was no more than 'A willow of the wilderness,
loving the wind that bent me', and warned the Senate that I would
have to bow out as soon as I had succeeded in negotiating an
agreed set of proposals.

But in fact, although very few in the university seemed to realize
it, or to be much concerned, the most urgent priority was not
whether or how to reform the federal constitution but whether,
with its existing financial arrangements, it could survive at all as a
university of the first rank. The colleges in fact had set their minds
and were focusing their energies on the wrong question.

In examining the constitutional options I gradually became

aware that the way ahead was fraught with legal difficulty because the existing statutes were governed by the terms of the Hilton Young Report of 1926 which, on my reading, led to the daunting conclusion that a new enabling act of Parliament would be needed before any major change in the statutes, including even the creation of a full-time vice chancellorship, could be brought about. To my surprise, however, Jock Logan, backed by the chairman of the University Court, Lord Scarman, took the optimistic view that an immediate, special appeal to the Privy Council would probably elicit prompt support on practical grounds for that essential change in the vice chancellorship, so after taking Counsil's advice, which supported that view, we made the attempt. Had the Privy Council shown any willingness to look beyond a purely legal evaluation we might have got away with this necessary practical step to open the way to stable leadership, but from the moment a committee of three law lords was appointed to give a verdict I feared the outcome. In the event, when speed was of the essence, the Privy Council took so many months in reaching a decision that it left both the university and me personally in limbo.

A degree of tension and instability is endemic in all federal systems, and responsible in part for this long delay was a sudden upsurge among a small number of academic staff of opposition to the course the university was taking, the initiative being seized by a group in the LSE led by John Griffith, professor of public law, who called on the Privy Council to reject the university's petition altogether. Thinking that a face-to-face explanation of the university's financial dilemma and the evident need for assured full-time attention at the centre might moderate their challenge, I persuaded the newly appointed director of the school, Dr Ralf Dahrendorf, to arrange for me to meet that school's academic board, which in fact happened to consist of most of the staff. From their patient, puzzled silence it was clear not only that much of what I was saying, especially on the financial crisis, was news to them but that the opposition at LSE went far beyond the matter of the vice chancellorship, which they obviously regarded as merely the tip of the iceberg, and in reality extended to the whole effort I had been making over the last year or so to introduce some form of rational planning and financial control at the centre. In the following weeks it gradually emerged, too, that Griffith and his supporters even preferred the maintenance of the existing constitutional status quo, despite its manifest weaknesses, and in disregard of the approval already expressed by the governing body of the LSE for the federation in a revised form.

As vice chancellor I was pretty well constrained into working directly through the senior councils in the Senate House, although I would have wished to visit and discuss the constitutional future directly with the academic staffs in the schools. But this would have constituted a mammoth task and, although meetings with the staffs of Westfield and Queen Elizabeth Colleges proved mutually cordial and helpful, the duty to inform and initiate debate in the colleges clearly rested not with me but with the respective heads of schools. But it was not until several years later, in 1974/5, that some heads, including those of Imperial College and LSE, where disquiet among the academic staff about the university's policy appeared strongest, actually took action to form collegiate study groups to study the implications of the university's move to seek a new enabling act, a tardiness which reflected the debilitating weakness in communications within the federal system as a whole. In the meantime the monthly bulletin to keep all university members abreast of developments did create some interest, but I suspect remained unread by most.

This was all the more frustrating because in the senior councils and committees within the Senate House I had succeeded quite soon after the rejection of the Murray Report in achieving both formally and informally a good degree of understanding of the university's situation and immediate needs. This was fortified by frequent reconnaissances, usually in the form of congenial, buoyant working lunches with the chairmen of the Academic and Collegiate Councils, then Professor Randolph Quirk of University College and Dr Bryan Thwaites of Westfield, the more enjoyable because both shared a rich, sardonic sense of humour. In regular meetings, too, I briefed Lord Scarman, the chairman of the Court.

By the summer of 1972 sufficient common ground was established to enable me to draft a comprehensive first working paper charting the constitutional way ahead. Nevertheless, only too well aware that the three chairmen and I carried relatively little weight in the important large multi-faculty colleges, I thought it essential that in the critical months ahead one of the powerful and influential heads of these colleges should take on at least the chairmanship of the Collegiate Council, later leading no doubt under the new enabling act to the permanent, full-time vice chancellorship, but much to my chagrin, one after another turned the idea down. Especially in the light of their known wish to have their own large colleges separately funded by the UGC, their refusal at this critical stage made me wonder about the extent of their commitment to the federation.

Outside the Senate House altogether, and in effect more widely influential than the central councils, there existed a small coterie of heads of schools to which I belonged. Initiated soon after his appointment by the provost of University College, Noel Annan, it had for several years past been meeting monthly over lunch at which the conversation more often than not turned on the university's future. Deliberately from the start no attempt had been made to include Jock Logan or Hamish Stewart, and the small group remained as a mix of heads of both large and smaller schools, representing in fact a new generation of leadership, more managerial in style than its predecessors and more determined to bring about radical change. Its early members included Lord (Bill) Penney of atom bomb fame, rector of Imperial College, followed later by his successor Lord (Brian) Flowers, also Sir John ('Shan') Hackett, principal of King's College, formerly commander-in-chief in Western Europe and well known for his wartime escape from captivity after the Battle of Arnhem. Later Dr Dahrendorf, the newly appointed director of the LSE and Dr Ron Tress, the master of Birkbeck College, joined the group.

It would have been difficult to find two more strongly contrasting heads of schools than Bill Penney and Noel Annan, Bill priding himself on a pragmatic down-to-earth approach, seemingly not all that interested in matters academic, and Noel, always fascinated, sometimes carried away by new ideas. Widely read and consummately civilized, animated and sharp in discussion and even livelier with the pen, Noel was passionate in his likes and dislikes, occasionally for effect throwing into his conversation a flurry of expletives, a curious lacuna in a mind normally so fastidious.

To all our lively, often hilarious exchanges Shan Hackett brought a measured, classical precision in thought and language, suavely bent on feeling his way from soldiery into academic life. In his students I think he found a substitute for his former troops, even deliberately willing to endure debates in the LSE's students' union, trying to puzzle out what among the militants was really causing such agitation and, on one celebrated occasion, joining in a students' protest march, all too obviously finding it difficult to keep in step with that slouching crocodile. When I visited King's College, his introduction of the student president as 'My favourite president' encouraged the latter to put an arm familiarly round Shan's shoulders while responding 'And this is my favourite principal!'

As the head of a college that already in effect enjoyed separate funding from the UGC, Brian Flowers could afford to take a relatively detached view of the federal university's future. Coming from Manchester to London, already with a wealth of experience worldwide, he brought a refreshing ingenuity and toughness into our debates, thus confirming in the eyes of one of our colleagues his reputation as a whizz-kid, although others thought he more resembled 'a cowboy'. For my part, I found him genial and supportive, and shared his fun in invariably referring to me as 'The Boss'.

When taking on the formal responsibilities of vice chancellor I naturally found myself within this informal group in a somewhat delicate position, aware that, as a clique, its existence and purpose were regarded with suspicion and some annoyance, especially in the medical and other small schools. But in my view its undoubted value as a 'think-tank' and influential pressure group outweighed this drawback and, as its members evidently wished me to continue as one of their number, we were able to get along with a vague, tacit understanding that whatever major aspect of constitutional reform in the federal university was brought forward and agreed on, each in our respective areas of university activity would seek to promote or at least not oppose it. Nevertheless, in the cavalier, rumbustious, enormously enjoyable spirit of fun round the lunch table, cultivated and adorned in particular by Noel Annan and Shan Hackett, it was all too easy in discussion to slide over real difficulties and I never felt certain that, when the chips were down, we would hold together. What, for instance, would be the attitude of the heads of the larger schools towards the federation if the UGC offered them separate funding, and was Dr Dahrendorf sympathetic towards the views of those members of his own college who apparently wished at all costs to maintain the existing constitutional status quo?

Nevertheless, when in the early autumn of 1972 I formally presented a working paper to provide an alternative to the Murray proposals in the form of a thorough reorganization of the university's constitution, it was accepted in its entirety in both senior councils and in committee after committee, and initially to my surprise, widespread through the university, virtually without comment or discussion.

Essentially in this paper I argued that the university would need a new act of Parliament to replace that of 1929, ensuring an escape from the straitjacket of the Hilton Young Report, and not only enabling the university to put in place a new set of statutes, but also in future permitting significant change without always having to go through the laborious business of first approaching Parliament. Such an arrangement incidentally had long been enjoyed by most of Britain's unitary universities.

Since the schools had already agreed on the matter, I proposed to retain a Court, small in size, to manage and divide the university's resources on a fair, confidential basis linked directly to a Senate, which would remain the sovereign body. In the latter, while ensuring the representation of all important interests, I sought to strike a balance between the managerial concerns of schools and the academic interest of teachers, so that all heads of schools as of right would have a place along with elected members of staff representing academic colleagues both from the schools and from the 66 university boards of studies. This new Senate would therefore be more than doubled in size with well over 100 members and would be joined by some members to be elected by Convocation, the influential body representing former students, and also some student members.

My expectation was that this enlarged Senate would gradually metamorphose from the existing, rubber-stamping, inert body of record into a genuine forum of debate on academic and financial policies, providing a university-wide sounding board of views, and a source of information on university proceedings to the public at large.

Translating these readily agreed principles and practices into acceptable rules in the form of draft statutes to be submitted at the same time as the proposed new act of Parliament, and doing so after consulting the governing bodies and academic boards of the schools, was bound to prove a lengthy process, which I judged might well extend over four years, certainly beyond my own term, though others, including Jock Logan, optimistically thought it would be much less. But immediate *démarches* for representation on the proposed Senate from those trades unions which were already active in the university and from Convocation seeking to maintain its proportionate strength and threatening, if thwarted, as it had done once before with marked success in 1951, to mount a petition to Parliament, revealed that the ride would be not only lengthy but decidedly rough.

* * *

At this juncture I had to put the whole business behind me because my wife, Dorcas, had become seriously ill with what turned out to be cancer. The bottom dropped out of my world.

An early sign that something was amiss had occurred in the late summer of 1972 when, along a mountain track on Great Gable in the Lake District, Dorcas suddenly lay down, quite unable to move another step. Back home, however, she appeared to recover quickly and a severe stomach upset later that year also seemed no more than an isolated incident. But, in the spring of 1974, she suffered a recurrence and the trouble was soon diagnosed as cancer of the bowels. From several successive operations in University College Hospital she made spirited recoveries, but each in turn proved more apparent than real, requiring yet further operations, so that it slowly became obvious that she had not long to live.

Dorcas believed in the dignity of making a fight for life, refused to stay in bed and insisted on getting up every day. Just as during the war we had decided to remain together as long as possible, so now, proud of her role as homemaker, she was determined to die at home. Meg, our daughter, and I nursed her until her death on the morning of 15 August.

So, without fear and with dignity she went into 'death's dateless night'.

When you have got into the habit of hopeful expectation, looking to a modicum of planning for the years ahead, and when that process is rudely shattered, an alternative of some sort or other has to be found. Grief cannot be assuaged, time deadens rather than heals and all that remains is to move through the days as they come, letting time pass, noting simply what happens, yet dimly clutching the hope that somewhere on the way there may still be a new harmony and balance to find, a golden mean to seek.

Against all advice I went off on my own to our beloved Lake District where together Dorcas and I had spent so many happy holidays. Matching my mood, the clouds gathered and the rain fell, but whether trudging up Borrowdale or drifting down to the gloom of Wastwater, it suited me to stay out and brave the elements.

At the end of the week I dragged myself back to our empty home in Mill Hill, where I had already disposed of Dorcas's clothes, only to find when I reached the flat on the university campus that I had to repeat the same miserable business.

* * *

While one's own life may seem to have come to a standstill, the world grinds on and by this time, and not before time, the boards and governing bodies of the colleges had at last begun systematically to explore the federal future. Meanwhile relative calm reigned in the Senate House, giving me an opportunity to take a first cautious look at some of the preliminary steps that would have to be taken if any significant rationalization and practical restructuring of the university were to take place. But one by one, with ominous repetition, my tentative reconnaissances came to nothing — whether it was the attempt, starting with geology and the classics, to halt and cut back the proliferation of subject departments in the colleges, or a move to persuade the senior members of the medical faculty to initiate a review of recent excessive development, or my effort to nudge the School of Slavonic and East European Studies into joining with Queen Mary College in creating an all-European programme. The same fate met my suggestion of closely associating the university's famous external degree system with the Senate House's existing overlarge extramural department to form a new distance learning programme. I felt like a moth trapped against a window pane.

The conclusion to be drawn was inescapable, that any policy of restructuring by persuasion alone without the prior sanction of strict financial constraint would get nowhere, and that reform capable of yielding the necessary short-term economies and the longer-term hope of major reorganization would have to await the new act of Parliament. At long last, too, the Privy Council confirmed this by announcing, as I had anticipated, that the federal constitution set up under the terms of the Hilton Young Report of 1926 must be adhered to until a new act of Parliament was obtained, ruling out any significant change, including even the creation of a full-time vice chancellorship. With this news, having already more than fulfilled my personal understanding when first accepting the two-year term as part-time vice chancellor, and despite calls to carry on and a unanimous indication by the Senate that it would reselect me until at least 1976, I resolved to find the earliest, suitable moment to resign and return to my work at my own college. But the chairman of the school's governing body, Lord Radcliffe, who had earlier himself served as deputy chairman of the Court, took the view that there was still time for me to rescue and reinvigorate the existing federal system, and that one more heave also might well complete the process of putting a proposal for an enabling bill to Parliament. With this encouragement, though without his optimism, I agreed to carry on, perhaps for another six months, in which period I hoped also to find a successor to the principal, Jock Logan, who was shortly retiring.

As soon as we began to look for a new principal the manoeuvring for influence and advantage, inseparable from a federal body, landed me with an overlarge search committee of 16 members, each of whom seemed to have a quite different idea of what was needed. Although the job description I had drafted, defining the relationship between the vice chancellor and principal as similar to that of a minister and senior civil servant, commanded ready assent, sharp differences of interpretation emerged as soon as interviewing began. Despite the rapidly changing circumstances affecting the role of the Senate House, some members, notwithstanding their protestations, were quite evidently still looking for another Jock Logan; some, though a minority, wanted to see Hamish Stewart, the clerk of the Court, succeed, but most were agreed and adamant that above all we needed a fresh face. In an over-elaborate trawl through the worlds of higher education and central and local government and business, several precious months went by before we were able to bring to interview seriatim ten candidates, including one from Australasia, but not one, however, not even Hamish Stewart, succeeded in commanding majority support.

Amid this heavy pounding there occurred the occasional lighter moment. From the paper qualifications our highest expectation rested on a candidate from Australasia, with whom, over tea and before the interview, I had an informal chat. Donning my Oriental persona, I served this in some style from an elegant Chinese tea set, a gift from the Chinese University of Hong Kong, and courteously in the best Peking manner presented a bowl of jasmine tea, his own choice. He took it and, as if it were a can of Castlemaine, drained it in one gulp, smacking his lips, saying as he passed it back, 'I'd like another jar of this stuff.' Clearly G. K. Chesterton's advice that

> Tea, although an Oriental
> Is a gentleman at least

had passed him by, and it would be less than honest of me to say that I was sorry when the committee later rejected him.

No doubt exasperated by this succession of failures, Bryan Thwaites along with several other members further muddled the debate by submitting a paper arguing that, after all, we did not need a principal, that in the past few years I had shown the capacity to cope with both jobs and should therefore be asked to carry on in that mode. Flattering though the suggestion was, bitter experience had already shown that the strain involved in trying to move and unite the sluggish federation and to convince the staffs of the constituent colleges was too great to be carried alone for much longer, and, without a second thought, I rejected the idea outright.

So urgent had the need to appoint a new principal become that finally, in some desperation, I managed to resolve the impasse by bringing forward the name of Dr Glenn Wilson, recently appointed as warden of Goldsmiths' College, who had made an excellent impression there. With a background of senior teaching and administrative experience in Britain, Africa and the United States he seemed just right for the job and, with the support of the majority, was appointed. But with much still to learn about his new role, he could give me no immediate relief from the absurdly heavy burden I was still carrying, and a nasty fall down a bank while out jogging compounded my growing general exhaustion and put me out of commission for some weeks.

Half a century earlier at a crisis of my fortunes, I had been suc-coured by the girl to whom until her death I had remained happily married. Now, seeing that I was in trouble, a senior woman administrative officer in the Senate House, Joan Marshall, whom I had recently got to know in her capacity as organizer of distance-learning programmes for London's external students, came to my rescue, soon helping to put me back on my feet.

Both of us having served in the army through most of the war and subsequently in the university, we shared many interests. At the time of the Hungarian revolt against the Russians in 1956 she had rendered great service as secretary of the Lord Mayor's Fund in placing and then nursing the careers of nearly 1000 Hungarian students in British universities. Although by nature forming an attraction of complementary opposites, I being a sceptical compli-cator while she was a candid simplifier, we found pleasure in each other's company and, with tolerance born of experience, soon fell in love and some months later were happy to get married.

With her timely aid and in renewed health and vigour, I was determined in the few months I was prepared to give to the vice chancellorship to bring fully into operation my proposed system for collective planning and financial control, which piecemeal I had steadily been putting into place. Without it I knew that no radical reorganization of the Senate House and its role would be feasible, and I feared the university might founder before it even got its enabling act. But in the meantime the sharp deterioration in the national finances had begun to unhinge the UGC's quinquennial system of funding, so suddenly even the already agreed London recurrent grants for 1972–7 had to be scaled down and the quinquennial system itself seemed certain to disappear. Although this underlined the need for central planning and firm financial control in the federation, it further deepened its immediate financial crisis.

In what I saw as my last task in preparing the way for an enabling bill, for some months past I had been sounding ministers (and their Opposition shadow members) and, at the same time, pressing the UGC to support the inclusion of just such a bill within the government's own forthcoming programme of legislation, trusting that the urgency of the matter and the importance of London's place in higher education would earn some priority, but was bitterly disappointed in the early summer of 1975 to be told that there was no room for this and that, therefore, the university would have to make its own private submission. This was bound to prove a much more laborious, time-consuming process because notice for a private bill in any given legislative session had to be given before the previous 27 November to allow time for petitions to be lodged, which, in practical terms, had the effect of ruling out any possibility of arranging an agreed London submission before the year 1976.

No doubt as a sign of a growing unease about the federation's future, serving members of the LSE in both the Collegiate and Academic Councils took the opportunity to challenge the need for any timetable at all, but the majority, who shared Noel Annan's alarm that 'This would condemn us to another 20 years of futility,' rejected the move, so by the early autumn an overwhelming majority of schools in the university had given formal backing to the terms of the proposed enabling bill I had presented and the statutes already drafted to go with it. But at the final confirmatory stage in the Senate, which by custom was purely formal, Dr Dahrendorf tried one last throw in again altogether challenging the need for the bill and calling instead for the maintenance of the status quo. Spotting that in the terms of his motion he had made no reference whatsoever to the future retention in any form of the federal university, which necessarily raised questions about the LSE's ulterior motives, I queried the omission, on which he hastened to reassure the Senate but in the outcome still found himself in a minority of one.

It was difficult to determine the precise motives which lay behind the successive efforts over many months by members of the LSE to halt the process of constitutional reform. No doubt they were mixed. Ever since the prewar period when Sir William Beveridge had simultaneously been director of the school and vice chancellor, resentment at the LSE and antagonism towards the federal centre had kept coming to the surface. At this final stage a strong case could have been made either to restructure the federation or even get rid of it, but the LSE had ignored this line and simply sought to preserve the status quo *in toto*, which had already been shown to be defective and hopelessly out of date constitutionally, managerially and financially. To my mind this smacked of an obscurantism, surprising in so distinguished a place.

With the Senate's decision at the start of 1975 to proceed for an enabling bill it was evident that the university had reached a turning point in not only having put behind it the débâcle consequent on the rejection of the Murray Report's proposals, but also in presenting a generally acceptable alternative that might offer a promising future for a reorganized and scaled-down federal system. In the full knowledge that in turning the fully drafted bill into the new act a fresh phase was beginning, which might well extend over several more years, I decided that this was the right moment for me to give up the vice chancellorship and return to my full-time job at the school.

Accordingly, I dropped a note to Jock Logan telling him that I would announce this to the next meeting of Senate, only within five minutes to find him bursting into my room, angrily banging on my desk, bellowing, 'You can't do this, you can't do this, not now when you've got all the reins in your hands!' But the reality was that I had fulfilled my original undertaking and there was no job for me, no real authority, and a late approach I had made to the chairman of the Court to make good my position had produced the bleak response that all the university could offer was a letter of intent. It was high time to depart.

In the often haphazard way in which the federal centre had grown accustomed to manage important matters, no settled procedure had been established in arranging for an outgoing vice chancellor's successor to be brought forward. It therefore fell to me personally to recommend to the Senate a name or names, so on my long-held conviction that the head of one of the large multi-faculty schools would be placed strategically and with the necessary authority to pilot the university confidently into the new era, I approached first Lord Annan and then Lord Flowers, only to find that neither felt able to take on what was still only a part-time appointment, although subsequently after the new act came into force both did serve terms in a full-time capacity. But time by then for the restoration of the federal university to anything like its former glory had plainly run out. When my term ended I turned for a successor to my deputy, Dr (later Sir) Frank Hartley, whom I knew to be a dedicated federalist with an advantage over myself of being able in retirement to give his full time to the vice chancellorship.*

Although by the time of my withdrawal early in 1976 the Senate had shown that it was virtually unanimous in seeking an enabling act, that particular measure in the form of a private bill did not receive Parliament's approval until 1978, and a further three years were to pass before the associated new statutes became effective in the university.

In the period since the establishment of the Murray Committee in June 1970 and amid the ever-increasing turmoil, setbacks and delays, the federal university went steadily downhill, the best chance of radical reform long since gone. A large number of senior members began to take advantage of the government-sponsored

---

* An appreciation of my term as vice chancellor is printed in the *University of London Bulletin*, No. 32, March 1976.

policy of early retirement, a development which in particular disrupted the standing of my own school; the morale of staff generally sank low and the once busy Senate House began to look like a morgue. The time came when there was evidently no longer even a role for the full-time vice chancellorship for which we had fought so hard.

When resigning the vice chancellorship in 1976, my own thoughts about the future prospects for the university were sombre. Why had every established constituent authority and an overwhelming majority of members at first voted so resoundingly to maintain the federation, only afterwards to stand back and, presumably taking it for granted that time must be on the federal university's side, tamely watch the process of disintegration begin? Were these the years the locust had eaten?

Although it was no mean achievement out of the disaster of the Murray Report to have mounted a rescue for the federation, my verdict subsequently on it would have differed little from that of Robert Southey's old soldier, Kaspar, when asked about the outcome of his last battle,

> 'But what good came of it at last?'
> Quoth little Peterkin,
> 'Why that I cannot tell,' said he,
> 'But 'twas a famous victory.'

245

10
Policing the Police

It all began in a deceptively quiet way one morning in early December 1977. Working in my study, I was surprised to get a call from the Home Office. 'It's the permanent secretary, Robert Armstrong, speaking; I don't think we've met but we have several good friends in common. I'd like to call on you, if I may, to put a proposition.' When we met, without beating about the bush, he asked whether I would be willing to take on the chairmanship of a Royal Commission which the Labour government under Mr James Callaghan had decided to set up. 'And the subject?' I asked. 'Pre-trial criminal procedure,' he replied. With only the vaguest notion what this meant, I responded woodenly that I knew absolutely nothing about it. 'For us,' he said, smiling, 'that's part of your attraction. We're certainly not looking for a lawyer!' Offering a few explanatory details, he suggested that before making up my mind I should have a word with the home secretary, Mr Merlyn Rees.

Although quite uncertain anyway about my personal capacity to handle a subject of this sort, there could be no doubt of its rising importance in the public mind. Against a background of increasingly violent street crime in the big cities, accompanied by an outbreak of IRA bombing on the British mainland, which posed questions about the adequacy of the police, scarcely a day passed without these matters being raised in the media and in Parliament. In debate attention was drawn to notorious incidents, including the Confait case, and to frequent allegations that in London the police were systematically misusing the 'sus' law in dealing with black people, which, it was said, indicated that sections of them were already running out of control. Calls were made, too, for a fresh root-and-branch enquiry into the service as a whole, the last having taken place as long ago as 1960.

However important the subject, what I found personally attractive was the idea of handling a Royal Commission and perhaps producing a report that might stand comparison with those influential state papers which, in my earlier work on India and East Africa, and also on British higher education, I had so much used and admired. Moreover, in recent years the reputation of the Royal Commission through political misuse of its role and governmental procrastination in implementing reports had fallen in public esteem and I valued an opportunity to do something to restore it.

When we met, the home secretary, brisk and businesslike, straightaway assured me that the government was intent on reforming the criminal justice system and that he would see to it that the proposed commission's terms of reference were precisely, yet broadly, drawn to open the way for later government action; also, in reply to my specific request, he said that ample research funds would be available and as an immediate step there would be consultation on the balance of membership. With these readily given and satisfying assurances I agreed to become chairman. Reflectively sitting back, the home secretary added that his own decision to have a commission had been triggered by a particularly heinous abuse of police powers by detectives in the Metropolitan Force in the recent Confait murder enquiry in which three youths, including a vulnerable, mentally handicapped boy, had been bullied by a senior police officer into confessing to a murder, of which incidentally it later turned out they were innocent.

As we parted, he stood up smiling, evidently about to offer a last piece of advice, and then pointing in what I took to be a westerly direction, declaring with some vehemence, 'If you want inspiration look beyond the border.' In my ignorance of the criminal justice system, I took it that he was jokingly referring to the fact that we were both Welshmen and that he must have in mind the Welsh border, and, although puzzled because I thought that the English and Welsh criminal systems were identical, dutifully shared a quiet laugh, only later to realize that he must have been alluding to Scotland, whose system of criminal justice was in general well regarded. My Welsh connection, however, seemed to have gained a new and valuable dimension, for a few days' later Lord Elwyn Jones, the Lord Chancellor, with a twinkle in his eye, went out of his way to welcome me 'to the Taff-ia'.

The commission's terms of reference as announced soon afterwards to Parliament by the prime minister, Mr Callaghan, provided for an enquiry into the ways in which police in England and Wales went about investigating and prosecuting crime; they called not only for a scrutiny of their powers but also for an investigation into how the position of suspects and those charged with crimes could be properly protected.

Simple and prosaic though these terms appeared to be, they nevertheless invoked one of the central enduring themes of British history, reaching right back to the struggle between king and Parliament in the seventeenth century, between the freedom of individuals, the authority of the state and the safeguarding of society, and in effect raising the question of whether and how an acceptable balance or equipoise is to be found and maintained. The subject formed part of the core of British democracy and was certainly worthy of any Royal Commission's devoted attention.

Although the subjects of law and order, especially in the criminal field, are often popularly supposed to be above politics, they have always formed a highly politicized, controversial area and in first reconnoitring what had recently been written on the subject I realized that I was moving into a legal and political minefield. Indeed, a couple of years previously, following a report from the Criminal Law Revision Committee, an attempt by government to strengthen police powers in the investigation of crime had created uproar and deadlock in both Houses of Parliament, ending in the abject withdrawal of the proposal. Since then, and with growing acrimony, the gulf between the parties had widened and appeared unbridgeable, and the likelihood of finding proposals that would satisfy the main political parties seemed remote. Had the move to set up the commission, I wondered, begun to indicate a will in government for radical change, or did it really represent the traditional ploy of removing a thorny subject from the immediate political agenda? I recalled A. P. Herbert's remark that, 'A Royal Commission is generally appointed not so much for digging up the truth, as for digging it in; and a government department appointing a Royal Commission is like a dog burying a bone.'

However, my immediate tasks were to make sure that the membership of the commission composed the right mixture of relevant expertise and general experience to do the job and, equally important, to find a general secretary capable of managing our business. For the latter, Sir Robert Armstrong strongly urged me to consider one of his colleagues at the Home Office, Christopher Train, who after a period of teaching classics at St Paul's School had joined the Home Office as a late entrant and quickly made his mark in running the crime policy-planning unit. On first acquaintance I found Train's directness and vigour in discussion impressive, reflecting in equal measure a mastery of the subject and enthusiasm for the task, and usefully salted with a pinch of dry humour. Much to the point, bearing in mind that we had to produce and write a report, a brief analysis of the relevant literature, which at my request he readily drafted, showed that as a draughtsman he possessed an admirable command of both structure and language.

In forming a strong nucleus it was straightforward to bring together a well-balanced group of four from the legal fraternity, and to add from the police Sir Douglas Osmond, widely considered to be the most thoughtful, effective chief constable of the day, along with Dick Pamplin, who had recently rounded off a varied career in the service with a successful term as president of the Police Federation. To these vested interests Professor Michael Banton was recruited to bring an essential objectivity and experience in research and, through long study both at home and abroad, a close understanding of relations between the police and public. Further lay experience, both relevant and powerful, was provided by Jack Jones, who had recently retired as the secretary of the Transport and General Workers' Union, and by Sir Arthur Peterson, who enjoyed the unique advantage of having already served both as chief executive of the Greater London Council and permanent secretary at the Home Office.

Just before the prime minister's formal announcement of the commission a note reached me that 'No. 10 wishes further to strengthen the progressive side of the membership' and was therefore putting forward a short list of names from which I was asked to choose and, although somewhat reluctant to increase the size of the commission to 16, I was glad to take the opportunity to add a couple of younger members, Dianne Hayter and Walter Merricks, both in their thirties. As a quite unexpected bonus it then turned out that half of those chosen were already serving as magistrates and were therefore well acquainted with that particular part of the court's system through which, nationwide, over 90 per cent of all criminal cases currently passed.

As a useful preliminary before running the risk of getting buried in detail, I took the trouble to glance through some of the reports of recent Royal Commissions, greatly surprised to discover how little basic research most had undertaken. The two most recent and relevant by subject, for example, the Thomson Report of 1975 on pre-trial criminal procedure in Scotland and the Royal Commission on Legal Services, had relied on descriptive surveys rather than investigatory research, and the last major report on the police in 1961 had done little more than take a single sampling of public attitudes, which can have yielded little that was not already well known. This last report was typical, too, in adopting what I could see had become the traditional classic mode of operation and presentation followed by most commissions — first a general appeal for written evidence, followed by an invitation to all and sundry to give oral evidence, and culminating in a structure of argument which in effect took the form of 'Some say this; some say that; and we believe this and therefore so recommend.' Such a process may well happen to reflect the state and mixture of current public opinion, but obviously suffers in doing little or nothing to encourage a radical enquiry, or in producing and testing new factual evidence as a basis for projecting and exploring fresh lines of thought on the subject.

Just after accepting the chairmanship I happened to meet Victor Rothschild, former director of the government's 'think-tank', who invited me to dinner, at which he went out of his way to deplore the lack of official action on many recent official reports, including the one on gambling, which he had chaired, and also the most recent on legal services. Angry at such a waste of time and money, he challenged me to say whether 'the sweat of a Royal Commission was worthwhile?' He may well have been right, but to my mind it did not necessarily follow that the idea had lost its public value. Provided the subject under review was appropriate for such treatment, that is reflecting an important issue on which differing value judgements were at work, and was not simply a matter of sorting out 'nuts and bolts', such as for instance the recent enquiry into the organization of the law courts, the Royal Commission to my mind still commanded the freedom to enquire systematically and comprehensively and to conduct any necessary research well beyond the scope of a civil service department or government policy unit. Further, if the commission did its job properly and presented a full range of important, relevant arguments, well and purposefully illustrated by research, its report, whether later acted on by government or not, would still serve as an enduring basis of reference and ideas for subsequent public debate.

However, when soon after we had got down to work and Mrs Thatcher had succeeded Mr Callaghan as prime minister, and had lost no time in publicly expressing her conviction that 'policy units' suited her purpose much better than Royal Commissions, I really did wonder whether the discredited reputation of the Royal Commission could be restored, and anyway whether any Royal Commission report would be acted on by her government.

Two early decisions I was called on to make on what I thought were no more than matters of routine turned out later to exert a decisive influence. First, despite the misgivings of both the Home Office and the Law Society, I set the target date for completion at three years, which in effect soon began to exert a far-reaching healthy discipline on the whole of our planning. Second, in full awareness that the public impact of many recent commission reports had been blunted and subsequent government action delayed or absorbed by the growing tendency of commissions to produce one or more minority as well as majority reports, I got the members at an early meeting to agree to accord the formal status of a minority report only to a submission supported by a quorum of no less than five. Individuals of course would still retain the right to express a note of dissent, although in effect enjoying a lower level of significance. In large measure through these decisions and despite the controversial political and legal nature of the subject, we not only delivered our report within three years, but did so by unanimous agreement, thus greatly strengthening the likelihood of early consequential government action.

In the debate, which had been set going by the public announcement of the commission, many lawyers and police officers, in particular, had rushed into print to offer their prescriptions for change, the majority eager to cite their own personal experience to substantiate their arguments, though rarely were they able to produce empirical evidence gained by research. Thus many obvious yet important questions went unanswered. What, for instance, in police investigations of crime was the precise extent of the use of detection and the questioning of suspects? How many persons were taken into police stations for questioning and how many then released without charge? How prolonged was the questioning? How many suspects claimed the right of silence? To these and a host of other related questions practical, precise answers were missing and the necessary factual base seemed certain to remain the same unless a programme of research was urgently mounted, a course which might well extend over a period of some 12 months.

While we were considering how to mount this, the commission was sharply reminded of the folly of proceeding without first establishing a factual base. Coincidentally, because the matter had happened to create a storm in the Commons, the home secretary as a matter of urgency referred to the commission the vexed question of official telephone-tapping, asking for early advice on a policy of control, on which it hoped later to produce a White Paper. But we suffered a severe disadvantage in not having received any relevant evidence on this and in not possessing any first-hand knowledge of the sophisticated technology. Moreover, the Home Office, for reasons of security, declined to provide a detailed breakdown of the warrants authorizing interception, so we did not even know what proportion was used in purely criminal investigation.

With hindsight I realize that, lacking this information, my response as chairman ought to have been to decline to handle the matter altogether. Nor did it help that when the commission hurriedly met to draw up its answer I happened to be abroad on university business, so the advice that went forward to the home secretary, in my opinion, if put into practice would have proved cumbrous, confusing and politically divisive. In the event little use was made of our advice, but this episode served as a warning that in approaching our main task we must take care to establish an adequate factual base for subsequent discussion, in short, that research and its purposes had to come first.

If we were to make sure of reporting within three years, it was obviously imperative, without even waiting for the written public evidence, that we should start on the research programme.

I therefore brought together a small working party, particularly making use of and benefiting from the mature experience of Michael Banton and the youthful research energy of Walter Merricks, moderated by the practical know-how of Douglas Osmond, to create a substantial programme. Any reservations about having to make such heavy demands of the 20 or so chief constables within whose forces our research teams would have to operate were instantly removed by the Association of Chief Police Officers' two senior representatives, Barry Pain at Kent and Ken Oxford at Merseyside, both of whom showed marked readiness to welcome new ideas.

This eagerness to cooperate came as something of a surprise because when the commission was first announced ACPO, the Association of Chief Police Officers, had gone out of its way to challenge the need for it, formally denying 'that any case existed for a radical overhaul of procedures'; and the Police Super-intendents' Association had greeted the news 'with almost universal pessimism. ... Rightly or wrongly,' it said, 'we view it as an attack on the limited powers already possessed by the police.' The service, in the words of its spokesman, 'felt at bay in the face of the big guns of every minority group and sociological agency, many with doubtful motives propounding the theory of a violent and unfeeling police service.'

In the search for new solutions it was obviously essential for the commission to complement its research with first-hand experience by paying visits both within Britain and abroad to study procedures different from those in England and Wales, and also to discover new experiments which might be relevant to the English system. An old friend, Dame Kitty Anderson, with wide experience of government committees, including the famous Robbins enquiry into higher education, helpfully went out of her way to warn me that a great deal of our time would be wasted unless the preparation of visits was purposeful, citing as poor examples several of the visits she herself had made with the Robbins Committee. Thus prompted, we focused our attention on those common law jurisdictions that offered a genuine comparative base, notably those of Canada, the United States, Australia and Scotland, arranging also for members of the secretariat to prepare the ground so that the commission's members could concentrate on what was strictly relevant.

On the west coast of the United States, in the district of San Diego, we saw how some procedural innovations that had found favour in some of our evidence, especially the extensive use before trial of both charge-bargaining and plea-bargaining and the strengthening of suspects' rights, were clogging that system and reducing the trial itself to a secondary place, in effect turning the adversarial system on its head. By comparison, in British Columbia in Canada we were able to study a criminal justice system very similar to our own, which had recently and successfully introduced the tape-recording of police interrogations and also removed the subsequent responsibility for prosecution from the police, changes which at first sight offered a feasible, promising model, deserving of further study.

Some of the written evidence we had so far received had exhorted us to copy the Scottish procurator fiscal system, which in fact happened to be an object of strong interest to two of our members with first-hand experience, Bill Forbes, a Scotsman, and Mrs Gask, who had been brought up in Edinburgh.

But study on the spot revealed that the picture of Scottish pre-trial procedure presented to us in written evidence did not closely reflect what was actually happening on the ground. In practice, for instance, we found that the fiscal usually accepted the case presented by the police and that the line between investigation and prosecution was often blurred and not drawn nearly so sharply as had been asserted. Moreover, the relatively lower esteem in Scotland usually accorded to the police, as compared with lawyers, made for significant differences in practice from the role performed by the former in England and Wales.

Within England and Wales most of the commission were easily able to make frequent visits to watch how suspects were handled in police stations; I personally paid at least one visit to each of the 42 forces, occasionally — particularly in the West Midlands — coming across rumours of oppressive police behaviour, though hard evidence was difficult to find. My main effort went into discussing investigative methods with squads of detectives in an effort to discover how useful their training had been. This usually provoked on their side categoric, at times passionate, insistence that training had little to contribute to improve detection, which they maintained could only be learnt 'on the job'. Working within an adversarial system, they saw the method of interrogation as largely intended to obtain confessions, and to my frequently repeated question on the distinction between 'robust' and 'oppressive' questioning, no one ever offered an answer.

In one of these discussions I happened to refer to the need for detectives to acquire the skill to make use of 'a cumulative series of questions', promptly being challenged to produce an example. I was only too happy to cite a report of a case conducted by the famous barrister, Norman Birkett, when prosecuting a cockney cab driver whose passengers were claiming damages. To their allegation that he had driven recklessly, the cab driver retorted that he had been 'going slow', on which Birkett started his cross examination:

Birkett:	You say you were travelling quite slowly?
Driver:	Yes.
Birkett:	Not fast at all, but quite slowly?
Driver:	That's right.
Birkett:	And you drew out to pass another vehicle?
Driver:	Yes.
Birkett:	Still not going fast?
Driver:	Yes.
Birkett:	(pausing) Let me see, you skidded slightly?

Driver:	Yes.
Birkett:	Mounted the pavement?
Driver:	Yes.
Birkett:	Hit a plate-glass window and smashed it?
Driver:	Yes.
Birkett:	Knocked over two stalls loaded with fruit?
Driver:	Yes.
Birkett:	Knocked down a pedestrian?
Driver:	I'm afraid so.
Birkett:	And finally hit the lamp-post?
Driver:	Yes.
Birkett:	(pausing) Well now, I wonder if you'd like to indicate how much more damage you might have done if you'd been going fast?

Most of the senior detectives had attended one of the existing four specialist training schools, where the curriculum evidently consisted largely of criminal law, a lot of it, including much that was irrelevant, being learnt by heart. Very little attention was paid to methods of interrogation and to the art of detection generally, a manifest absurdity when deterrence against crime so obviously lies in the threat of detection. Police training in general appeared to be scattered almost haphazardly among the forces, each separate centre competing for custom against the others, and it was difficult to avoid the feeling that the system from top to bottom needed to be overhauled and replaced by a more coherent national rather than regional or force by force structure. However, this dimension lay outside the commission's direct responsibility and, after making attempts to broach this matter informally in senior police circles and in the Police Department of the Home Office and receiving little encouragement, I let the matter rest.

In a mixture of personal visits I covered the spectrum of police personalities and attitudes from 'Andy to Aldy', from the forceful, God-fearing James Anderton at Manchester to the smoothly discreet advocate of community policing, John Alderson at Exeter, having to keep pace with the former as he energetically bounded up flights of stairs to his grand, new command headquarters, and being taken aback when the latter, in response to my casual reference to visits, which as chief constable he no doubt made to consult the chairman of his police authority, retorted, 'I don't go to see him, he comes to see me!' Nor could I fail to be surprised at being met at the railway station by one North Country chief, resplendent in a dark, pinstriped morning suit, relieved by a natty bow tie and a red rose in his buttonhole, carrying a bowler hat and beautifully rolled umbrella. Later, at lunch, plainly not wanting me to engage in direct conversation with the chairman of his police authority, who happened to be a publican, his reaction whenever the latter showed the slightest inclination to speak was unceremoniously to thrust one more can of beer at him, a ploy which repeatedly worked like a charm.

For my part it would have been naïve not to recognize that to the police and possibly also to the Home Office a professor of Oriental history, empowered to enquire into their work and descending suddenly on them, must have appeared an irritating, if not absurd, oddity; but accustomed daily to cope with the unusual, they always took me in their stride, so that in their stations, on the beat, in the pub, in training centres and at conferences, I had every opportunity to become familiar with their distinctive, defensive subculture infused by the old-fashioned virtues of comradeship and loyalty, reinforced by an obstinate determination to get on with the job. But in conversation with senior officers, with Sir Ken Newman at Scotland Yard and Sir Philip Knights at Birmingham, the latter in a file- and book-cluttered office with not an inch of space to sit on, more like a professor's than a policeman's, it became abundantly clear, in a society rapidly fragmenting and becoming more criminal and less supportive, that they and their forces felt increasingly isolated, beleaguered and betrayed.

However, when the police service took me by surprise in awarding me the rare and prestigious James Smart Police Medal, I took it as signifying that as a friendly, constructive critic I had been tried and not found wanting.

Meanwhile, in a couple of intensive weekend sessions in a quiet retreat near Northampton, the commission had rounded off its second year's work, bringing together for the first time the several strands of our enquiry and thoroughly digesting the findings of our research. Rather like a lawnmower steadily refining the height and precision of the cut, our discussion always went backwards and forwards over the options for change, greatly eased by the extent and frequency to which the results of research were steadily reducing areas of potential disagreement.

By this stage two strongly opposed groups in the commission were actively manoeuvring for dominance. On the one side Jack Jones, with at the outset five or six others in support, perhaps reflecting the working man's traditional antagonism to the police, asserted that, as they were the enforcers of authority on the streets, the advantages in the existing system lay disproportionately with the police, and that the cards were stacked against suspects and defendants, who anyway enjoyed insufficient safeguards. By comparison, Arthur Peterson and Douglas Osmond were seeking to put at the top of the agenda the struggle to protect society by bringing criminals to justice. They emphasized that the police were embattled, shackled by laws and procedures that favoured the criminal, perhaps already losing the struggle against increasing crime. Above all, therefore, they put their emphasis on the need to strengthen police powers of investigation.

These differences came to a head in considering the central place of the right of silence in pre-trial procedure which the suspect in an adversarial system traditionally enjoys, that is the right not to have to answer questions either before trial or at the trial itself. Early on I had come to realize that the government, in deciding to make use of a Royal Commission, ought to have directed its attention first to the accusatorial nature of the trial itself rather than to the pre-trial procedure because manifestly it was the former that dictated the framework and course of the system as a whole. Moreover, the focus of public attention was already shifting to defects in the trial itself, in which a growing volume of serious miscarriages of justice, possibly through police misbehaviour, were beginning to come to light. As it was, the cart had been put before the horse, leaving my colleagues and myself handicapped in being precluded, except for the purpose of discussion, from dealing with and perhaps proposing significant modifications to the accusatorial framework not only before trial, but at the trial itself.

Since we had to maintain the existing accusatorial form, the majority of us had reached the conclusion that it was only fair and

logical to retain the right of silence, though few were willing like
Jack Jones to treat it as an absolute right, not in any circumstances
to be touched. Several members were willing to see it modified in
one way or another, either at the pre-trial stage or even,
preferably, at the trial itself, or both, as our barrister, Bill Forbes,
urged. My own position was that we simply did not know to what
extent and how the right was currently used in practice, and that
before reaching conclusions on such a pivotal matter we should
await our research findings, on which four or five of the
programmes still in progress had a direct bearing.

In the event the findings from several of these projects exercised
a decisive influence. Barrie Irving's 'fly on the wall' study of the
process of interrogating suspects at Brighton police station
revealed how persuasive, even on occasion demoralizing, was the
effect brought about by confinement in a police cell, usually inducing suspects to talk, so that the great majority, including even
professional criminals, did not in fact choose to exercise the right
to remain silent. This at a stroke took the heat out of the debate,
confirming most members in the view that the presumption of
innocence and the right of silence should together be maintained
as forming the core of the existing accusatorial system.

Since there is no adequate substitute in the investigation of crime
for police questioning, our experiment in tape-recording interviews was bound to be of critical significance. Throughout the
previous decade, opinion among the police had been so strongly
sceptical about its usefulness and desirability that the Home Office
had been discouraged from pursuing the matter, even though in
both Australia and the United States, which enjoyed similar
jurisdictions, this method had already been successfully introduced. One experiment carried out with the Kent force confirmed
this, demonstrating beyond question not only that a suitable,
tamper-proof recording machine could be constructed, but also, to
the surprise of many, that the use of taping actually provided as
much help and protection against abuse to the police as to the
suspect. Virtually overnight those initially sceptical police officers
who were engaged in the experiment became converts.

To apply this system generally was bound to be expensive, but
an unexpected finding showed that most of the expenditure would

be incurred not, as we had first assumed, for the taping itself but for the subsequent transcription; and since it was likely that the majority of interviews would not be subsequently challenged in court, only those actually at issue at the trial itself would need to be transcribed. The total financial outlay could therefore be kept under control and there was no reason except cost why the system should not be universally established.

Our inclination therefore was to have taping applied throughout the service immediately, but to honour our terms of reference, which cautioned us to have regard for cost, we finally recommended a modest start in only a couple of forces, with later gradual extension; but when the subject reached Parliament, it came as a relief to me that consideration of cost was sensibly put aside to enable the taping system to be applied countrywide.

Unlike these vexed, controversial areas of police investigation and questioning, there was little difference among members on whether the police should retain the responsibility of prosecution, all readily accepting that in principle these functions should properly be separated. Whether the policy of creating a new prosecution service of lawyers would later be adequately supported by the legal profession (and the financial costs publicly acceptable) was less clear; but our own exercise in operational research decisively removed any lingering reservations on these matters among the commission's own members.

But in seeking to replace a system which for over a century had gone on growing haphazardly without clear rationale — each new change of rules in turn having been added on its own merits regardless of its effect on the system as a whole — the majority of members came to the conclusion that it would raise the level of debate and give greater validity to the system as a whole if we were able to establish some standards, perhaps even construct a simple framework within which not only to evaluate the adequacy in general of existing procedures but also to compare and justify our own new set of proposals. But strong doubts were expressed about whether this was either feasible or sensible, Douglas Osmond arguing that the procedures applying both for police and suspects were too much at the mercy of political expediency to be governable in this way, and others maintaining that anyway they were already too complex to allow it. There was no alternative in their view but, as in the past, to go on changing the procedures piecemeal.

To accept this, however, would be to go on clinging to the comfortable, even hallowed, customary English practice of refraining from declarations or setting standards of principle, which incidentally had been the line followed by the great bulk of the evidence already presented to us, including that of the police. When the commission appeared to be reaching a stalemate Arthur Peterson, like a knife through butter, cut through all further argument by pointing out that in mounting our experiment in tape-recording we had in fact already applied three primary standards or tests. Were the methods we were proposing fair to all parties, to the suspects, to the police and to society in general? Also were they open to scrutiny? And were they so arranged as to be publicly accountable? If the answers, he concluded, were in the affirmative, then the extended use of these tests or standards was justifiable and calculated to give extended legitimacy to the whole system.

At a stroke this settled the argument and the commission went on to use that simple framework of ideas within which to evaluate and present its package of proposals.

Some months after the report appeared I was invited to introduce it to a gathering of professors of law of British universities and, in justifying the commission's decision to use this simple conceptual framework for its work, found that they were not overly impressed or persuaded of its usefulness, some even expressing a preference for the English tradition of treating each separate case or change 'on its merits', which surprised me for it had been my understanding that social scientists, among whom I included the academic lawyers, usually sought the rigour of developing and justifying their own work within some such framework.

Although myself accepting the usefulness of making use of such a framework I was under no illusion that, within it, permanent or final solutions could be established, for as the incidence of crime varies, public attitudes to police powers and suspects' rights always tend to shift, now up, now down, rather like a seesaw, posing not a simple conundrum like putting together a jigsaw, which when done is solved once and for all, but rather a series of questions on which from time to time varying value judgements in society are at work, requiring, as they change, some adjustment, large or small, to the balance of the system.

* * *

Our report, in its final published version, formed the first general review of pre-trial criminal procedure undertaken in England since 1845; offering, in place of the existing hotchpotch and wide variety of laws and practices which govern police powers and suspects' rights, a rational, intelligible and organic framework. As a practical guide for the police in operating this new system, we prepared also a detailed series of codes to govern their handling of suspects, well aware that the police would grumble about the paperwork necessarily involved in maintaining a system of report which, at the trial stage, could be seen to be accountable.

A decade later, when asked what in general had done most to change and improve the police perception of their job and their behaviour, especially in criminal investigation, one of the leading chief constables without hesitation replied, 'The Royal Commission and the PACE Act which followed.'

Our package of proposals, covering both the investigation and prosecution of crime, was also calculated to command wide enough support both from the public and police to enable Parliament to give it early statutory effect; so for the first time in their history the police would know exactly what they were entitled and bound by duty to do, and the public would be aware of what exactly were the suspects' rights. If given statutory form, we had no doubt that it would go some way to protect the public against the gross excesses and misbehaviour in police investigation which had occurred in the 1970s — and have only recently begun to be revealed to the public — and in fact, as soon became apparent, it came just in time to save their bacon and give the service a fresh chance of restoring health to its methods.

What unfortunately we had not been allowed to address was the basic question of whether the accusatorial nature of the system of the trial itself should be changed, and in the light of the serious weaknesses and miscarriages of justice which were beginning to be exposed in criminal trials, it was plain that even if early action were taken on our proposals, fresh scrutiny of the whole trial system could not long be deferred.

Ten years on, as I write, the Police and Criminal Evidence Act (PACE), to a remarkable degree in our volatile and fast-changing society, appears to have stood the test of time.

At the commission's final meeting, when the members came together to put their signatures to the report, there occurred at the moment when Jack Jones's turn came one of those sudden, unpredictable silences to which such gatherings are subject. Throughout our work he had maintained an inflexible opposition to any strengthening of police powers and, as we moved from topic to topic, he had been able, though only piecemeal, to gather support from one member or another, so many thought he would at the last make a gesture by refusing to sign the report. But the cumulative effect of our research findings had steadily undermined absolute and inflexible positions, and to the line the majority of the commission had taken no significant, general alternative had emerged, not even from his side. When the document reached Jack he hesitated briefly before remarking with a smile, 'Well, Chairman, you've been very fair to our views both in debate and in draft, so I'll sign.' Subsequently, in discussing the completed report with Sir Brian Cubbon, the permanent secretary at the Home Office, it amused me that his first, surprised reaction was 'How on earth did you get them all to sign?'

* * *

Our euphoria was short-lived, for in the week preceding the day of publication several of the civil liberties' groups, which somehow or other had got hold of the completed text in draft, launched a carefully prepared, pre-emptive strike in journals and the daily press aimed at undermining the report, claiming that it represented a craven acceptance of police demands, that it constituted nothing less than a policeman's charter and was, in the gibe of Lord Gifford, chairman of the Legal Action Group, little more than 'a cop-out'. In an article in the *New Statesman*, Harriet Harman, legal officer of the National Council for Civil Liberties, one of the most persistent of our critics, even went so far over the top as to claim that the report 'would make general and permanent the sort of powers the police were given allegedly on a temporary basis under the Prevention of Terrorism Act'.

A few hours before the press conference to launch the report, Jack Jones, who for some reason could not himself be present, released a personal letter to the press emphasizing his strong disagreement with those of our proposals that extended police powers. 'The majority of the commission', he wrote, 'failed to appreciate the acute social problems in the deprived areas. In particular I feel that the recommendations of the majority are insufficient to safeguard the rights of the young, the mentally-handicapped and the ethnic minorities.' However, this one-sided demurral was soon overtaken and discounted by the more detailed and measured assessments in the press generally, which on the whole, along with the Law Society, the Bar Council and the police, the last albeit somewhat cautiously, welcomed the balance of the report as acceptable.

But of all the many public commendations, the one which as chairman I personally most appreciated appeared in Malcolm Dean's review in the *Guardian*. 'Whatever happens to the Commission's report,' he concluded, 'it is already assured of one considerable political achievement: the rehabilitation of the reputation of Royal Commissions. The systematic approach with which the Commission tackled its subject is bound to be regarded as a model for the future.' Mr Merlyn Rees, who as home secretary had initiated the enquiry, told a colleague that setting up the commission was one of his best decisions.

The commotion which greeted the report soon reached the hurly-burly of the political arena, where, with crime rates still rising and the role of the police increasingly being subjected to widespread questioning, there was little danger that it would be sidelined. It appeared that every university and polytechnic, every law society and police force wanted to arrange a conference on the subject, in the majority of which, usually with one or two of my colleagues, I readily participated.

Well aware that the commission had been established by a Labour government and was now reporting to a Conservative prime minister, whose scepticism about the value of such bodies was well known, I and my colleagues kept our fingers crossed about the likelihood of future action by government, and meanwhile, over a period of two years went on meeting periodically to reassure ourselves that the political will in Westminster to take action was maintained. It therefore came as a relief but no great surprise when the home secretary, Mr Whitelaw, in 1982 announced that, based on the proposals in the report, he would seek an early opportunity to present two new bills: one to reform the investigation, the other the prosecution of crime.

11

The Police Complaints Authority

As chairman of the Royal Commission there was one important area of police procedure within our remit which I regretted not having been able at the time to investigate in detail. This was the sensitive subject of the adequacy of arrangements to enable members of the public to lay formal complaints against police officers for alleged misbehaviour. In its report, the commission had been able to do little more than recognize the important role an effective system of this kind should serve in encouraging good relations between the public and the police. But disquieting incidents kept occurring and, despite three *causes célèbres*, the Kelly, Blair Peach and Liddle Towers cases, which raised questions about police behaviour, the police associations in their evidence to the commission had blandly contented themselves with expressing satisfaction with existing arrangements for complaints.

Shortly after the Royal Commission's work was completed the home secretary, William Whitelaw, surprised me by asking if I would be interested in taking over from Lord Plowden as part-time chairman of the Police Complaints Board, the statutory body responsible for 'policing the police'. Although given not the slightest hint that he was looking for change in the system, I accepted the invitation as an opportunity to make good one of the gaps in the commission's report and from the start set out to evaluate recent public criticism, and, if possible, to seek to redress any faults in the complaints' system which might come to light.

First introduced by act of Parliament in 1976 by Roy Jenkins, the then home secretary, in the face of strong police opposition highlighted by the dramatic resignation of the well-known Metropolitan commissioner, Sir Robert Mark, the role of the proposed new Police Complaints Board had emerged through some highly contentious parliamentary debates as an uneasy compromise, allowing the police themselves to continue to investigate complaints by members of the public, and the director of public prosecutions to retain the decision whether to charge an officer with any criminal offence, merely empowering the new board to receive reports and to deal with disciplinary complaints about officers below the rank of chief superintendent. Even within this restricted sphere the board's performance since 1976 had been far from convincing, for in the three years from 1978 to 1980 it only managed to justify charges against officers in about 1 per cent of cases, an outcome many critics and the public found incredible.

Moreover, the process of investigating complaints had proved exasperatingly slow, each case on average remaining 160 days in police hands and 30 in those of the board, figures all the more questionable because the great bulk of complaints were not at all serious but minor, often involving little more than road traffic irregularities and obscene language.

Against this low level of achievement the case for reform looked strong, and as chairman I at once began to use the board's annual reports and interviews with the press to raise the need for reform, in order to make sure that in the new act of Parliament (PACE) then in active preparation, a section to redress the handling of complaints would also if necessary be included.

From Lord Plowden I had gathered that, in the light of initial police opposition, the board in its early years had deliberately decided to maintain a low public profile, in which purpose it had unquestionably succeeded, for on an early visit to the Hendon Police College (which happened to coincide with the first day in office of the new commandant, Geoffrey Dear) I discovered that very few of the staff there and none of the police students had ever heard of the board. So low was the profile that it led me to remark publicly that 'it had crawled into a ditch', a comment which caused anguish in both the Home Office and the police associations, and led to questions in Parliament. It did not seem likely that the existing arrangements could readily or quickly be changed for the better because nearly all the board members were part-timers, few of whom in my opinion were pulling much weight, leaving the experienced deputy chairman, Sir George Ogden, and myself to carry a disproportionate load. Changing and strengthening the composition in the short term was impossible and anyway uncertain for, as I soon discovered, party political considerations played a very large part in the minister's approval of new members.

A short time after my appointment as chairman a senior official in the Home Office, in some embarrassment, telephoned to inform me that on the instruction of the prime minister it had been decided that persons in my position, if already receiving a pension drawn from public funds, would be paid no more than one-third of the recognized salary, which in effect reduced me to the lowest paid member of the board. Putting on one side the fact that the college funds from which my pension arose included a substantial element from private not public sources, I was disinclined to argue because I was doing the job not for money but out of a sense of public service, and in order to make good a gap in the proposed Police and Criminal Evidence Bill. It was some consolation, however, to find that the Home Office's subsequent, lame letter of justification had to be drawn in such civil service gobbledegook as would have earned it instant inclusion as a prime example of how not to write in Sir Ernest Gowers's classic guide on *Plain Words* for that service.

In that unusually hot summer of 1981, it was the so-called race riots erupting in the inner cities of Bristol, Liverpool and Brixton, and involving alleged police brutality, especially towards black people, which really raised and kept the subject of complaints against the police before the public. Later, in officially reporting to the government on the Brixton riots, Lord Scarman pointed to bad economic and social conditions in the inner cities as probably forming the primary cause, but throughout the attention of the media and the public remained obstinately focused on the more tangible role of the police and the extent to which their behaviour had been a contributory factor.

Against this background, the frailty of the Police Complaints Board presented an easy target to critics, notably the National Council for Civil Liberties, and it came as no surprise when in October 1981 Alf Dubs, a Labour Member of Parliament, put forward a bill seeking wholesale change to replace existing arrangements with a completely external, independent investigation of complaints.

This put me in a dilemma for, although already convinced of the need for substantial change, I knew from several first-hand encounters that the politicians, especially in the Labour Party, in their eagerness to calm the public with instant, simple solutions, were on the one hand exaggerating the prospective role of a complaints system and, on the other, failing to assess the full consequences either for the public or the police of what they were proposing. To try to raise the level of the debate and to heighten public awareness of its significance, I therefore wrote an article for *The Times* newspaper pointing out that a switch to a system of investigation independent of the police would not only in effect create a separate, second police force but also was quite likely to involve an annual extra cost of the order of something like £10 million. What did the public expect of a complaints system, I asked? How far, especially in the context of the riots, did it represent an understandable wish to punish offending police officers rather than the need to raise the general standard of police behaviour? Ought not the complaints system, I urged, be seen by the public not as the major control on police behaviour but simply as the final check in a series of constraints, all of which were intended to instil habits of behaviour among the police in keeping with the general spirit and character of our public life? If by these means the emphasis could be placed on improvement within a police system in which in any event discipline must rightly remain with the chief constable, then the argument for leaving the investigation of complaints in the hands of the police while putting it under some form of independent supervision obviously remained extremely strong. Moreover, if the investigation of complaints were concentrated on the really serious cases, leaving the great majority of cases, which were minor, to be dealt with by an informal method of resolution by discussion, the whole system could be made more efficient and speedy to the benefit of both police and public.

On the day it appeared, happening to meet a very senior official of the Home Office, I was taken aback when in greeting he called out, 'Bloody cheek, prescribing your own job!', but shortly afterwards was satisfied to find that the evidence given by the Home Office to the House of Commons' Home Affairs Committee, which was looking into the police complaints system, followed my line of thought and that the committee itself subsequently opposed the idea of independent external investigation.

Meanwhile, the public's attention remained focused on the evidence about police misbehaviour then being given to Lord Scarman's enquiry. As an old friend and working partner on University of London affairs, I saw no difficulty in approaching him confidentially to put my own suggestions for change, and as a result was satisfied to find later in his published report that while still bowing in the direction of the ideal of totally independent investigation, he finally came down in favour of the practical lines the board and I were promoting.

When therefore in 1983 the government brought forward its first Police and Criminal Evidence Bill, a new section, as the home secretary acknowledged, largely incorporating the proposals initiated by the Police Complaints Board to strengthen independent supervision and to concentrate on serious cases, was included, and when, through the incidence of the general election, it was lost, the second and successful bill again brought forward by the Conservative government maintained and even strengthened the proposals.

Few quangos or other similarly independent bodies are given or take the opportunity to initiate the statutory reform of the function they represent; and when in 1986 in the form of the Police and Criminal Evidence Act (PACE) the bill became law I viewed it as a satisfactory rounding-off of my two ventures into the world of criminal justice and as marking the appropriate moment for me to bow out of the Police Complaints Board. From the start of the Royal Commission in 1978 to the passing of the act in 1986, ministers, senior civil servants and legal advisers had arrived at and departed from the Home Office, giving me the satisfaction of being the only senior player to see the business right through.

12

'A Terror Watchdog'?

B ut disengaging myself from the general scrutiny of policing, to the study and reform of which I had already given the best part of nine years, proved by no means easy, for almost at once I was asked by the Home Office to bring to bear my recent experience and knowledge of police procedures by initiating an experiment for Parliament's benefit to monitor, and perhaps make suggestions for improvement in, the practical operation of controversial legislation, in this particular instance the highly important Prevention of Terrorism Act.

Introduced into law after 40 hours of agitated debate in Parliament in the wake of the notorious IRA bombings in 1974, this act had avowedly been designed as an instrument of arbitrary power to express political policy. It provided for the arrest and detention of suspects without showing cause for up to seven days and empowered the home secretary to impose exclusion orders in the form of what was aptly described as 'internal exile' within the United Kingdom. It gave the police the power to override civil rights whenever they had reason to suspect terrorist activity and, short of arrest, allowed a great deal of unreported stopping, questioning and searching. It therefore rightly remained a subject of anxious public and political debate.

For good reason, therefore, Parliament had made the act subject to annual renewal and, in seeking to keep in close touch with the way it was working, members in both Houses had called for an annual, eve-of-debate report to be prepared by an especially appointed monitor or independent judicial adviser, luridly referred to by *The Times* as 'The Terror Watchdog'. This was the experimental role I was asked to initiate.

Minded to accept because the home secretary had recently gone out of his way to state that he intended so far as possible to have the provisions of this act applied in the *spirit* of the recently enacted Police and Criminal Evidence Act, I interpreted this indication, especially in the context of the newly proposed Anglo-Irish agreement, as likely to open the way to gradual operational improvement in this sensitive area. It seemed to me feasible, both in police operations and in the protection of suspects, to introduce modest changes calculated to attract public support, for instance, by the tape-recording of interrogations, so I agreed for a period of one or two years to initiate the experiment.

On starting, a senior official in the anti-terrorist branch of the Home Office assured me that about six weeks' intensive effort annually would be required, but disconcertingly it at once emerged that the forthcoming renewal of the act was scheduled for February, only six weeks away, a period which also included the Christmas break, and it was small comfort to be hastily promised that 'this is a wholly unreasonable deadline' and 'it really will be better next year'. Directed to Scotland Yard, ostensibly to receive advice on how to look after myself, I got a cool, bewildered reception from officers who had never heard of the 'terror watchdog' and were patently sceptical of my role.

In the event, by dropping all my other commitments in order to include short but essential visits to Liverpool, Northern Ireland and Scotland, including meetings in each area with police and civil rights' groups, I contrived, with a bare 48 hours to spare, to get the report into the hands of ministers, and also of Members of Parliament. It was therefore with eager anticipation that I went to listen to the debates, only to find in each House a tiny handful of members present and those who spoke more disposed to complain about the late arrival of the report than to discuss it. It was a dismal, disappointing beginning.

For the second round in the following year, well ahead of the proposed renewal debates again scheduled for the month of February, I made sure that ample time was allowed. Even so, foul weather, a succession of deep winter gales, snowstorms and bitterly sharp frosts disrupted and imperilled my programme, leaving me with one poignant memory, in particular, of a night on the quayside at Stranraer awaiting the ferry from Northern Ireland beside the icy sea — smooth, grey and sullen as a sheet of lead — facing an onshore wind so chill as to freeze the tears on my numbed cheeks.

On this second round, however, there was no question that members of both Houses found my function and report helpful. But already I was beginning to have doubts about the practical usefulness and worthwhileness of what I was doing. Suggestions I had made to ease and improve the operation of the more extreme statutory provisions, for example by devising a means of gradually phasing out the objectionable but little used and not very effective 'exclusion policy', or in taking note of the continuing public concern about police behaviour in the Northern Irish interrogation centres, urging the desirability of experimenting with the tape-recording of police interrogations, were not taken up by ministers.

One incident to which I felt it right to draw attention concerned a widow of Irish extraction living in Birmingham who had made no secret of her support for the 'British troops out of Ireland' movement and whose house was raided by the West Midlands Police. In an orgy of ransacking they had behaved in a grossly destructive manner, the senior officer in charge meanwhile nonchalantly smoking in the garden outside. To my surprise, in debate no member of either the Lords or the Commons took up the reference. Had any of them, I wondered, read my report? Being already acquainted with the chief constable of the force concerned, I had thought it courteous before the day of debate to advise him by telephone of the item in question. Our conversation was brief. 'When is the report being discussed?' he asked. 'On Thursday next,' I replied. 'That's all right,' he said, 'I'm retiring on Wednesday!'

In the light of my experience as chairman of the Police Complaints Board I had also looked forward to a fruitful visit to meet the members of the similar board in Belfast, but although courteously received, I was shown no files and, despite my questioning, our exchanges remained bland and uninformative. Indeed

I got the feeling that it was an inert body functioning in an atmosphere like that of a morgue. To voice some concern I went out of my way to speak to the permanent secretary at the Northern Ireland Office, but so far as I could discover no change took place.

By no stretch of the imagination could the late night debates preceding the renewal of the act, attended by so pitifully small a number of members, be envisaged by me or anyone else as an appropriate context in which to consider desirable change, the more so since no alternative forum, such as a standing or select committee for Northern Ireland, existed. It had also become abundantly clear that as long as political policy remained the same, the act would not be changed; and it was an added irritant to witness the members of both Houses conspicuously failing to give the sort of attention to these matters they obviously expected of the police at the operational end. This second round also ended in a farcical mix-up in Parliamentary procedure, so that in effect no straight vote was taken on the act, making a mockery of both it and my own efforts. With this, my disillusion with the hypocritical nature of so much of Parliamentary activity was complete, confirming my view that in its own way it was in as run-down a condition as our inner cities and as badly in need of thorough rehabilitation and reform.

Among my priorities as monitor, I had been planning to enquire into the undoubtedly complex reasons for the very low rate of criminal charges — a mere 3 per cent ultimately preferred by the police in Northern Ireland — in relation to the large number of suspects they detained, anticipating that such a study would indicate where improvement was feasible in the pre-trial procedure, especially in the task of investigation. But in the light of experience, whatever findings might ultimately have emerged, I had to face the reality that in the prevailing political impasse ministers regarded the act as set in stone and that any effort by me to devise practicable and acceptable suggestions for change would be wholly disproportionate to the outcome. Having demonstrated that the role of monitor was feasible and that as and when the political policy changed it could become potentially useful, I had no wish to go on marking time and so withdrew.

Somewhat earlier, after the government had announced that,

based in the main on proposals in the report of the Royal Commission I had chaired, two new important statutes, one concerning the investigation, the other the prosecution of crime, would shortly be brought before Parliament, I received a letter from Sir Ian Bancroft, then head of the civil service, saying that it had long been the custom to ask the outgoing chairman of a Royal Commission whether as a memento he would wish to receive a silver replica of the seventeenth-century inkstand which rests on the prime minister's desk at No. 10. Much touched and pleased by this generous, imaginative gesture, I accepted, and in due course was invited to the Civil Service Department to collect it. Rather expecting, I must admit, to receive it from the hands of a senior member, perhaps in traditional style over a quiet, congratulatory glass of dry sherry, I was surprised at the entrance to be directed downstairs to an obscure storage room in the basement where a bemused junior official in a brown overall met me, first carefully checking my identity, then, without another word, thrusting into my hands an oblong, brown paper parcel, presumably containing the inkstand, before abruptly departing, leaving me to find my own way out.

So it ended, as it had begun, not with a splash but a ripple.

13
Finding a Golden Mean

Although in outcome generally beneficial, those ventures which from time to time I undertook into the sphere of central government made me thank my lucky stars that at the end of the Second World War I had not seized the opportunity to commit myself in that direction but had remained true to my first love, the world of teaching and research.

This recoil from a career in the civil service or possibly in politics, or even in the business world, was instinctive for I knew that I would never have found it tolerable to put myself at the beck and call of politicians, or to toe the line as a committed party political man, or to work in any branch of commerce or industry whose primary and dominant aim, discounting people, was the maximization of profits. Set against the prevailing disposition and greed of contemporary society, these choices at times made me feel something of a Simple Simon at odds with the world.

It is true that in such walks of life signal and worthy achievement, whether public or personal, is often gained, yet rarely it seems without bitter conflict and an atmosphere of acrimony and denigration; and any doubts which occurred or may have lingered on the wisdom of my choice were exorcized in so often witnessing at first hand the corroding, destructive effects on the behaviour and character of those many politicians and senior civil servants with whom I came into close touch; and also, I may add, in perusing their memoirs, which so often reach an end in 'dust and ashes'.

So far as I can judge, my own personal and public purposes and ambitions throughout life did not change all that much. Even from early days I felt most comfortable with a Confucian-like, at times almost stoic philosophy of self-discipline, self-reliance, moderation and service, no doubt driven at the start by a determination to escape from the poverty which had dogged my family and early life. In these endeavours, neither at the beginning nor afterwards did I feel attracted to any simple panacea purporting to govern the sum of human activity, or to any doctrine which pretended to answer all questions; and certainly not to communism or fascism which so dominated the 1930s in which I grew up. Neither did I see merit in committing myself to any one political creed or party.

Nor was it the thought of riches, of worldly success or of exercising power that took me into academia. Deep down, I suppose, after my grim boyhood in India and survival in war, the feeling grew overwhelmingly that it was enough to be alive, to be in the land of the living. There was still some way to go along the road of life before I discovered that the true measure of moral courage and personal integrity is to be able to carry on with fortitude despite personal failures and the tragedies that overtake the ones you love. These are the situations in which you discover that all that is left to stand up in is your character.

Largely through my varied wartime experience in the education corps, especially in studying the postwar reconstruction that would be needed, I began to appreciate the extent to which an active civic spirit backed by personal service is needed to foster sound public institutions and a free society. But turning this understanding into practical purpose and outcome is never easy. What does seem clear is that a society that will observe the laws of the land is not created by Parliament or police or judges but by the sense of moral responsibility, cultivated when young and reinforced throughout life.

In the academic workplace, no less than in the everyday give and take between people in general, there are so many differing value judgements continually in play, so many diverse objectives always being sought, many quite irreconcilable, that it makes good sense to accept that the safest method of achieving lasting change has to be piecemeal. Significant social and economic change achieved at a stroke, or for the individual simply by turning over a new leaf, is rare. Moreover, in public life it is usually achievement enough to promote and preserve what amounts to little better than an uneasy equilibrium, accepting that it is constantly threatened and in periodical need of reform, and only rarely likely to yield a long-lasting solution. Often of course this involves compromise, but sometimes not.

Great leaps forward, for instance in our own day in the biological and medical sciences and in discovering the human past, have rarely, if ever, come about overnight through some lone discoverer penetrating the truth after ages of error, some single flash of insight, but rather by the gradual, cumulative modification of positions previously held. Alexander Fleming's discovery of the mould of penicillin would have remained an interesting curiosity without the insight and endeavour of Howard Florey and his colleagues; and the much-studied mystery of the origins of Christianity is only now becoming clearer through the work of the many scholars piecing together the fragments of the Dead Sea scrolls.

For the ordinary individual, too, society presents so complex and haphazard a mass of jigsaw pieces that in determining his own way forward he is wise to seek to add one piece at a time; and to remember that in finding agreement with people, in being a co-operator not a conqueror, it is often necessary to be willing to reconcile principle and expediency, ideals and policies. In this process we may hope to find an acceptable physical and spiritual balance, and perhaps even harmony.

With persistence, differences of degree, suitably and cumulatively ordered, may well in the course of time produce major and long-lasting differences of kind. These were among the important lessons which, through trial and error, I had to learn and bring to bear in devoting a large part of my adult life in creating new British schools of Asian and African history and then in transforming the School of Oriental and African Studies itself into an influential and permanent force in the British system of higher education.

Moreover, as the era of Western colonialism faded and non-occidental societies the world over gained the freedom to reaffirm themselves, Britain itself was going through the painful process of becoming a multi-ethnic society, offering the opportunity to explore through education the terms of peaceful understanding and coexistence between cultures as, for instance, between the Arabs and Jews, Hindus and Muslims, which had long been at war in their homelands. With staff and students drawn for the purpose of study from more than 100 nations, nowhere could have provided a better crucible for experiment and study.

* * *

At the close of my periodical ventures into public service, despite disappointments and at times frustration, I accepted an invitation from the Lord Chancellor, Lord Hailsham, to become chairman of the Council on Tribunals, largely because of its close links with consumer complaints' systems in that it supervised the procedures of over 70 major, rapidly growing tribunals which, by comparison with the courts, were providing the public with a relatively quick and cheap service.

The council, as I soon realized, if rightly developed, could provide a much-needed focus and lead for the myriad of organizations springing up to defend customers' interests, not least in the privatization of big utilities like gas, water and electricity.

First, however, it was necessary to bring the council's statutory powers into line with the role the council was already beginning to play, and therefore to persuade Lord Mackay, who had succeeded Lord Hailsham, to initiate appropriate yet modest legislative action. But, although on assuming office he had made much of his opportunities as a reformer, it became clear that in any event it would be some years before this step would be taken. Rather than simply mark time, I therefore in 1990 withdrew gracefully into retirement.

It was a decision hastened, too, by a spell of poor health. Those early years under the tropical Indian sun finally took their toll in the onset of skin cancer, which fortunately yielded to early treatment. But soon afterwards I suffered a pulmonary embolism, which struck me as I was walking down Kingsway in London. Fortuitously, as I subsided breathless to the pavement, a taxi quite by chance drew up alongside me, so that with an effort I was able to scramble aboard and got myself taken to the University Health Centre in nearby Gower Street, an institution incidentally which 30 years previously I had largely been responsible for founding. There I was resuscitated and set on the slow path to recovery. Not long after this, however, I had another spell in hospital, this time for an operation for cancer of the prostate, followed by five painful weeks of X-ray therapy, happily once again restored to health through the skills of the doctors and nurses at the Middlesex Hospital, and the loving care of Joan at home. While writing these words I await a replacement to the lens of my right eye, now looking forward to a new lease of sight and the means to go on reading and writing; and out of doors to roam the beaches and hills of the Isle of Purbeck where we have a new home, to watch the scurrying dunlins on the silver sands of Shell Bay and keep a look out for the rare Adonis Blue butterflies on the Swanage heathlands; there also to listen to the soaring song of the skylarks over Durlston Head, where far below the dinosaurs once roamed.

Now in sight of the last ascent, worldly passion almost gone, cultivating stillness and repose, not simply in peace of mind but also in suspended judgement, it more than suffices to view the public arena in the ironical whimsy of Ogden Nash as:

> A rolling, rattling, carefree circus
> Of mammoth Polkas and Mazurkas,
> Pterodactyls and Brontosauruses
> Singing ghostly, prehistoric choruses.

in which, with him,

> Amidst this mastodonic wassail,
> I caught the eye of one small fossil.
> 'Cheer up, sad world,' he said and winked,
> 'It's kind of fun to be extinct.'

Index

281

Index

285

Index

Index

Index

Thomas, Jimmy, 2
Thompsons, the, 138
Thomson Report, 250
Thorn, Jules, 220
Thornham Magna, 86
Thwaites, Dr Sir Bryan, 233, 240
Tiberias, 119
Tigre, 135
Tomlinson, Sir George, 174
Towers, Liddle, 266
Train, Christopher, 249
training and education, HM Treasury, 123–5
Tranmere, 4, 25
    Tranmere Rovers, 4, 25
Transport and General Workers' Union, 249
Trasimene, Lake, 111
Tremayne, Joe, 85–6
Tress, Dr Ron, 225, 234
Trevelyan, G. M., 29
Trinity College, Cambridge, 40, 65
Trotsky, Leon, 67
    Trotskyites, 198
Turkey, 45
Turner, Clarrie, 17, 26–7
Turner, Sir Ralph, 42, 45, 48, 55, 56, 157, 175–6, 179–80, 187
Twain, Mark, 111, 113
Tyre, 119

Uganda, 126, 143, 145, 198
Ullendorff, Professor Edward, 193
Unilever, 201
United Africa Company, 133
United Nations, 148, 150
United States of America, 69, 124, 134, 159, 164, 176, 182, 188, 190–3, 196, 203, 206, 213, 241, 254
University College, 163, 184, 189, 215, 220, 230, 233, 234, 244
    Hospital, 237
University Court, 209, 214, 222, 223–6, 228, 231–2, 236, 239
University Grants Committee, 93, 155, 157, 181, 187, 200–6, 216–19, 223–4, 227, 230, 234–6, 242
University History Board, 162
Uruguru mountains, 135
USSR, 195; see also Russia

Uttar Pradesh, 171

Valetta, 130
Valhalla, 16
Vatikiotis, Professor, 193
Veitch, Professor George, 33, 35–6
Vesey-Fitzgerald, Dr, 41
Vesuvius, 99
Vick, Sir Arthur, 201
Victoria, Lake, 133, 137
Victoria, Queen, 1, 23
Volkswagen Foundation, 192

Wa Chagga, 133, 142
Wa Pare tribe, 142, 144
Wakefield, 129
Wakefield, A. J., 83, 130
Wales, 125, 248, 254, 255
Wales, Prince of, 8, 173
Walker, Ken, 189
Wallasey, 54, 72, 74, 76–7
War Office, 65, 71, 74, 75, 80, 81, 86, 87, 93, 95, 96, 104, 122
Warburg Institute, 184, 215
Ward, Dr Ida, 42
Warrington, 69
Wartski, Mr, 59
Warwick, University of, 202
Washington, 196
Washington, George, 109
Wastwater, 142, 238
Waterloo, Battle of, 32, 58
Webster, Professor Sir Charles, 53, 160, 163
Wellington, Duke of, 23, 32, 97
West Africa(n), 42, 146, 149, 150, 187; see also Centre for West African Studies
West Indies, 36
West Midlands, 255
    West Midlands Police, 273
Westfield College, 215, 233
Westminster, 126, 142, 265
Westmorland, 131
Whitelaw, William, 265, 266
Widnes, 69
Williams, Bill, 95, 125
Williams, Shirley, 196
Wilson, David, 192
Wilson, Dr Glenn, 241